Dictators

and
Diplmats

A Special Agent's
Memoir and Musings

Robert W. Starnes

Published by

NOBILITY
P R E S S

Nobility Press
P.O. Box 589
San Marcos, Texas 78667-0589
www.nobilitypress.com

Cover, interior design and eBook conversion by
Rebecca Finkel, F+ P Graphic Design
Back cover copy by Judith Briles

Dictators and Diplomats: A Special Agent's Memoir and Musings
Robert W. Starnes.—1st ed.

Hard cover ISBN 978-0-9979703-0-2
Paperback ISBN 978-0-9979703-1-9
eBook ISBN 978-0-9979703-2-6
Audio book ISBN 978-0-9979703-3-3

Library of Congress Control Number: 2017918496

*To my wife and soulmate, Pam,
and my children—Jacob, Zachariah, Rachel, and Caleb.
The bravery and encouragement you exhibited
while traveling with me to war zones and
dangerous assignments abroad make you
the true unsung heroes in my life.
Without you all, my lifelong dreams,
and destiny would have never been fulfilled.*

*To my mother, Angie,
thank you for your perseverance.
Your life example continues to be
a blessing to us all.*

*Above all, thanks to my Lord Jesus Christ
for eternal salvation and a lifetime full of adventures*

CONTENTS

Preface..vii

SECTION 1: The Early Years...xv
    CHAPTER 1: Road Roaches...1
    CHAPTER 2: Don't Tread On Me...................................17
    CHAPTER 3: DSS: Men in Black...................................25

SECTION 2: The Butchers, the Takers, and the Coup d'état Maker..35
    CHAPTER 4: Paraguay's Black Berets............................37
    CHAPTER 5: The Car Bomb is Enroute............................45
    CHAPTER 6: The Barbie Effect..................................61
    CHAPTER 7: A Queasy Terrorist.................................77
    CHAPTER 8: Stranded with Hezbollah............................91
    CHAPTER 9: Assassination of a Fledgling Nation...............101

SECTION 3: In the Teeth of Civil War................................117
    CHAPTER 10: Let's Get Our Man!...............................119
    CHAPTER 11: True Grit..135
    CHAPTER 12: Chariot of Fire..................................149
    CHAPTER 13: Andean High......................................155

SECTION 4: Island Life..161
    CHAPTER 14: Kiwis Who Protected a Tiger......................163
    CHAPTER 15: Dr. Moreau Meets Lord of the Flies...............173
    CHAPTER 16: The Bearded Tree.................................191

SECTION 5: Domestic Dens....................................201

   CHAPTER 17: Love Bandit 203

   CHAPTER 18: Operation Wurstfest...........................217

   CHAPTER 19: Capone-ized 223

   CHAPTER 20: A Walter Mitty Complex.......................235

   CHAPTER 21: The King's Winetasters.........................243

   CHAPTER 22: Texas Treasure Burning.......................249

SECTION 6: To The Shores 261

   CHAPTER 23: Libya or Bust...................................263

   CHAPTER 24: Gaddafi's Regime 269

   CHAPTER 25: Ancient Lands 275

   CHAPTER 26: A Diplomatic Time Capsule...................283

   CHAPTER 27: Stayin' Alive....................................293

   CHAPTER 28: Into the Cuckoo's Nest.........................305

   CHAPTER 29: Benghazi 315

   CHAPTER 30: From the Shores of Tripoli.....................321

   CHAPTER 31: Left But Not Forgotten........................325

Epilogue 331

Acknowledgments...335

Photographs and Inserts 337

Index 347

Endnotes 353

About the Author 359

Dictators and Diplomats is written in honor of the faithful men and women of civilian law enforcement and uniformed military services, who daily improve our world through their unselfish sacrifices with valor in service to Americans to protect life, liberty, and the pursuit of happiness.

I will forever appreciate the men and women who courageously engage in the age old struggle between good and evil. No matter how overwhelming the bad in people manifests, dedicated members of law enforcement and the military make our world a better place, one good deed at a time.

In late August 1966, the City of Dallas, and our nation, was still recovering from President John F. Kennedy's assassination at the hand of Lee Harvey Oswald (November 22, 1963). The very heart of Texas was deeply wounded (August 1, 1966) by Charles Whitman's crazed sniper murder rampage from atop the University of Texas "Tower," killing 14 people and injuring at least 31 that fateful day. Our nation was embroiled in the Vietnam War, and coming to terms with the momentous Civil Rights Movement.

I was a skinny, barefoot 5-year-old boy visiting my grandmother during summer vacation in Fort Worth, Texas. I anxiously waited to exchange the two pennies in my hand for a piece of bubble gum at Georgie's neighborhood convenience store. Next to me at the counter was a Fort Worth police officer who took time out of his busy day to smile and spend a few minutes in conversation with me, a youngster who longed to sink his teeth into the sweet bubble gum.

Then the police officer reached into his pocket, pulled out a dime, and slid it across the counter to the cashier. The cashier lifted the lid from a cookie jar and encouraged me to take a chocolate chip cookie.

"My treat," said the officer.

In the words of Carl W. Buehner, "They may forget what you said-but they will never forget how you made them feel."[1]

Whether practicing community policing or performing a personal act of kindness, I often remember how my new friend in blue made me feel special that day.

Thanks to this officer's simple gesture of goodwill decades earlier, the taste of kindness from his ten-cent cookie resonates with me to this day.

His good deed influenced my career that included multiple international tours-of-duty and spanned six continents over 29 years as a Special Agent with the U.S. Department of State, Diplomatic Security Service (DSS), and the Texas State Troopers.

I have had the privilege of working alongside and knowing well truly exceptional men and women, including the cherished time I spent in Normandy, France, in June 1994, during the 50th anniversary remembrance of D-Day. I was assigned to Pointe du Hoc while conducting executive protection security site advance for a planned visit by the U.S. Secretary of State. I had the distinct honor of interacting with and looking into the eyes of those aging heroes from arguably the United States' greatest generation. Stories of their and other veterans' struggles, experiences, and sacrifices continually strengthen my and many other people's characters spanning multiple generations.

Late in my career, I spoke at a luncheon for the Hostel Elders Program. Seated next to me was a wheelchair-bound, elderly man. The soft-spoken gentleman thanked me for my government service.

After chatting over our meal, he shared that he had served in World War II and belonged to the U.S. Army's 29th Infantry Division. My first response was, *Wow! I'm sitting next to a real-life hero!* The 29th Infantry Division sent the initial wave of soldiers to Omaha Beach in Normandy, France, during D-Day's Operation Overlord. I asked this WWII veteran if he had shared his experiences with others. He responded that his family had repeatedly encouraged him to write down his experiences. Obviously, still haunted by the experiences of war, this gentle warrior could not bring himself to relive those experiences with those closest to him.

In this book, I have written about events and historical perspectives never before shared. I believe history should not be locked away within the depths of one's memory, but shared with current and future generations. For if our experiences that make up historical events are never shared, generations that follow will be denied opportunities to learn from, and hopefully avoid similar pitfalls, or be inspired by past successes.

I believe that community and public service are the social threads of which America's fabric is woven.

To the servicemen and servicewomen who protect our country; to the men and women who protect our communities; and to the loved ones who support them in public service—even to the point of making the ultimate sacrifice—victories for humanity are won on a daily basis.

In this book, I share both serious and life-threatening historic events, as well as humorous instances and adventures of unique national security challenges on global fronts.

"Adventure" as defined by Merriam-Webster is "an undertaking usually involving danger and unknown risks."

For me, unknown risks from encounters with nature or humans are the spice of life. Born with an adventure junkie gene and spirit of exploration, I have a similar vein as Captain James Cook, Lewis and Clark, and Daniel Boone.

Just as the eyes are the window to one's soul, I believe discovery is the window to imagination. I long to discover new places, new experiences and learn from diverse cultures, in a quest to uncover 'what lies around the next bend', all while living on the ragged edge.

I share the famed outdoorsman and survival expert Les Stroud's *Survivorman's* philosophy:

> *In the adventure known as life, there are those who live it vicariously, and enjoy the ride from the safety of an armchair; and that's good. There are those who have a few chances to realize incredible and life-changing experiences; and though they don't repeat them, they carry with them a growth and personal philosophy for the rest of their lives. And there are those for whom a taste is never enough; for whom the lust of adventure is nearly insatiable. And if you add to that the overwhelming desire to create, and to share, then you get where I reside. For the end of one adventure only signifies the beginning of another.*[2]

I remain humbled to have been given one of the rarest and prized gifts any government can offer: opportunity. I believe opportunity is likened to a stage. Regardless of the skills and talents possessed by individuals, it is opportunity that allows one to participate in, and hopefully fulfill, their life's destiny on that stage.

Adversity has afforded the U.S. opportunities throughout history to reveal the exceptional character of Americans during times of need. The valor of Admiral Chester Nimitz, Lt. Audie Murphy, and Major General James Earl Rudder likely would have never been fully revealed without real opportunity.

During my 23 years of service with the DSS, I received world-class training in counterterrorism, counterintelligence, criminal investigations, and executive protection that allowed me to travel to exotic lands and become acquainted with truly inspiring people.

While I have written about dignitaries and events I observed during my career, I have been careful to not violate the unwritten executive protection code of divulging instances that might bring harm or embarrassment to those whom I protected.

Whether countering international terrorists and spies or trading chess moves with criminals, each encounter brought a new and potentially exciting adventure.

I hope you enjoy a brief journey through snapshots and snippets comprising my life's international "wild-ride."

What a wonderful ride it has been!

"It is not the critic who counts; not the man who points out how the strong man stumbles, or where the doer of deeds could have done them better. The credit belongs to the man who is actually in the arena, whose face is marred by dust and sweat and blood; who strives valiantly; who errs, who comes short again and again, because there is no effort without error and short-coming; but who does actually strive to do the deeds; who knows great enthusiasms, the great devotions; who spends himself in a worthy cause; who at the best knows in the end the triumph of high achievement, and who at the worst, if he fails, at least fails while daring greatly, so that his place shall never be with those cold and timid souls who neither know victory nor defeat."

—Theodore Roosevelt

SECTION ONE

THE
EARLY
YEARS

grandfather (x3) Joseph Peter Crider protected Texans living in the frontier as a Texas Ranger. As the legend goes, Ranger Crider was returning from chasing a band of Comanche Indians in the Texas hill country. The thirsty Ranger stopped for a drink of water at the Pedernales River, near Fredericksburg, Texas. There, along the river, Joseph Crider came upon and captured a fourteen-year-old Comanche girl. The Ranger took his young captive back to his community where years later, he married Paulina Lunday, his Indian captive. This amazing story is commemorated by songwriter/singer Austin Ladd Roberts in his song, "The Water."[3]

Robert W. Starnes, Texas Highway Patrol.

Because highway patrolmen spend countless hours crawling across their state's highways and byways, patrolmen sometimes refer to themselves as "Road Roaches."

Growing up in the farming community of Manor, Texas, near Austin, I had driven by the Texas State Police Academy in Austin many times. Located close to the University of Texas, the DPS Academy, managed by former U.S. Marines, had a reputation of stringent physical training akin to a military-style boot camp. The five-month-long academy was both physically and academically challenging. Cadets were pushed to their psychological limits, often times jostled from sleep to take spelling exams at 2:00 A.M., participated in a boxing tournament without weight classes using worn boxing gloves, performed countless sit-ups and push-ups, and run endless miles to build endurance.

Joseph P. Crider, Texas Ranger, and wife Paulina circa 1860.

Discipline for slacking required the offending cadet to wear a necklace made up of a rope tied to a gold painted brick. Repeated daily, the DPS instructors' mantra was, "the more you sweat, the less you bleed!"

As a cadet, I enjoyed stories and lore shared by senior troopers visiting the academy. One trooper and his partner on patrol inspected an area under a bridge where they discovered a young couple making out. Having a bit of fun, the troopers informed the couple that what they were doing was illegal and gave them two choices: Either go to jail or get married. The couple opted for marriage. Using a state traffic law book, the troopers recited a mock wedding and departed.

Did the couple discover the joke or did they go through life believing that a state trooper married them off under a bridge? Frankly, I believe this story was more lore than fact, but I found it amusing just the same.

Peeping Anne

At the DPS Academy, the cadet barracks were divided alphabetically into two dormitories. The windows of my dorm looked out onto the loading dock area at the back of our building, while the other side faced Austin's heavily traveled North Lamar Boulevard. The recruits shared a common bathroom and showers. Personal clothing and toiletries were stored in each recruit's locker located next to his cot. The cots were lined up next to each other, similar to a military barrack.

Texas DPS headquarters building in Austin, Texas.

One night, a recruit noticed someone across the street peering with a telescope into our dormitory. Our drill sergeant, using binoculars, determined the "peeping Tom" was actually a "peeping Anne." A young woman was apparently taking visual "eye candy" advantage of her location to the recruit barracks. The drill sergeant decided to teach the ogler a lesson.

The following night at shower time, the sergeant handed out binoculars and lined up recruits on the barrack's roof, where we fixed our binoculars on peeping Anne's apartment. Like clockwork, peeping Anne pulled back her curtain and focused her telescope lens.

However, instead of catching bare-backed recruits in the showers, peeping Anne got a different kind of eye-opener—two dozen young men staring back at her from atop the building. In a near panic, she quickly closed her curtain and was not seen peeping into the dormitory again. I chuckled at the adventurous sergeant and his creative and effective solution.

Speeding Broomstick

Early in my highway patrol assignment in Rosebud, Texas, my field training officer told me that a career in law enforcement is ninety-nine percent utter boredom and one percent sheer excitement. For most, it is the adrenaline rush from the one percent of excitement that attracts and retains men and women in law enforcement.

One Friday, I was on duty alone during a night shift. Just south of Marlin, Texas, on State Highway 6, I stopped a vehicle for speeding. Inside were a male driver and female passenger. Highway 6 was a heavily traveled two-lane road that connected Waco to Bryan-College Station, and was frequently used by students from Baylor and Texas A&M universities. When the vehicle rolled to a stop, a 6'8"-tall man, scrawny as a broomstick, quickly exited the large Chevrolet Monte Carlo and walked back to my patrol car. I smelled alcohol on his breath and noted other signs of intoxication. I arrested and handcuffed the driver after he refused to submit to a field sobriety test.

At that time, state trooper vehicles did not have the prisoner metal mesh separator between the front and rear seats. Standard procedures required prisoners be handcuffed and seat-belted in the front passenger seat. Just before I buckled the prisoner's seat belt, he began screaming at his female partner to take off. Before I was able to buckle his seat belt, I ran to his car's window to seize the keys to prevent her from leaving the scene. The woman put up a struggle, scratching at my arms. Meanwhile, the prisoner got out of the patrol car and began to walk toward the Monte Carlo. I released the woman, ran back, and pushed the prisoner down, causing him to roll down the ditch. I immediately ran back to the woman, but it was too late. She was speeding toward College Station.

I have no memory of how I accomplished the feat, but I was somehow able to lift the prisoner, place him in the patrol car, and buckle his seat belt before I began the chase. I called a state trooper from the adjoining county to join the chase. The trooper was driving a newly issued 6.0-liter Ford Mustang, with a 160 mph factory speed rating. Now, followed by two patrol cars, the woman was traveling in excess of 95 mph.

I radioed ahead to request municipal police departments to block side street traffic while we sped through their towns. A moving road block was positioned near College Station in an effort to stop the runaway vehicle. Unfortunately, one of the three patrol vehicles provided a slight space between the moving road block where the suspect was able to shoot the gap. A College Station police car rammed the Monte Carlo, causing it to swerve into the center median. The dust from multiple patrol cruisers skidding into the median reduced visibility.

I slowly approached the dust cloud only to observe the woman's vehicle emerging, followed by two patrol cars. Now third in line, I cautiously joined the chase. My prisoner became visibly upset and screamed that he was a state employee and would have my job. The woman had wrecked the car while exiting the controlled highway. Within seconds, the prisoner and I rolled into the area with rotating police lights resembling the final scene of The Sugarland Express. Troopers and police officers surrounded the wreck with weapons drawn. But one trooper was standing in front of my patrol car, with his weapon aimed at the suspect.

Before I was able to put my patrol car in park, the prisoner began head-banging my shoulder. Each time he struck me, my foot slipped slightly, causing me to nudge the trooper with my front bumper. With my window rolled down and my vehicle in park, a pair of arms reached

1924 New York Yankee baseball team.

While patrolling Texas highway 77 near Chilton, Texas, my traffic radar began beeping, alerting me to the oncoming speeding vehicle. I turned my overhead lights on and stopped the vehicle along the dry winter grass. An elderly man wearing a maroon Texas A&M University shirt and sporting a large grin exited his vehicle. The driver's license introduced this grey-haired man as Patrick Olsen. I asked the driver if he happened to be related to the Olsen for which Texas A&M's baseball field is named. The kind gentleman paused a moment before quietly sharing that the university's baseball field was named in his honor. Being a baseball fan, I spent the next twenty minutes talking baseball with him. His eyes lit up as he shared his experiences and participation with college baseball. He seemed especially proud of his record of consecutive attendance at the college world series in Omaha, Nebraska. I sent Mr. Olsen along his way with a warning that day. Years later, I learned that Patrick Olsen was a member of the 1924 New York Yankees, making him a teammate of Lou Gehrig and Babe Ruth. Despite his extraordinary sports accomplishments, I will always remember the positive impression Patrick Olsen imparted through his humility and optimism.

I also became acquainted with Texas A&M University head football coach Jackie Sherrill during his football scouting trip to Baylor

University in Waco, Texas. Travelling 69 mph in a 55 mph speed zone, I stopped and cited coach Sherrill for speeding on Highway 6

near Marlin, Texas. Just recently hired at Texas A&M, coach Sherrill was still driving under his Pennsylvania driver license.

An accomplished college gridiron player and coach, Mr. Sherrill

Jackie Sherrill, Texas A&M football coach.   played fullback and linebacker for

the University of Alabama from 1962-1965, winning two national championships under coach Bear Bryant.

Sporting an impressive 180-120-4 record as a head coach, Jackie Sherrill served as the head coach at Washington State, University of Pittsburgh, Texas A&M University, and finally at Mississippi State University. Notably, coach Sherrill had recruited and coached Heisman Trophy winner, NFL Hall of Famer, and Dallas Cowboy legendary running back Tony Dorsett.

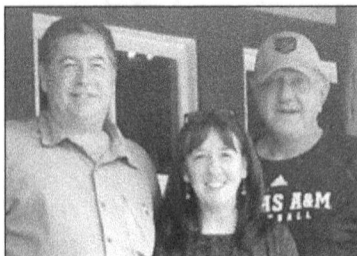

During the early 1980s, a person who received a traffic citation by a state trooper had the option of paying a fine or contesting the

Robert W. Starnes (L) and wife Pam (C) are reunited with neighbor and former coach Jackie Sherrill (R), 35 years after the issuance of a speeding citation.

citation in court. In the event a driver failed to do either, troopers were required to attempt to make contact with the violator by calling them three times. If after the third phone call the matter remained unresolved, the trooper would request the judge issue an arrest warrant.

Given his extremely busy coaching schedule, Mr. Sherrill did not pay the fine or contact the judge. Twice, I was unsuccessful in contacting coach Sherrill. I was one call away from requesting the justice of the peace to issue an arrest warrant. For the third and final phone call, I contacted the Texas A&M athletic department, and informed the university of the situation. Within fifteen minutes of my call, the judge was contacted and the fine paid. Fortunately, the third phone call proved to be the charm.

Had an arrest warrant been issued, I pondered at the theoretical options of serving a warrant on a head football coach of a major university in a state where football is king. Perhaps the warrant could have been served on the sidelines during the annual Aggie-Longhorn football game in College Station. Of course, as witnessed in 1981 by the sword-wielding Aggie cadet who protected Kyle Field from the intruding Southern Methodist University cheerleaders, I would have had to rethink serving an arrest warrant within the confines of Texas A&M's hallowed football stadium for fear of inciting a riot.

Now working as a sports commentator, coach Jackie Sherrill is a true gentleman who lives on his ranch in Wimberley, Texas, just 15 miles from my residence in San Marcos, Texas.

BURNT ORANGE EXPERIENCES

It's almost a rite of passage for folks raised in Austin, Texas, to grow into Longhorn sports fans. My father was the ironworker who hung the original University of Texas seal to Memorial Stadium's end zone north gate; now remodeled, the seal remains there today. During junior high school, I spent two years walking up and down the stadium stairs selling concessions and watching great football games during the Longhorn glory years. Naturally, my blood turned from red to burnt orange.

Robert W. Starnes standing in front of the University of Texas stadium seal.

During my first highway patrol assignment in Falls County, Texas, living on a small ranch a few miles outside of Rosebud, Texas, I was honored to have befriended the Texas athletics Hall of Fame legend, Howard Clifford "Bully" Gilstrap. Bully was a retired University of Texas football and basketball coach. An accomplished player and coach, Bully led the Texas Longhorn basketball team to their first NCAA Final Four appearance and worked alongside legendary coach Dana X. Bible. I enjoyed my visits to Bully's ranch and listening to his college sports stories.

Bully" Gilstrap, University of Texas Hall of Fame coach.

During a visit to Bully's ranch, I noticed small numbered tags affixed to his wooden cattle corral. Bully told me the seasoned lumber was the original wooden bleachers from Memorial Stadium in Austin, during the days of Bobby Lane, Tom Landry, and Tommy Nobis. I sorely my friend Bully.

How Bout Them Cowgirls

Though not directly a sports figure, although sporting a figure, I stopped a different sort of speeder. While working radar on Highway 6, I pulled over a Camaro that was traveling in excess of 70 mph. The words, "Dallas Cowboys Cheerleader" were scrawled across the entire rear window. I informed the attractive driver why she was stopped and that she would be issued a speeding citation.

When I inquired her occupation to record on the citation form, now indignant, she shook her head from side to side and responded in an haughty tone, "Can't you read? I am a Dallas Cowboys Cheerleader!"

Clearly, this young woman had an inflated ego. In order to give her the attention she sought, I responded that I needed her autograph on the citation and she could be on her way. I must admit that justice prevailed that day.

A Pink Raccoon

On Texas State Highway 7, I stopped a speeding vehicle and told the driver to sit in the patrol car while I conducted the appropriate record checks. When all checks were clear, I gave the driver a warning and advised him to slow down in the future. Though I smelled a hint of alcohol on the driver's breath, I did not believe him to be intoxicated.

As with many drivers suspected of drinking and driving, this driver gave the typical response as to the number of alcoholic drinks he had consumed: only one. While I was writing the warning, I saw peripherally a raccoon crossing from left to right in front of the driver's car.

The man became excited when he saw the raccoon, pointing his finger and insisting that I look at the animal. I intentionally waited a few seconds while the raccoon made its way in front of the vehicle before I looked. By then, it was out of view. I asked the driver whether he was sure he had only one drink. Intent on proving his innocence, the man became more insistent.

As I lowered my gaze, the raccoon cleared the vehicle and made its way across the ditch toward the foliage. Again the driver pointed at the raccoon and insisted I look. Again I waited a moment as the raccoon became hidden from sight. I looked up—there was no raccoon. In a serious tone, I asked the driver if the raccoon was pink. He didn't appreciate my jest and drove off, vexed that I did not see the wily raccoon.

The Claps Man!

Law enforcement can be a dirty and unpleasant occupation. I stopped a vehicle on Highway 7 near Marlin, Texas, and arrested the driver for intoxication. While inventorying his vehicle, I found a club (illegal weapon) and a small U.S. Postal scale, often used by drug dealers to weigh their illegal products. The suspect refused a breath test but agreed to a urine test. I didn't have one of the large plastic bottles normally used for collecting urine samples, so instead, I emptied the anti-coagulant powder from a blood sample test tube. Technically, rules of criminal procedures required an officer to hold the container while collecting samples. Given the drunken state of the driver, the ordeal was quite messy.

Urine sample in hand, we drove to the jail. While completing the booking documents, I overheard the jailer ask the prisoner questions about his medical condition. At first, the prisoner's mumbled responses were inaudible. The frustrated jailer asked the prisoner to repeat his response. The prisoner again mumbled a response. Sternly, the jailer insisted that the prisoner speak clearly.

The now equally frustrated prisoner clearly replied, "The claps, man, I have the claps!"

Having just handled his urine sample without gloves, my first thought was to cut my arms off at the elbow and thus avoid any unspeakable disease I may have contracted from the ordeal.

A Spanish Lesson

Early in my highway patrol tour, my partner stopped a car for running a stop sign. Given the driver's clumsy driving skills, my partner suspected him to be an unlicensed migrant worker. I suggested to my partner that the driver probably did not speak English, to which he answered that it would not be a problem as he spoke Spanish. Excited at this knowledge, I told my partner that I wanted to learn Spanish. My partner said "no problem" and I followed him to the driver's car where he knocked on the window.

The driver lowered the window and my partner demanded, "I need to see your el driver license-O."

Shaking my head at his prank, I told him that he was not speaking Spanish. His response was that speaking Spanish was easy. All a speaker has to do is add an "el" to the front of a word and "O" to the end of the word. Insult was added when the driver actually produced an identification document, making mockery of my partner's Spanglish.

Beware of OJ

One of the most comical and memorable experiences I had while working as a Road Roach was when my highway patrol partner bartered with a Marlin (Texas) police officer for a birthday gift for his father. The Marlin police officer was an accomplished artist who specialized in gold-leaf paintings, artwork quite popular during the late 1970s. The officer agreed to paint a West Texas windmill scene on a glass pane with India ink, backed by 24-karat gold leaf. In return, the officer asked my partner for a half dozen live rattlesnakes. He would use the skins to make wallets and headbands.

With a burlap sack containing six Western Diamondback rattlesnakes and a homemade snake snare, my partner and I drove from Rosebud to Marlin. I still thought it odd that the police officer wanted the snakes alive.

We knocked on the Marlin police officer's apartment door. The officer, dressed in his dark blue police uniform, greeted us. I noticed his small apartment was especially void of furniture. The officer told us that burglars had recently broken into his apartment and made off with sofas, chairs, beds, and chest of drawers.

With the bag of squirming snakes, the officer walked cautiously to a back bedroom, also without furniture, and emptied the lively snakes onto the tile floor. The officer sarcastically quipped of the unwanted surprise burglars would receive if they entered this bedroom, now equipped with a "living alarm system."

Adjusting to their new environment, the snakes quickly sought refuge in an empty closet. Feeling compassion for the officer, my partner left behind our snake snare.

A few days later, while patrolling near Marlin, my partner and I met up with the Marlin police officer to inquire about the status of the bartered artwork. With eyes widening, the officer shared how he was almost killed by one of our rattlesnakes. Garnering our full attention, the officer continued: He planned to euthanize one snake at a time by snaring and placing the live snake into his freezer. This kept the other snakes "fresh," and seemed a more humane way to eventually remove the valued skin.

The officer had placed a snake in his freezer just before beginning a night shift. The next day, awaking from his previous night duty, the tired police officer staggered from bed and went to the kitchen and opened his freezer for a can of juice concentrate.

Speaking more loudly now, as if reliving his near-death horror, he recounted that when he opened the freezer door, the rattlesnake's head struck him on the forehead. Shaking from the memory, the officer pointed to his would-be wound.

When he recovered from the shock and horror, the officer discovered that the rattlesnake had wrapped itself around the freezer door food rail. There it froze solid, with its head and body set about six inches from the rail. On reflection, the Marlin police officer realized that when he had opened the freezer door, the now-frozen snakehead swung with it—the door—and struck him right between his eyes.

My partner and I were amused at first, but then mostly amazed at the officer's stunning snake battle. Who knew the perils inherent in the quest for a drink of orange juice?

It was time to restock our rattlesnake inventory.

CHAPTER 2

DON'T TREAD ON ME

Creeped out by the oddity of this place,
we continued within the Snake Farm's bowels.

The five-foot long PVC-pipe snare arched like a fishing pole hooked to a prize-winning large-mouth bass. Unlike a few seconds of relaxed excitement for a handsome game fish on the end of a monofilament line, consequences of a misstep for the six-foot Western diamondback rattlesnake at the end of our homemade snare garnered our complete attention and respect.

The troopers move hay to capture snakes.

Just minutes before, my fingers, protected by my leather ranching gloves, grasped the two wire strands bundling the bale that concealed the serpent lying before me inside of the dilapidated barn. Years of layered dead grasses carpeted the wooden floor planks. Opposite, Terry Vance, my highway patrol partner, dug his boot soles through the loose hay, hoping to reach a more stable platform from which to negotiate the granddaddy snake slithering for its freedom.

Terry Vance uses a homemade snare to capture reptiles alive.

The frost from our heavy breath floated for a few seconds before dissipating into the frigid central Texas air. Winter had come early on this still January morning in 1983, near Rosebud, Texas.

Vipers' reflexes are much slower during the cold winter months because of their cold-blooded nature. Yet their venom remains consistently toxic despite the cold weather. Seeking protection from the freezing conditions, we discovered a large rattlesnake den sheltered beneath the warmth of the hay. A systematic, orchestrated team extraction would be needed to prevent losing one of these prized reptiles—sold by the pound—while preventing an unwanted bite in our newly discovered "glory-hole."

"Ready?" I asked. Wearing a bright white football jersey with red letters and a baseball cap advertising an oilfield company, Terry nodded yes and quickly acted, securing the loop around the snake's neck. This snake was strong and unwilling to be captured without a struggle. Refusing to yield to the viper's rebellion, Terry widened his stance and exercised all his strength to hold the snake in place as it squirmed on the slippery hay. Instead of snakeskin belts or hatbands, our snakes were destined for the confines of the terrariums at the Snake Farm Zoo in New Braunfels, Texas.

Taking care to not strangle the now active snake by retracting the wire loop too tightly, Terry lifted the snake. With its index-finger–sized rattle and foot-wide girth, the coiled serpent could easily digest unsuspecting rodents and

Off-duty troopers inspect potential snake den.

The Rosebud News front page, Jan. 23, 1983, edition.

mammals. Rattles echoed as the reptile dropped to the bottom of our 40-gallon trash can used on this day as a temporary snake repository.

We both stopped to catch our breath. Six months since arriving at the Texas Highway Patrol substation in Falls County, Texas, my "adventure junkie gene" was at full throttle. The area was overpopulated with rattlesnakes that had begun infesting residences and endangering the peace and safety of its inhabitants, including children. The pleas from these neighbors convinced us to make their small portion of the earth a safer place to live. With the benefit of earning supplemental pay, Terry and I were determined to catch and sell as many rattle-snakes as possible.

An hour after the snakes' capture, a quick snap of the trash can lid signaled the end of a fruitful hunt. More than six snakes lay at the bottom of our trash can. *The Rosebud News* owner and editor recorded our adventures on film and printed an article titled, "What do off-duty

Animal World and Snake Farm Zoo, New Braunfels, Texas.

Texas Highway Patrol troopers do for entertainment in Rosebud?" on its front page.

A few weeks later, on a cold, overcast day, Terry and I made the 120-mile trek to the Snake Farm Zoo, which had agreed to buy our rattlesnakes in order to repopulate their "wishing well" attraction that was filled with various snake species.

Pounding on the front door of this off-season, exotic tourist haven, we saw an elderly woman appear. The door's unoiled hinges let off a high-pitched squeal as we and our prized catch were welcomed into the eerie confines of the Snake Farm. Stepping inside the doorway, the white-haired woman introduced herself as the business co-owner. Pausing, she pointed to a gallon jar containing a small amount of water and a live coral snake. The woman proudly boasted that the coral snake she referred to as her "baby" was shedding its snakeskin. It became clear that this woman loved her job and cared for caged animals.

Just as Terry and I entered the snake building, something exploded against the wall, sending soft, wet fragments our way. After a short fight-or-flight moment, we regained our composure and learned that, uncharacteristically, a large hairy adult orangutan, in solitary confinement was hurling fruit at us. He had lobbed an apple against the wall which caused the commotion.

Now thoroughly creeped out by the oddity of this place, we continued within the Snake Farm's bowels, past a cage of three intertwined anaconda snakes and another exhibit housing large alligators. Shortly we met the old woman's husband. Missing several fingers and a thumb, the square-jawed old man had a head full of white hair and stories.

Equally in love with his exotic creatures, the man gave us a nickel-and-dime tour of his "Shawshank" or "Shawsnake" palace. He smiled as he pointed out the poisonous scorpions and immense tarantula spiders. We entered a large room lined with terrariums stacked three levels high. I marveled at the many different snake species on display.

Coming to a gorgeous white albino rattlesnake, the man stopped, pointed his index finger on his thumbless hand, and declared that this snake had cost him more than five thousand dollars. In a moment, the old man had inflated our dreams of hunt-

Snake Farm terrariums.

ing, capturing, and selling expensive reptiles and realizing a large payday. Deflating our vision of financial grandeur, he explained that this white snake possessed both hemotoxic and neurotoxic venom. While handling this very snake, it had bit his wrist. Chuckling, the old man revealed an ugly scar on his right wrist and said the medical bills he incurred while tending to this snake bite cost him thousands of dollars. I was a bit dejected, but mostly fascinated at his ability to continue his trade, in spite of his near-death experiences.

The old fellow continued his tour, pointing to a few more snakes that had inflicted the scars on both of his arms. At the end of one aisle, we stopped in front of an inch-thick Plexiglas terrarium that protected us from a twelve-foot king cobra. The shiny black snake lay still, its beady eyes starring in our direction. Cobras have been known to inject enough venom to kill an elephant.

No longer smiling, the man clearly displayed respect for this Asian-born killer. His voice was deadly serious as he explained how his brother, who also owned a snake farm in Louisiana, was bitten by a cobra while milking its venom. After losing his grip, the cobra bit him, and within minutes his brother was dead from the lethal venom.

After a moment of reflection, the old man escorted my partner and me to the room containing a twelve-foot diameter wishing well. Here, I thought, countless wishes were made on the backs of squirming serpents. Mesmerized, I pulled a coin from my pocket, wished for a safe journey, and tossed it into the well.

Indian Spectacled Cobra staring at the camera.

My coin bounced several times before it rested on the concrete bottom. Like a scene from an *Indiana Jones* movie, the floor seemed to throb from the sound of many varieties of slithering snakes. Wiser and a bit more cautious at nature's beauty and danger, we bid the old couple good-bye.

Throughout my 29-year law enforcement career, my visit to the Snake Farm Zoo has often crossed my mind. Just like snakes in the wild, there are many similarities between varying venomous human criminal species.

Ribbon snakes, like traffic offenders, may initially evoke fear of the unknown. However, once identified and subdued, they are harmless.

Chicken snakes resemble egg-sucking pickpockets and fraudsters peddling snake oils that sometimes cause frustration and contempt with every bite of crime, but they are generally non-life threatening.

Coachwhip and racer snakes are similar to online scam artists who prey on victims over the Internet, traveling at great speed. They are difficult to capture.

Boa and anaconda snakes correspond to criminals who are not content with capturing their victims, instead, their satisfaction is to squeeze the life out of their victims through kidnapping, black-mail, and extortion.

Black mamba snakes closely resemble territorial street gangs who possess extremely toxic venom, and become quite aggressive when agitated.

Bushmaster snakes, whose long fangs impale vital organs, often killing their prey before their toxins cause paralysis, resemble psy-chopathic serial killers. They attempt to destroy their victims' very souls by heartless acts devised from their deranged minds, cutting deeply to the marrow.

Cobra snakes, echo the extremely deadly venom spewed by terror-ists and their hateful ideology, capable of calculating torment upon individuals, communities, and entire nations.

With the risks and rewards of snake hunting on those cold Texan days, little did I dream that my snake-wrangling adventures would be a prelude to another sort of viper hunt: A law-enforcement roundup of terrorists, would-be assassins, snipers, mafia members, fugitives, and other strange cases of criminals who possess venom far more deadly than the diamondbacks that once lay within arm's reach.

For these "criminal offenders," their weight is measured by the court of law, and their terrariums consist of prison cells.

I greatly enjoyed the three and a half years I spent as a highway patrolman. I will forever carry with me these adventurous and humorous experiences.

Seeking a change of pace, I transferred to the Texas Governor's Protective Detail in Austin. It was during this assignment that I became acquainted with the Diplomatic Security Service (DSS), the most diverse law enforcement agency in the world.

Let the international serpent roundup begin!

CHAPTER 3

DSS: MEN IN BLACK

"Who are the Diplomatic Security Service?"
asked the judge.

During the early morning hours on October 23, 1983, a group of Shiite terrorists made their final preparations. Once known as the Switzerland of the Middle East, Lebanon was at war with itself. Beirut had become a chessboard dotted with eighteen officially recognized religions, all vying for political power and influence. Competing political and religious stances from multiple nations, including Iran, Saudi Arabia, Syria, Israel, and others, empowered

Nighttime clearing operations at the U.S. embassy in Beirut. The arrow points to Ambassador Dillon's top-floor office, which he occupied when the bomb exploded.

multiple terrorist factions, most notably Iranian-backed Hezbollah's attempts to gain the upper hand in this small country, about one-third the size of Maryland, bordering Israel to the north. The sizable

multinational forces, including U.S. Marines and other U.S. servicemen, were inserted into Lebanon in a peacekeeping role to support
the U.S.-brokered ceasefire between the Palestine Liberation Organization and Israel.

Giving a final, prearranged
signal to begin an attack, terrorists
sent an explosive-laden dump
truck toward the building used as
the U.S. Marine headquarters
building. The determined suicide
bomber drove through three
guard posts, a barbed-wire fence,
and into the building's lobby,
detonating a bomb consisting of
approximately 12,000 pounds of
explosives.[4] The explosion collapsed the building, killing 241
Marines, sailors, and soldiers. For
the Marine Corps, it resulted in

Sgt Luis G. Lopez, of the Marine Security
Guard detachment, stands guard outside the
embassy immediately after its bombing.

the largest loss of life in a single day since the Iwo Jima battle during
World War II.[5]

Only six months earlier, a suicide bomber attacked the U.S.
Embassy in Beirut, killing 63 people, including 17 Americans. Although
the identity of the Marine Barracks attackers was never discovered,
many experts believe the Iranian-backed Hezbollah was responsible.

America, and the world, was facing an ever-growing threat from
Islamic terrorism. From 1979 to 1983, some 300 terrorist attacks were
recorded, ranging from the U.S. Embassy takeover in Tehran, attacks
against U.S. military and diplomatic installations, to airplane hijackings.
In 1984 alone, some 100 attacks were reported. The United States
security forces had to rise and meet the challenge of protecting U.S.
national security.

President Ronald Reagan, the "Great Communicator," had had enough of terrorist attacks against Americans abroad. President Reagan

Admiral Bobby Ray Inman (ret).

directed Secretary of State George Shultz to commission a panel to review, research, and provide recommendations on how to better secure and protect diplomats and facilities abroad. The security panel was chaired by retired Navy Admiral Bobby Ray Inman. This blue-ribbon panel published its report in June 1985, which included recommendations for boosting security ranks by hiring several hundred special agents.

On August 27, 1986, President Reagan signed into law H.R. 4151, the Omnibus Diplomatic Security and Antiterrorism Act of 1986, formally establishing the U.S. Department of State Bureau of Diplomatic Security (DS), and the Diplomatic Security Service (DSS).

Prince Charles and Governor Mark White at the Texas State Capitol.

It was a bright, sunny February day in 1986, and the crowd of 3,000-plus spirited people swelled onto the south grounds of the Texas State Capitol to celebrate the sesquicentennial anniversary of the Texas revolution for independence. Prince Charles greeted the exuberant crowd, many waiving small Union Jack flags.

Special agents with the Diplomatic Security Service (DSS) exuded professionalism and confidence while protecting the Prince of Wales. Vehicles and buildings were searched for hidden bombs, guest lists were checked and double-checked through multiple databases, press pens and greeting lines were cordoned and posted with agents, and local law enforcement officers were woven into the tapestry of a layered security web in Austin that day.

I was posted on the Capitol's south steps, slightly behind the podium where Prince Charles and Texas Governor Mark White spoke, poised to quickly respond to any uninvited persons who might want to rush the Prince. Only a thick pink granite wall, quarried in Marble Falls, Texas, separated me from the Capitol's foyer, housing the marble statue of Tennessee frontiersman and Alamo hero, Davy Crockett.

A special relationship with the Lone Star State has been created with England since the Republic of Texas gained its independence on March 2, 1836. In addition to DSS' primary protective responsibilities, the DSS special agents were on a recruiting mission, distributing pamphlets to the troopers who assisted them that day.

To the sound of roaring applause from both British expatriates and Texans, Prince Charles was whisked away in his Jaguar sedan. His

Walter Cronkite, former Texas Governor John Connally, Prince Charles, and Governor Mark White during the 1986 Texas sesquicentennial reception.

motorcade limousine left for an event boasting the world's largest cake, baked to celebrate Texas' 150th birthday. The Duncan Hines classic yellow cake with vanilla icing weighed 90,000 pounds. Of course everything is bigger in Texas.

I was intrigued with DSS. After Prince Charles' departure, I began researching the newest federal law enforcement agency. I discovered that DSS is a hybrid federal law enforcement and security agency with the distinction of playing an important role in the U.S. intelligence community. When forming the DSS, the recipe used by President Reagan's commission incorporated a mixing bowl within the U.S. Foreign Service, a cup of the U.S. Secret Service, a pinch of the FBI and U.S. Marshal Service, a dash of the CIA, a smidgen of the U.S. combat military and Army Corps of Engineers. Baked within the heat of counterterrorism and counterintelligence at some of the most dangerous places in the world, DSS was forged.

Overseas Mission (U.S. Embassies and Consulates)

- U.S. Ambassador's chief security advisor
- Counterterrorism
- Counterintelligence and technical security
- Operational supervision of the U.S. Marine detachment
- Operational supervision of a local guard force
- Criminal investigations
- Personnel investigations (security clearances)
- Executive protection
- Special events protection (for example, Olympic Games)
- Protection of U.S. government employees and dependents
- Protection of U.S. government buildings and facilities
- Emergency Action Plan and evacuations
- Protection of classified information

- Construction security manager for diplomatic facilities
- Residential security
- Chair of Overseas Security Advisory Council (OSAC)
- Coordinates Antiterrorism Assistance Program (ATAP) training
- Implements the Rewards for Justice Program, capturing high level fugitives

Domestic Mission

- Criminal investigations (passport and visa fraud)
- Personnel investigations for security clearances
- Special investigations
- Cybercrime investigations
- Executive protection—Secretary of State and visiting dignitaries
- Counterterrorism coordination
- Counterintelligence coordination
- Multifaceted training
- Security research and development

Having worked alongside the DSS special agents that day in Austin, observing their dark suits, dark sunglasses, radio earpieces, and listening to their overseas adventures, I was ready to commit to this unique law enforcement agency.

Just three semesters from completing my Bachelor's degree in education at Texas State University in San Marcos, Texas (President Lyndon B. Johnson's alma mater), I dedicated myself to becoming a member of the DSS, the most intriguing of all U.S. law enforcement agencies. DSS has the greatest global reach and an over-arching mission of providing a safe and secure environment for conducting U.S. foreign policy.

Raised a simple country boy from Manor, Texas, I had been content with being a highway patrolman, raising farm animals, fishing, hunting, and interacting with family and friends. This was the life I knew and the life I enjoyed. However, as I grew older, I felt a sense that there were people, places, and things needing discovery. A desire to spread my wings grew, and I increasingly wanted to fly to greater heights and over new lands. Like Charlie's golden ticket for a tour in *Willy Wonka & the Chocolate Factory*, the DSS recruiting pamphlets proved to be my life-changing ticket.

My time spent at the Diplomatic Security Training Center in Virginia was a long-delayed homecoming of sorts. Several of my family members can be traced back to America's ancient planters who helped settle and lived in and near Jamestown, Virginia, including Captain John Bond. Captain Bond served as a member of Virginia's House of Burgess as well as the sheriff for the Isle of Wight near Jamestown.[6] Who knows, I might somehow be related to 007 Bond—James Bond.

(L–R) General Alfred Gray, USMC Commandant (Ret.), Robert W. Starnes's wife, Pam, and Robert W. Starnes during DSS graduation ceremonies.

Service with the DSS elevated my view to a worldwide perspective and took me to new heights of experiencing unique and diverse cultures that I would never have known by remaining in Texas. I would miss the Governor's Protective Detail, and I hoped to someday give back to DPS for allowing me the opportunity to serve the State of Texas.

While posted overseas as the Regional Security Officer (RSO), DSS have operational command of the Marine Security Guard (MSG) and U.S. Navy Seabees assigned to embassies and consulates assigned to embassies and consulates. To my knowledge, DSS is the only civilian agency, other than the U.S. Commander-in-Chief, exercising direct operational command of active U.S. military units.

People are generally perplexed at how a relatively small U.S. federal law enforcement and security agency has such diverse global impact responsibilities. Partly because the DSS prefers to maintain a low profile and partly because most Americans are unaware of how embassies and consulates operate. Often, when introduced to people unfamiliar with the U.S. Department of State, a typical response received by a DSS agent is, "from what state"?

When the opportunity presented itself, I used the mystique to my advantage. Once, while assigned to the DSS office in Houston, Texas, on a typical Houston mid-morning, I could not help but to gaze at the Wyatt Earp–style handlebar mustache sported by the Houston municipal judge. He intently reviewed the parking ticket dismissal request form that lay before him. Although I received the parking ticket while conducting an official criminal investigation, the City of Houston's parking ticket dismissal process required someone to personally appear before the judge.

"Diplomatic Security Service?" asked the judge in an inquisitive tone. "I have never heard of this agency. Who are the Diplomatic Security Service?" asked the judge.

I nonchalantly responded, "Have you ever heard of the *Men in Black*?"

Reclining back in his leather chair, the judge stared at the ceiling and pondered this statement. Suddenly, a big grin crept across the judge's face. While shaking his head in wonderment, the judge chuckled, signed the ticket dismissal order, and bid me a pleasant ado.

The protocol of assigning executive protective details for all visiting foreign officials requesting entry into the United States is accomplished through diplomatic channels. If a threat analysis deems that protection is warranted, the Department of State determines which protective agency has jurisdiction.

The U.S. Secret Service is responsible for protecting visiting current heads-of-state, while the DSS protects former heads-of-state, official visitors below heads-of-state, and many other official visitors.

DSS excels in executive protection but is often overshadowed by the U.S. Secret Service, fostered by Hollywood movie portrayals and aided by the desire of the DSS to maintain diplomacy by remaining under the radar. In addition to visiting foreign officials, the DSS protects the U.S. Secretary of State domestically and abroad. Internationally, DSS protects U.S. ambassadors, American envoys, and other selected diplomats, oftentimes in postings deemed high in critical threats such as Iraq, Afghanistan, or Libya.

The confusion between the U.S. Secret Service and DSS is prevalent in popular literature and film. While providing protection for a visiting dignitary during a diplomatic reception, author Tom Clancy was approached by a DSS special agent who told the author of an error in his book, *Patriot Games.* In this book, Tom Clancy had written that the U.S. Secret Service protected a British prince during a visit to the United States. The DSS agent explained to the famous author that in real life, the DSS would have protected the visiting prince, not the U.S. Secret Service. A perfectionist, Tom Clancy excelled in accuracy.

In order to correct his error, Tom Clancy made a change in the *Patriot Games* movie adaptation. In the movie, while donning night vision goggles, IRA terrorists attack Jack Ryan's home, killing the protective security detail agents. In this attack scene, Jack Ryan (played by Harrison Ford) picks up an incapacitated agent's radio and calls for any DSS agent to assist.

A DSS special agent shared his experience after watching the *Patriot Games* movie with his wife at a local theater, he mentioned how a woman sitting directly in front of the DSS couple turned to her partner and asked, "What is the DSS?"

The partner confidently replied, "Department of Secret Service." No respect!

In 1996, nearing the completion of a domestic tour-of-duty as a supervisory special agent at the DSS Washington field office, I was offered the Regional Security Officer position at the U.S. Embassy in Asunción, Paraguay. I have always been drawn to Latin America and greatly appreciated an opportunity to serve in South America.

Paraguay, then known within the DSS ranks as a "sleeper post," was supposed to be an easy, laid-back assignment. This assignment

Map of South America, Paraguay highlighted

had become an unwritten award from the DSS Director for my efforts with transitioning the DSS Washington, D.C., field office from a predominately personnel investigative office to an exclusive criminal investigative and executive protection field office. Hours of mentoring newly assigned agents to the world of criminal investigations consisted of seemingly endless surveillances, the art and science of writing arrest and search warrants, and planning complex undercover operations had paid dividends in the way of my onward assignment to Paraguay.

Or so I thought!

THE BUTCHERS, THE TAKERS, AND THE COUP D'ÉAT MAKER

CHAPTER 4

PARAGUAY'S BLACK BERETS

Three other gang members went into action,
demanding the passengers' money and jewelry.

During my pre-departure out-briefings in Washington, D.C., I became increasingly aware that my assignment to Paraguay would be no easy tour-of-duty. I was repeatedly cautioned about the rise of Islamic terrorist operations emanating from Paraguay. The bombs used in the 1992 and 1994 terrorist attacks against the Israeli Embassy and Jewish cultural center in Buenos Aires, Argentina, were suspected of being assembled in Paraguay.

Undeterred by the rising terrorist threats in Paraguay, my wife Pam and I, with our children Jacob, Zachariah, Rachel, and Caleb, departed the safe confines of marble building facades lining the streets of our nation's capital to South America's wild west venue in Asunción, Paraguay.

During my flight from Ronald Reagan Washington Airport to Paraguay, at 30,000 feet above the Atlantic Ocean, I reminisced about my first run-in with an Islamic terrorist wishing to kill Americans.

A few years before my Paraguayan assignment in the late 80s, while investigating passport fraud at the DSS Houston field office,

I was assigned a case based on the fraud indicator of the passport applicant who had attested that he was born in the back seat of a taxi cab en route to the hospital.

This "Einstein" really thought his fantastical story would not generate suspicion.

Many seasoned terrorist groups excel in battle strategy, tactics, and execution. However, cultural misunderstandings and intellectual stretches can sometimes result in blatant missteps and miscalculations. Just like common street criminals, terrorists can become sloppy. Over-thinking their attempt to deceive can easily blow their cover.

Born in Rawalpindi, Pakistan, the subject of my investigation turned out to be a Pakistan Air Force jet fighter pilot who had gained entry into America using his official Pakistani passport containing a U.S. diplomatic visa for the purpose of absenting himself without leave from the Pakistani military. Working as a pizza deliveryman in Houston, this terrorist admitted to offering his services to fly military fighter jets for Saddam Hussein's Iraqi military in order to "kill American soldiers."

When his war offer was rejected by the Iraqis, he applied for and was accepted into the U.S. Army's Airborne. According to the Army's Criminal Investigative Command (CID), the U.S. Army background investigation on this terrorist failed to reveal his true identity and motives to kill Americans. Subsequently, this terrorist was merely two weeks from reporting for active U.S. military duty.

After serving a few months' jail time for passport fraud, this terrorist was deported back to his home in Pakistan.[7] The Pakistani government does not take military desertion lightly. I had heard through the grapevine that the Pakistani defector was eventually court-martialed and executed for his crime of desertion. To my knowledge, this was the first person in the world to have received capital punishment as an indirect result of passport fraud conviction.

The seriousness of this Pakistani terrorist's nearly successful attempt at infiltrating the U.S. Army hits closer to home when, 10 years later, on March 23, 2003, U.S. Army Sergeant Hasan K. Akbar killed two fellow Airborne soldiers and wounded 14 others in a grenade attack in Kuwait while they slept in their tents.[8]

Now, only hours before arriving in Paraguay, the airline captain's voice snapped my attention back to the moment at hand when he instructed passengers to fasten seatbelts in anticipation of inclement weather.

Paraguay gun shop with Nazi memorabilia.

Arriving at the Silvio Pettirossi International Airport in Asunción, Paraguay, I relished the excitement of South American adventures as the large jet engines began powering down. Pam, our four children, and I were happy to be at our destination. The green airport walls provided a governmental, clinical mood. The heat and long wait in the immigration and customs lines were nothing like the systematic yet professional processes back home. Dorothy and Toto were no longer in Kansas.

Although Paraguay has a history of providing refuge for notorious Nazi fugitives, Paraguay is historically pro-American and can trace its high-level ties back to 1878. U.S. President Rutherford B. Hayes negotiated a boundary dispute treaty between Paraguay and Argentina, resulting in Paraguay receiving 60 percent of their current land mass. As a result of the favorable treaty, President Hayes was elevated to hero status, and the largest Paraguayan state is named after the nineteenth U.S. President.

With a total population of less than eight million people, Paraguay is a subtropical nation of diverse landscapes, steeped in a warring history with an obvious tinge of Germanic culture through their foods, Alpine-style architecture, and an occasional question, "Sprechen Sie Deutsche?"

Paraguay's diversity was refreshing. Mennonites had first emigrated from Canada and colonized Paraguay's harsh Chaco (great wilderness) region in the early twentieth century. We observed Mennonite families, many visiting the capital city from Paraguay's hinterlands, wearing traditional farming overalls, cowboy hats, or fedoras. Occasionally you could see horse-drawn trailers amid the hustle and bustle of Asunción's city streets.

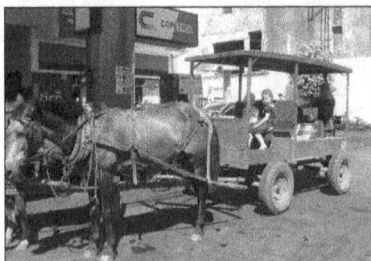
Paraguayan Mennonite children in San Juan Bautista, Paraguay.

We were greeted by three smiling staff members of the U.S. Embassy before loading our baggage onto an embassy cargo van in the mid-afternoon heat. Pam and I shared some anxieties of being so far from home and away from our extended family during our three-year tour to this subtropical, landlocked South American country. Trying to communicate with our taxi cab driver, we spoke in broken Spanish. The cab driver responded to us in Guarani, the local indigenous language. To us, the driver could have easily been speaking a language spoken on Mars. I knew that others may have easily thought the same thing about my accent. It was difficult enough communicating with other Americans with my thick, Texan accent.

Paraguayan riot police surround U.S. embassy in Asuncion.

When I first pulled up to the U.S. Embassy, I noticed armed and physically fit Paraguayan police officers dressed in khaki uniforms wearing German-styled army field hats. They were stationed around the park-like compound, scattered across its fifteen acres where the terra cotta-tiled Chancery building, the U.S. Ambassador's residence, and the Marine Security Guard's detachment's residence were located.

A few days into my assignment, I became aware that Paraguay closely resembled Hollywood's version of living in the Wild West. A U.S. consular officer escorted a young Peace Corps Volunteer (PCV) to an embassy's second-story conference room for a situational interview. At the time, the Peace Corps had assigned 400-plus volunteers in country, making Paraguay the single largest PCV contingency in the world.

Still shaken from his life-threatening event, the young, slender PCV's hand shook when he reached for the glass of water. Taking a deep breath, the PCV began to describe his experience as a crime victim.

The driver of a rickety blue bus, a part of Paraguay's public transportation system, acknowledged a uniformed Paraguayan national police officer. The police officer boarded the bus for the long trip from the hinterlands near the Jesuit Ruins in Itapúa Department to the capital city of Asunción. The once powerful South American Jesuit order was the inspiration for the movie *"The Mission"* starring actor Robert De Niro.

The police officer made his way to the rear of the crowded bus, not realizing that a fellow passenger was a Peace Corps Volunteer who was also traveling to Asunción.

The bus engine consistently whined, as if it were in pain from the grinding floor-mounted stick shift. It bounced and swayed along the rough rural roads. The warm air rushed through the bus windows, relaxing and almost hypnotizing the passengers. The bus driver occasionally broke their trance and down-shifted the gears for a routine passenger pickup stop. At one stop, four young men in their early twenties got on and scattered throughout open seats in the front of the bus and remained quiet.

After traveling several miles down the road, the leader of the four newly arrived passengers stood up, brandishing a handgun, and began yelling at the bus driver, ordering him to stop the bus. A look of fear overtook the startled bus driver's face as he quickly complied and stopped the bus along a grassy embankment.

The three other gang members went into action, demanding the passengers' money and jewelry. Just as the three men began to collect their booty, the gang's leader, still standing beside the bus driver, focused his gaze toward a young man seated along the aisle, several rows behind. For a moment, the gang leader struggled to place the young man. Lost in thought, and in his own wild trance, he connected the face of the young passenger as being the son of the mayor from a nearby town.

The PCV paused and looked at me and the consular officer, before taking another drink of water. After his last gulp, the PCV regained his composure and continued.

Like a scene from a slow-motion horror movie, the driver and passengers sat stunned as they watched the gang's leader walk to the young man, point his aging revolver at the mayor's son's head, and pull the trigger. The gunshot shattered the therapeutic winds of the peaceful drive. The warmth set in heavy as blood spilled. Amid gasps and screams, the young man's body went limp on the floor.

The Paraguayan police officer, who was mentioned by the PCV as entering the bus early on, was taking personal leave to visit family members in Asunción. He removed his revolver from his holster and opened fire at the four gang members. Some passengers immediately hit the floor while others, including the PCV, escaped the "kill zone" by crawling out of a bus window during the height of the shootout.

Paraguay, a financially challenged yet developing country, could not afford to pay for the ammunition of its police officers. Instead, it was up to the police officers to purchase their ammunition and ensure their own firearm proficiency. Fortunately for the other bus passengers, this police officer was quite the marksman.

The bus, leaning slightly from its uneven perch, caused a bit of a distortion as the police officer now faced down the barrels of four handguns aimed directly his way. Within the span of seconds and still maintaining his position at the rear of the bus, the police officer displayed incredible calm and accuracy when he shot three of the assailants, even while being critically wounded himself in the hail of gunfire. Equally stunned at the events that had unfolded, three of the thugs exited the bus while the fourth lay dying on the bus door steps.

The bus driver picked himself off the floor, quickly threw the bus in gear and sped away. Some passengers who had escaped through the windows jumped back onto the moving bus, while others fled the area on foot. Cries from children and mothers now joined the whines of the bus engine. The bus driver drove to a safe distance of about a kilometer down the road. Partly fearful and partly angry, the driver stopped the bus, opened the door, and kicked the wounded gang member out of his bus before driving on to the nearest police station.

The PCV concluded the interview by stating simply, "That police officer saved my and many others' lives."

The police investigation revealed that the gang leader who had murdered the mayor's son and another gang member both died as a result of gunshot wounds. A third robber was found lying under a nearby tree, also wounded by the police officer.

The Paraguayan police officer was rushed to the hospital located directly across the street from the U.S. Embassy in Asunción. On learning of the officer's feat that saved our PCV's life, the Deputy Chief of Mission, the Foreign Service National Investigator, and I visited the injured police officer. The brave man was small and slender with dark black hair and piercing brown eyes. His left arm was wrapped with bulky gauze, and drain tubes and IVs pierced his skin. The police officer was barely strong enough to speak to us. Speaking in Spanish, we thanked and congratulated him for his heroic, life-saving actions.

Politely accepting our gratitude and slightly wincing from pain, the police officer spoke in a weak voice, asking me if I would support him to participate in a police training course sponsored by the DSS Antiterrorism Assistance Program, so that he could join the Paraguay Fuerza de Operaciones Especiales (FOPE).

FOPE? Who or what is FOPE? I thought.

I would later become very well acquainted with FOPE during my three-year tour in Paraguay. This highly trained police unit resembles a military-style Special Forces unit possessing extraordinary tactical skills to address high-risk threats, including counterterrorism.

FOPE members proudly wear distinctive black berets with a black jaguar patch, the rare South American feline representing strength and stealth. The jaguar is the world's only large cat that kills prey by crushing its skull with a devastating bite.

CHAPTER 5

THE CAR BOMB IS ENROUTE

I noticed that the captain jokingly winced
while peering over my shoulder at the passing vehicles
through my office window.

On arriving at the embassy in Asunción one October morning in 1996, the bright American flag fluttered in the soft warm breeze. Paraguay, nestled between Brazil and Argentina, known as the tri-border area (also known as the Triple Frontier), where an aura of corruption permeates the soil, water, and air.

The tri-border has a history of harboring undesirables. At the conclusion of WWII, Schutzstaffel (SS) officer Josef Mengele, known as the "Angel of Death," escaped Nazi Germany and moved to Hohenau, Paraguay, about 145 miles from modern-day Ciudad del Este (city of the east).

While serving as the chief medical officer at Auschwitz concentration camp from 1943

South American tri-border area.

Left: "Angel of Death," (SS) Nazi Josef Mengele. Right: Children survivors of the Auschwitz concentration camp liberation.

to 1945, Joseph Mengele's mission was to establish a master race for Hitler's Third Reich. He was responsible for the deaths of over 1.1 million people, mostly Jews. Mengele's brutalities included injecting dye into children's eyes in an experiment to change eye color, and once ridded a lice outbreak in a cell block by ordering all 750 women to their gaseous death.

While residing in Brazil in 1959, Josef Mengele became a Paraguayan citizen, and temporarily lived in Paraguay[9] under his true name. He enjoyed the protection of Paraguayan President Alfredo Stroessner until his death in 1979.

Ciudad del Este is Paraguay's largest city located within the tri-border. Formerly known as Puerto Alfredo Stroessner, named after Paraguay's dictator of thirty-five years, the city is riddled with corruption. Ciudad del Este is connected to Foz do Iguaçu, Brazil, by the Friendship Bridge spanning the Paraná River. Ciudad del Este is a magnet of commerce and illegal activities, due in part to its trade in tariff-free goods.

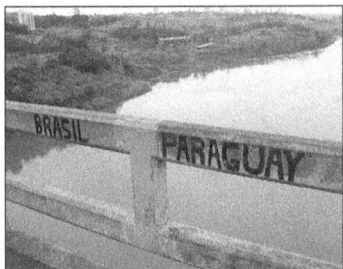

Paraguay and Brazil border on the Friendship Bridge.

The proximity of the tri-border and the U.S. Embassy was of absolute concern to me. "Like Casablanca during WWII, Ciudad del Este is an oasis for informants and spies; peddlers of contraband (largely cheap East Asian goods) and counterfeit products;

Morning view over Ciudad del Este

traffickers in drugs, weapons, and humans (prostitutes, including women and children forced into prostitution); common criminals; mafias; undocumented Arabs; and terrorists."[10]

Ciudad del Este, Paraguay, and Foz do Iguaçu, Brazil, are epicenters of South America's Islamic terrorist support and activities. According to Paraguayan intelligence officials, in 1994 Sayyid Muhammad Hussayn Fadlallah, the spiritual leader of Hezbollah, traveled undercover to Ciudad del Este on an Iranian passport to bless the local mosque.

Moreover, as reported by the Brazilian newspaper *O Estado de S. Paulo*, the Brazilian intelligence services, Agência Brasileira de Inteligência (ABIN), there was evidence that Osama bin Laden himself visited Ciudad del Este in 1995. During his three-day stay he purportedly met with the members of the Arab community in the city's mosque, where he talked about his experience in the Afghan war against the Soviet Union.

Khalid Sheikh Mohammed, formerly the third-highest ranking member of al-Qaeda (captured by the United States in Rawalpindi,

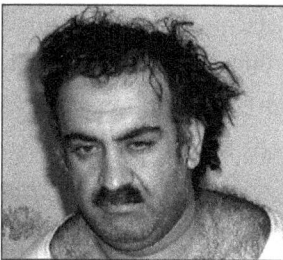

Left: Khalid Sheikh Mohammed. Right: Osama bin Laden

Pakistan, in March 2003) and believed to have been the organization's treasurer, had reportedly spent about 20 days in Foz do Iguaçu, the Brazilian sister city of Ciudad del Este. According to Brazilian Federal Police and the Brazilian section of Interpol, Khalid Sheikh Mohammed entered Brazil on December 4, 1995, as a tourist with a Pakistani passport (though he himself is a Kuwaiti national) through Aeroporto Internacional de Guarulhos. He left on December 24 for Holland from the Aeroporto do Galeao en Rio de Janeiro.[11]

On March 17, 1992, a car parked in front of the Israeli Embassy in Buenos Aires exploded, killing 29 people and injuring 250. Two years later, on July 18, 1994, also in Buenos Aires, another car bomb attack almost destroyed the Jewish-Argentine community center building (Asociación Mutual Israelita Argentina, AMIA), killing 87 people and injuring more than 200. Both attacks have at least two characteristics in common. Evidence in both cases, including an intercepted telephone call from the Iranian Embassy in Argentina, confirmed the attacks were carried out by Hezbollah.[12]

Secondly, the thread in both cases followed by the investigators led them to the area from which the attacks were staged in Ciudad del Este, Paraguay.[13]

Of specific concern to U.S. national security, the U.S. Embassy in Asunción, Paraguay, was the closest American diplomatic presence to the tri-border and Ciudad del Este. The security office was severely understaffed, especially in light of its close proximity to the tri-border and the radical terrorists that supported their livelihood of hate from this lawless area.

The U.S. Embassy's security program in Paraguay consisted of a small U.S. Marine Security Guard detachment, a well-trained unarmed local guard force headed by Joe Bibb, a retired U.S. Green Beret Sergeant Major, a locally hired Foreign Service National Investigator, and two Paraguayan police officers assigned to protect the U.S. Ambassador. In addition, dozens of uniformed Paraguayan police officers, of which the embassy reimbursed the police department via a monthly stipend, were assigned to protect the embassy's outer perimeter.

Acclimating to the overwhelming workload, I was determined to upgrade the embassy's physical, technical, and procedural security posture and enhance emergency reaction planning, especially in light of Paraguay's near successful coup detat in 1996. The coup was purportedly orchestrated by the small but fiery former Paraguayan general, Lino Oviedo. This attempted coup had resulted in serious threats against the staff assigned to the U.S. Embassy.

Only three weeks into my assignment to Paraguay, I had received a routine criminal passport fraud investigative lead from the DSS Chicago field office, requesting assistance to locate a fugitive using the alias of Ibrahim Malmood Awethe, who had a Paraguayan connection.

When processing a criminal investigative lead at an embassy, it is routine to check records with compartmentalized databases with various U.S. agencies assigned to that specific mission. On being buzzed into the embassy's counterterrorism analytic office, I inquired from the division chief if he would conduct a database check for the subject of my investigative lead, Ibrahim Malmood Awethe. I laid a copy of the passport application and the fugitive's passport photograph on his desk.

Imposter Ibrahim Malmood Awethe

The photograph was of a middle-aged man, thinning hair, full face and large nose with a serious and nervous look on his face. Picking up the photograph, the division chief's eyes widened as if he had seen a ghost. Recognizing the passport photograph of the person claiming to be Ibrahim Malmood Awethe, the division chief stated, "Oh s**t, that's the same guy who is planning to bomb the embassy!"

What were the odds? The criminal fugitive sought by DSS in Chicago was the same terrorist planning to bomb our embassy in Paraguay. Startled, it took me a few seconds to absorb this new revelation, especially since RSO's primary congressionally mandated responsibility while serving abroad is to protect U.S. diplomats and diplomatic facilities.

After a "come to Jesus meeting" of jurisdictions for protection of U.S. diplomatic interests, the counterterrorism division chief quickly made a secure telephone call to his headquarters. Based on his apparent one-sided conversation, I deduced his superiors ordered him to cooperate. Hanging up the telephone, the chief relented and shared his cards. The division chief explained how a team of known Shia Islamic terrorists, mostly from Lebanon's Al Beqa'a Valley (30 miles east of Beirut), had recently arrived to Paraguay's tri-border area and were planning to bomb the United States Embassy and/or Israeli Embassy in Asunción.

Our fugitive had operated under multiple identities throughout the world, including Marwan al-Safadi, Marwan Adnan al-Qadi, and Ibrahim Malmood Awethe. At this time, the U.S. government believed his true identity to be Marwan Abid Adam Kadi.

Adding to his radical Islamic terrorist credentials, Marwan al-Safadi was serving a nine-year sentence in Canada for smuggling drugs from Brazil (the precise details of which are unavailable in the open source). Finally, with the help of Hezbollah elements in that area, al-Safadi escaped from a prison in Montreal and fled to South America with a false U.S. passport[14] in the name of Ibrahim Malmood Awethe.

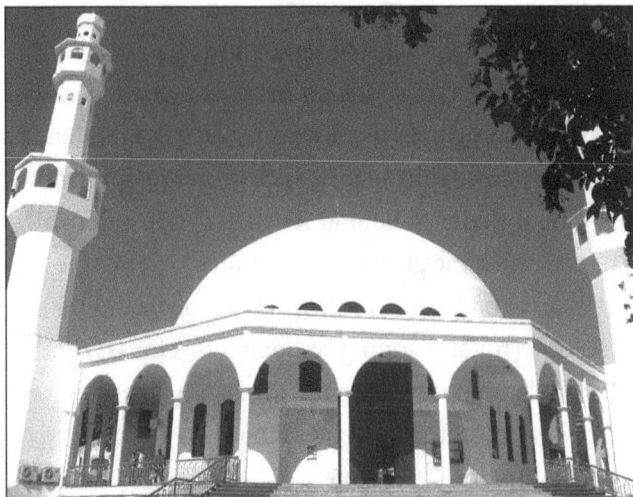

Foz do Iguaçu, Brazil.

In 1996, the Brazilian Federal Police discovered the Lebanese explosives expert Marwan al-Safadi, who participated in the 1993 World Trade Center attack in New York, also resided in the tri-border in the 1990s (*Epoca-O'Globo,* Rio de Janeiro, 2006).[15]

Marwan al-Safadi was eventually arrested by Brazilian authorities for possession of cocaine before escaping custody and fleeing across the border to Ciudad del Este. Asked about the alleged bombing plot, Robert Service, U.S. Ambassador to Paraguay stated, "there was enough corroborating information to suggest that there was a plan against the U.S. Embassy." Service, who retired after completing his tour of duty as U.S. ambassador to Paraguay, said U.S. concerns about the presence of Islamic terrorist groups in the Iguazu area "was one of the considerations" behind President Clinton and the First Lady's decision not to visit Iguazu in October 1996.[16]

Whatever identity he chose to use, Marwan al-Safadi was suspected of leading a violent Iranian Shiite-sponsored terrorist group. He was a bad man, with a bad past, who undoubtedly harbored bad intentions against the Western powers, including a planned attack against our embassy to coincide with the first anniversary of the bombing of the Saudi National Guard headquarters in Riyadh, Saudi Arabia.[17]

The United States and Israel suspected Marwan al-Safadi's initiated threat was made against facilities of both nations.[18] Believed to be working for an organization that belongs to the shadowy network of terrorist organizations sponsored by Iran, such as Hezbollah, a U.S. Department of State statement warned of al-Safadi's plans for an attack against American targets in Paraguay.

A suspected Lebanese bomb-maker, believed to have lost a hand in a bomb-making accident in the Middle East, had been identified as a member of Marwan al-Safadi's attack team, now hiding in Paraguay's tri-border.

While working a late night at the embassy, flipping my government-issued cellular phone open, I detected anxiety in the caller's voice.

The embassy's counterterrorism chief desperately proclaimed, "The bomb is on the road and en route to the embassy!"

Although the intelligence about the imminent car bomb attack proved to be a false alarm, time was of the essence to neutralize the threat. The U.S. government knew Marwan al-Safadi and his collaborators were in Paraguay, and would soon carry out pre-attack surveillance leading to a car bomb attack against our embassy.

In times of crisis, when counterterrorist resources are needed at embassies and consulates, RSOs turn to the DSS Mobile Security Division (DSS commando force). These highly trained special agents have served as embassy security officers during their career, greatly assisting them with understanding the foreign diplomatic environment. Due to limited staff availability as a result of terrorism fires ignited throughout the world, headquarters was unable to provide a DSS Mobile Security Division. Given the Mobile Security team's advanced counterterrorism capabilities and experiences working in and around diplomatic facilities, their unavailability was especially disheartening.

It was during this crisis that I became acquainted with FOPE on a firsthand basis. During the initial moments of this terrorist crisis, FOPE deployed their counterterrorism specialists and bomb detection unit around the U.S. Embassy, 24 hours a day. Dressed in their khaki police uniforms with machine guns draped from their necks, FOPE created a foreboding, ninja-type, Special Forces visual deterrent that played a key role of enhancing our outer layer of protection during this crisis.

During a U.S. Embassy Emergency Action Committee (EAC) meeting chaired by the Ambassador, I shared the unwelcome news of the unavailability of the DSS Mobile Security team. Understanding my predicament of operating with limited American law enforcement support, after the meeting, the embassy's U.S. Military Liaison Officer (MLO), a full-bird Special Forces colonel with significant military accomplishments—including exhibiting extraordinary leadership during the U.S. invasion of Panama—Operation Just Cause—stopped by my office and made an offer I could not refuse.

The MLO colonel politely offered to re-assign an elite U.S. military unit that was on a training mission for the Paraguayan military, directly under my operational command during this crisis. How does one truly thank another for placing such a powerful and accomplished elite unit under my command? I humbly accepted.

In light of their grueling jungle training and advanced survival skills, U.S. Special Forces have earned the nickname of "snake-eaters."

I now commanded security assets that included the Marine Security Guard detachment and a platoon of elite "snake-eating" U.S. Army soldiers. For hours, this U.S. Army team and I devised surveillance detection and counter-attack strategies. The unit was commanded by an energetic captain from Washington state. The captain shared that his rite of passage to manhood was achieved when his dad rubbed bear's blood on his face from his first bear kill in the great Northwest. The captain's positive attitude and excitement of overcoming dangers and challenges was contagious.

Rarely have I seen—let alone led—a group of dedicated men who never once complained about surveilling from positions within

U.S. Embassy in Asunción, Paraguay.

parked vehicles where the heat exceeded 110+ degrees Fahrenheit in the subtropical environment. Resembling the television series *The A-Team*, this elite military unit and I created concealed elevated building-top observation points on the embassy compound from which to spot any suspicious activity or a perceived car bomb attack. Any surveillance detected of the hostile terrorist group would be captured on government-owned video surveillance cameras. This would be essential in order to provide much-needed evidence for criminal prosecution that would hopefully lead to the capture and aid in our disruption efforts.

I secured approval from the Paraguayan police to post a wrecker tow truck 24/7 near the embassy. The wrecker truck might be able to quickly react and remove a suspected car bomb from the embassy's building structure located close to a heavily-traveled public roadway. Unfortunately for me, the closest building to the public road happened to be my office.

I remember the U.S. Army captain attending a morning briefing in my office. I noticed that the captain jokingly winced while peering over my shoulder at the passing vehicles through my office window. When asked about his jittery demeanor, the captain responded light-heartedly about our vulnerability of a car bomb if detonated near my office. I encouraged the captain to put on his bear-hunting face, noting that in the event of a car bomb attack outside my office, he would not feel a thing.

Although we had received general information that Marwan al-Safadi's terrorist team was located in Ciudad del Este, I presumed the terrorists would conduct pre-attack surveillance prior to detonating a car bomb in front of our embassy. Based on this premise, my surveillance detection plan was simple: identify the terrorists and collect photographic evidence during their most vulnerable state of pre-attack surveillance, to be used for their prosecution in U.S. courts.

The counter-attack strategy was a bit more complex. In the event that sources and methods employed by intelligence agencies were

Market in Ciudad del Este, Paraguay.

unsuccessful in neutralizing a planned attack against the embassy, the final backstop option for the U.S. Embassy security team would likely be armed intervention on possibly very short notice. We might have only seconds to attempt to neutralize the terrorists before they could detonate a car bomb targeted for our embassy. One huge advantage working in our favor was the fact that the terrorists had lost their element of surprise. They did not know that we knew of their presence and motive.

Tensions remained high as the crisis twice escalated to the point of deploying the Marine Security Guard detachment along with the U.S. Army unit augmentation in counter-attack roles. I received two false alarms based on inaccurate source intelligence that the terrorist car bomb was on the road and en route to the embassy.

Ramping up to a state of high alert for the false alarms, not knowing the terrorists' exact whereabouts or their time of attack, the minutes passed like hours. After a few days had passed, based on assessments by intelligence experts, the embassy finally received reliable information of the terrorist's location in Ciudad del Este.

The U.S. Embassy security team and Paraguayan police assigned to counter this threat needed two additional days to prepare to disable the terrorist network. At this moment in time, the U.S. Presidential election between incumbent President Bill Clinton and Republican Senator Bob Dole of Kansas was only a few weeks away. Given the high political anxieties, the Deputy Chief of Mission informed me that the White House had directly instructed our embassy assets to request the host government to immediately disrupt Marwan al-Safadi and his terrorist group. Working with the Paraguayan police's counter-terrorism unit, truck-loads of police officers were transported to Ciudad del Este under the cover of darkness to execute multiple search warrants.

Infiltrating trusted sources within the tight-knit Arab community in Ciudad del Este proved to be quite difficult. Information about the planned police raids had mysteriously leaked the following day, resulting in the disbanding of Marwan al-Safadi and his terrorist group into the tri-border's murky nooks and crannies.

The Paraguayan police quickly established road blocks around Ciudad del Este. I was momentarily stunned when I received the dreaded news that a retired Paraguayan military colonel had collaborated with al-Safadi by donning his former Paraguayan army uniform and smuggled al-Safadi through police road blocks.

Marwan al-Safadi had again escaped!

The Paraguayan police raid of the apartment used by al-Safadi in Ciudad del Este discovered it filled with explosives, pistols equipped with silencers, double-barreled rifles, false Canadian and U.S. passports, and a large amount of cash.[19]

U.S. Embassy personnel remained on edge, knowing that a nasty scorpion was on the loose. Did al-Safadi and his band of killers still possess the capability to attack our embassy? Where was the car bomb? Might the terrorists change their bombing plans to an assassination plot? These were the protective security questions I posed during the aftermath of al-Safadi's most recent escape.

A team of DSS agents from the United States were dispatched to Asunción to supplement my security program. Special agent Michael Hudspeth of the DSS Protective Intelligence Investigations (PII) was a member of this much-welcomed team. Special Agent Hudspeth, a DSS investigative legend, provided me with valuable cloak-and-dagger support for several off-site meetings with confidential informants in an effort to locate al-Safadi and disrupt an attack. Agent Hudspeth excelled in blending into the local environment while positioning himself for rapid reaction in the event our security posture was compromised.

Paraguay police captures suspected terrorist Mar-wan al-Safadi.

A few days later, the Paraguayan police developed intelligence that al-Safadi was hiding only two blocks from the U.S. Embassy, in the residence owned by the retired Paraguayan colonel who had facilitated al-Safadi's escape.

FOPE officers surrounded and locked down the retired colonel's stately residence until a court-ordered search warrant was obtained. The law enforcement–secured perimeter came as a complete surprise to al-Safadi and his retired colonel collaborator. On finally receiving the arrest and search warrants from the judge, Marwan al-Safadi, an accomplished prison escape artist, peacefully surrendered himself to the custody of FOPE. Wearing blue jeans and a short-sleeved collared shirt, Marwan al-Safadi was escorted under heavy police protection to court appearances.

Extraditions can sometimes drag out for a year or more. Given al-Safadi's track record of escaping from Canadian and Brazilian prisons, I was hoping to avoid a lengthy extradition for al-Safadi's return to the United States. Fortunately, the Paraguayan government agreed to expel al-Safadi from Paraguay to the custody of DSS agents. A U.S. Air Force C-141 airlifter, in-country on an unrelated military mission, was parked on the tarmac at Paraguay's airport. The Department of State's coun-

Paraguayan police securely transports Marwan al-Safadi to DSS custody.

terterrorism staff office authorized payment of $25,000 to the U.S. Department of Defense to keep the aircraft in Paraguay for an additional day in order to transport al-Safadi to the United States.

I traveled to the airport to ensure the U.S. Air Force pilots were clear on their change of orders to stay in-country for an additional day. While briefing the pilots, I noticed several elderly, retired U.S. military veterans who were on board the aircraft as vacationing "jump flight" passengers. These men seemed excited about the evolving security situation. However, their excitement quickly turned to disappointment on learning that they would be required to sleep inside the aircraft for the night while awaiting the arrival of a dangerous terrorist passenger.

After receiving a Paraguayan presidential decree, Marwan al-Safadi was transferred to United States custody. The sun hung low when DSS agent Michael Hudspeth and I escorted al-Safadi, under heavy police protection led by FOPE, onto the fueled and waiting U.S. military aircraft. I retreated to the tarmac and watched the large Air Force transporter lift off the runway and fly toward Brazil. Once the plane entered international air space, Marwan al-Safadi, still suffering from

DSS agents and Paraguayan police escort Marwan al-Safadi to awaiting U.S. military aircraft.

a wrist injury sustained during his dramatic Brazilian helicopter-aided prison escape, received his *Miranda* warnings from DSS Special Agent Hudspeth.

While on the tarmac in Brazil during a refueling layover, a determined Brazilian government official serving with the equivalent rank of the FBI Director requested permission from the DSS RSO assigned to the U.S. Embassy in Brasília to board the U.S. Air Force plane to speak with al-Safadi, the man who embarrassed his government by escaping from his prison. Sharing an excellent relationship, this high-ranking Brazilian officer assured the RSO and Special Agent Hudspeth that he would not interfere in the prisoner's escort rendition and jokingly stated he would not shoot the prisoner.

With the Air Force pilot's permission, the Brazilian official boarded the aircraft, leaving his large security entourage on the tarmac. The official walked up to al-Safadi, wagged his index finger in his face, and emphatically stated that once the Americans and Canadians were finished with him, Brazil would be waiting next in line. According to Special Agent Hudspeth, al-Safadi fidgeted and appeared quite uncomfortable during the Brazilian official's chastisement.

In the grand scheme, it sometimes becomes more important to protect highly valuable, irreplaceable sources than to seek prosecution for specific crimes. In lieu of risking the cover of informants, the difficulty of proving the elements for a terrorist conviction, and years of unserved prison sentences in Canada and Brazil, the United States government chose to prosecute al-Safadi for passport fraud charges only.

Marwan al-Safadi was eventually sentenced to 8 months in federal prison for the U.S. passport fraud case.[20] After serving his time in the U.S., al-Safadi was deported to Canada, where he was sent to serve the remainder of his Canadian sentence.

CHAPTER 6

THE BARBIE EFFECT

Within minutes, the mobster was singing like a fat canary.

L ooking directly at Pedro Martinez, I said, "No way will we find him." Pedro was the U.S. Embassy's Foreign Service National Investigator (FSNI) assigned to the Regional Security Office (RSO) in Asunción, Paraguay.

I had just received a criminal investigative lead from DSS headquarters in Washington, D.C., by way of the U.S. Marshal's Service. This lead instructed my office to liaise with the Paraguayan national police to locate, arrest, and extradite William Fourie, a 48-year-old South African native who had jumped bail from the Federal District Court in Austin, Texas.

Pedro Martinez, Foreign Service National Investigator

Mr. Fourie was a seasoned criminal. In 1987, Mr. Fourie, unlicensed to trade or export rough diamonds, was previously convicted in South Africa for illegally dealing in raw diamonds. There are laws aimed at curbing the violent diamond trade, sometimes referred to as "conflict" or "blood" diamonds.

I thought it coincidental how I had just traveled some 4,600 miles from my previous assignment in Texas to Paraguay, only to locate a fugitive from Texas!

William Fourie was indicted in 1997 on U.S. federal charges ranging from money laundering to wire fraud, to misuse of travel documents, all revolving around financial crimes of bilking millions of dollars from at least 32 victimized individuals and businesses throughout the United States, Switzerland, and Malaysia. His main *modus operandi* used against his victims was to offer security-backed loans and investing clientele monies while promising 200 percent returns.

Based on Mr. Fourie committing U.S. immigration fraud and relying on her own experiences and intuition as a seasoned federal prosecutor, Assistant U.S. Attorney (AUSA) Lilly Travis pleaded with the federal district judge to deny bail for Mr. Fourie on the basis that he presented a flight risk. Failing to grasp Lilly Travis' concerns that Mr. Fourie was a flight risk, the presiding federal judge ordered Mr. Fourie held pending a $100,000 bond.

Posing as a jet-setting cardiac surgeon, Mr. Fourie conned his new fiancé of three weeks, maxed out her credit card at $30,000, and convinced his fiancé's parents and his ex-wife to put up their homes as bond collateral to secure his release. Adding icing to his cake, Mr. Fourie had gotten the phone number of

William Fourie

an Austin businesswoman from a cellmate, and he convinced her to pay for his attorney fees. Mr. Fourie was indeed a con man's con man.

Mr. Fourie sent the Austin-based federal judge a letter requesting he be allowed to withdraw his previous guilty plea against these charges, accusing his "faulty lawyers"; he also accused his co-defendant, Ms. Lydia Kennedy, of functioning as a CIA operative and pretending to be related to the famous Kennedy family. The federal judge responded, "It astonishes me that a person with your intellect would go to such extremes to make such outlandish claims."

Assistant U.S. Attorney Travis' flight risk hunch proved to be right on the mark. On June 15, 1998, on the day of his trial, William Fourie failed to appear, and two days later, his vehicle was found abandoned near the border town of Laredo, Texas. Using his corrupt powers of persuasion, Mr. Fourie had swayed the U.S. federal district judge to discount AUSA Travis' motion for no bond. Mr. Fourie had notched another victim on his belt. This time it was a federal judge.

The U.S. Marshals Service's Fugitive Task Force went into action and unfurled an electronic dragnet over Mr. Fourie's world. Shortly after his disappearance, Mr. Fourie called his fellow friend in crime who was living in the Philippines. This friend collaborated with Fourie's flight from justice by holding two phones together, mouth piece to ear piece, in order to conceal the locations of Fourie's initiated contacts. Similar to Pablo Escobar, Colombia's former drug cartel leader, Mr. Fourie became complacent, dropped his guard, and compromised his concealment. Mr. Fourie began directly calling the bail bondsman who had put up the money for his release.

Fourie's location was still unknown, but he was now back on the grid. Mr. Fourie's lax attitude allowed the U.S. Marshals Service to intercept a telephone call he had made to the Hotel Cecilia in Asunción, Paraguay. The Marshals' meager investigative lead to my office in Paraguay consisted only of a single telephone number for the Hotel Cecilia.

In a "glass-is-half-empty" state of mind, I thought this lead would quickly fizzle. I believed that short of a significant injection of financial resources, technology, and expertise, the Paraguayan police were ill-equipped to locate a seasoned and elusive international fugitive.

Pedro Martinez's national pride was partially wounded by my negative attitude about his nation's police force. He was now doubly motivated to prove me wrong.

After finishing a lunchtime plate of chicken schnitzel, Pedro Martinez and I made our way to the Hotel Cecilia. Pedro parked along the busily traveled downtown street named *United States*. The six-story, pale-yellow rectangular hotel building reminded me of a bird cage that sat on several exposed concrete columns.

Hotel Cecilia

The Hotel Cecilia was managed by a Paraguayan of Germanic descent. I provided the hotel's general manager William Fourie's name and a range of dates. The general manager disappeared for a moment, and to my amazement, he returned with a drawerful of neatly organized index cards. Thumbing through the index cards, within seconds, the hotel manager produced a three-by-five dog-eared reservation check-in card, yellowed from age. The card listed our fugitive's name along with the name of the local Paraguayan citizen who had made the hotel reservation.

A slight smile grew on Pedro's face as he confidently proclaimed William Fourie was as good as captured.

Although pleasantly surprised at the hotel's record-keeping efficiency, I was still a "doubting Thomas." After all, we had merely collected the name of another stranger whose participation with Mr. Fourie was stale. I struggled with the dilemma of just how much time I should spend on locating an internationally elusive fugitive when priority number one was countering terror threats against our embassy.

During the return trip to the embassy, I meditated on this newly discovered stranger, Fourie's accomplice. Who and where is this elusive stranger who had collaborated with our fugitive to secure his lodging months earlier? Had he also disappeared to remote corners of the Earth? Several days had passed as Pedro and I waited for a response from the Paraguayan police investigator to identify that all-elusive hotel reservation-maker.

On a sultry subtropical day, just before lunchtime, on September 1, 1998, with a serious gaze, Pedro Martinez looked me straight in the eyes. His stoic look quickly turned into a broad smile. Pedro excitedly announced that the person who had made the hotel registration for Mr. Fourie had been identified, located, and was being detained by the Paraguayan police. Wow! I was truly impressed. The police investigator scheduled a meeting with Pedro and me for later that day.

Pedro and I drove to a police building located not far from the U.S. Embassy in Asunción. The Paraguayan police investigator divulged that the detained man who had collaborated with our fugitive was known to be a small-time mobster involved in petty crimes and small-time confidence scams throughout South America. The police investigator informed us that the mobster was claiming ignorance as to the whereabouts of William Fourie.

In order to initiate psychological tactics against the detainee, the police investigator asked me to enter the holding cell, walk up to the jail bars, and look the mobster from head-to-toe while shaking my head in an affirmative action. The investigator was confident that the sight of an American diplomat would implant fears of CIA involvement in the mobster's mind.

I marveled at the advanced Paraguayan police tactics of using a spy-type "bad cop" fear against a suspect to achieve a positive outcome. How could a small police agency have such forward-thinking officers? I followed the investigator's instructions to the letter.

The caged mobster resembled a Hollywood movie character. His dark, greasy black hair was slicked straight back. His eye sockets were dark and sunken deep into his skull. He wore a dark, pin-striped suit and sported a mean and frightening expression.

On seeing me enter the room, the mobster quickly arose from his jail cell's bed. Before walking to the steel bars that separated us, I spoke English loud enough for the mobster to deduce that I was an American from the U.S. Embassy. I made my way to the jail bars, stopped, looked the mobster up and down, nodded my head in the affirmative, and promptly departed the room.

Within minutes, the mobster was singing like a fat canary.

Several days later, I learned that the police station used to detain this criminal thug was actually a very prominent building that was historically used by security forces to torture political prisoners during the Alfredo Stroessner dictatorship era. Born to German immigrants, this Paraguayan dictator brutally ruled from 1954 to 1989 as an anti-communist.

World War II Gestapo SS officer, Klaus Barbie

Just a half-century prior, Stoessner hired the infamous former World War II Gestapo SS officer, Klaus Barbie, as his nation's anti-communist security consultant. Known as the "Butcher of Lyon" during his Nazi assignment to France, Klaus Barbie perfected his skills of torture. These included: needles under the fingernails; bone-breaking sessions by repeatedly slamming a door on knuckles; screw-levered handcuffs that cut through flesh when tightened; hanging prisoners from the ceiling; near drownings in bathtubs filled with ice-cold water; performing mock executions; breaking a spine with a spiked ball; and multiple beatings leaving a prisoner's face an unrecognizable pulp.[21]

A U.S. Embassy Foreign Service National employee shared how as a child, she would sometimes hear loud music emanating from this same building in an unsuccessful attempt to drown out tortured screams. To this day, this same employee walks several blocks out of her way in order to avoid close proximity to this building. It still evokes fear in her, as well as the older generation of Paraguayans who are haunted by Paraguay's turbulent history.

During a brief respite, Pedro Martinez, now in his fifties, proudly showed me a black-and-white photograph of himself leading his army detachment as the unit's flag bearer during a military parade when he was a younger man. Viewing the military units as they passed their elevated perch, Stroessner and Chilean President Augusto José Ramón Pinochet Ugarte are clearly visible in this memory of Pedro's past. Pedro said that although his father served as an Army colonel during Stroessner's era, he no longer had access to Stroessner, who was living in exile in Brazil after his government's 1989 overthrow in a violent coup d'état led by Stroessner's friend and confidant of 35 years, General Andrés Rodríguez.

Proud of his military service to his country, Pedro asked if I might be able to use my DSS magic and help him contact the former dictator to autograph his prized photograph. Wanting to do Pedro a favor, I contacted the DSS RSO in Brasília, Brazil, to determine if he would be able to send a runner to get the autograph for Pedro. The United States

Pedro Martinez army military parade.

had confronted Stroessner for years over suspected human rights violations, and RSO Brasília responded that due to the political sensitivities, an American diplomat seen conversing with ex-President and dictator Stroessner could easily cause a political dust-up.

I knew there had to be another way to skin this cat. I had become acquainted with retired Paraguayan Colonel Estanislao Lesme Martinez, who formerly served as Stroessner's chief of security. After his retirement, Colonel Lesme became an ordained Christian pastor. I asked Colonel Lesme if he continued to stay in contact with Stroessner. He responded that he had not, but he did see Stroessner's daughter on occasion. I asked the retired colonel if he would pass along Pedro's photograph to Stroessner's daughter who could in turn pass it to the former Paraguayan president during her next trip to Brazil. Colonel Lesme gladly agreed.

Several months later, while I was on personal leave, retired colonel Estanislao Lesme Martinez visited the embassy to drop off the autographed photograph for Pedro. During Stroessner's reign, the mere mention of the name of Colonel Lesme evoked fear, in a similar way that Heinrich Himmler's name evoked fear during WWII. The embassy's Marine Security Guard called and informed Pedro that the colonel was in the visitor's lobby and wanted to talk to him. Pedro later jokingly shared how his heart stopped beating on learning that Stroessner's ex-chief of security wanted to speak with him. Although appreciative of my assistance with attaining Stroessner's autographed photograph, Pedro said my act of kindness may have shaved off a few years of his life.

Paraguay had come a long way from the earlier torture years to psychological police tactics. The interrogators achieved complete disclosure of our fugitive Fourie's location. No waterboarding, no electric shocks, no rubber hose beatings. Police-initiated psychological operations carried the day. Within a few hours, the mobster broke his silence and revealed that he was harboring William Fourie in a garage apartment next to his modest single-story personal residence located near FOPE's headquarters building. If the mobster was aware of that building's history, it would be enough to get him talking.

On September 5, 1998, the Paraguayan police entry team arrived, busted through the apartment door, and arrested Mr. Fourie. In order to minimize unwanted public notoriety of American involvement, I intentionally remained in the shadows during the raid. One Paraguayan police officer received medical attention when the mobster's wife, who appeared to be on a "concubine loan" to Mr. Fourie, sunk her finger-nails deep into his lower lip, causing tissue damage.

The police seized Fourie's South African passport, two Brazilian identification cards with different aliases, fourteen credit cards, sixteen computer disks, and a 12-gauge shotgun. Weighing almost 300 pounds, William Fourie did not resist and was promptly transported to the infamous Tacumbú Prison to await his formal extradition to the United States.

Tacumbú Prison

An entire book can be written about Tacumbú Prison. I had pre-viously visited Tacumbú Prison with a Bostonian Christian missionary on Sunday. Its courtyard resembled something out of the Mayberry jail from television's *The Andy Griffith Show*. Family visitors were allowed to bring potluck dinners and mingle with all the prisoners inside the prison's courtyard. An entire prison wing was dedicated to transvestites.

Prison guards managed an on-site hotel room used for conjugal visits. Of course, only the prisoners who could meet the prison guards' high financial rates were allowed access to Tacumbú Prison's hotel room. What a wild place!

I profusely thanked the Paraguayan police officers for locating the mobster who was aiding our fugitive, and for the raid that captured Mr. Fourie. In essence, pulling off a seemingly impossible locate and arrest.

However, my elation would be short-lived.

Charlie, a fellow Texan from Houston, was the ranking U.S. consular officer at the embassy. Charlie asked me if I would be interested in accompanying him to the Tacumbú Prison for his weekly visit to American citizen prisoners. Always open for an adventure, I agreed, under the proviso that Charlie allow me to check in on Mr. Fourie.

Prison guards escorted Charlie and me into a small, dark room used as a prisoner visitation room. It took me a few minutes to comprehend Fourie's appearance. The once portly fugitive had lost about 100 pounds. Due to his prison-initiated diet, Mr. Fourie sported an active, wrinkled dewlap that hung low and jiggled when he spoke. Somewhat subdued, the South African asked Charlie Smith if he would mind bringing him flea repellent during his next prison visit as his body was being eaten up by the Paraguayan parasites. It's ironic how a bloodsucker can feed on another bloodsucker. Frankly, I felt greater compassion for the prison fleas.

A prison escape by Fourie weighed heavy on my mind since the infamous February 28, 1998 violent prison break of over half the inmate population at the Emboscada maximum security prison about 45 minutes from Asunción. So serious was this Emboscada prison break, the entire embassy staff was placed on lockdown, pending the success of the police and military roundup of over 100 violent convicted criminals.

On December 31, 1998, while awaiting extradition to the United States, William Fourie purportedly conned two Tacumbú prison guards with the promise of rich financial payments. With the prison guards'

Paraguay Police arrest three escapees from the Emboscada Prison.

aid, William Fourie simply walked out of the prison's front gates. Now on the lam, intelligence was developed that Mr. Fourie was planning to sneak out of Asunción via the public bus transportation system. I mischievously thought how fitting it would be for Mr. Fourie to catch the infamous blue bus previously used by the Peace Corps Volunteer.

Pedro and I accompanied the Paraguayan police in a stakeout of the main bus terminal. On January 4, 1999, wearing a long-sleeve shirt and blue jean pants, just like clockwork, Mr. Fourie shuffled into the bus terminal, to the ticket booth, and finally into the waiting arms of the Paraguayan police. William Fourie was returned to Tacumbú Prison, minus the two prison guards who had been relieved of their duties for collaborating in Mr. Fourie's escape.

In a fortuitous move by the prison warden, Mr. Fourie's new cellmate was a recently captured mega-mobster from Argentina possessing equally advanced con skills as Mr. Fourie. The Paraguayan government became increasingly embarrassed when the local press began reporting that Mr. Fourie and his jail mate were operating criminal scams from prison using their cell phones. After several

Bus terminal in Asunción

months passed, the prison warden intercepted information that William Fourie was attempting to bribe a Paraguayan Supreme Court clerk to "misplace" his extradition file in order to buy him time to plan another prison escape.

According to the prison warden, William Fourie and his mega-mobster cellmate had organized a protest of 200+ inmates in the prison yard to object to previously unwarranted security crackdown. This planned protest was believed to have served as a distraction for another escape by Mr. Fourie. William Fourie must have thought his stars were again aligning.

By now, William Fourie had worn out his Paraguayan welcome. He had become a national liability. The Paraguayan president, embarrassed by the havoc this South African fugitive had caused his government, accelerated the fugitive's extradition and ordered him removed to the United States. Another big-time viper destined for a Texas terrarium.

To secure Mr. Fourie from a third escape plan leading to his formal extradition, I devised a two-option strategy: 1. Transport Fourie to the U.S. Embassy, where Pedro Martinez and I would secure the fugitive for a few nights until we could arrange his transportation to the United States, or 2. ask the host government to transfer custody of Fourie from the Tacumbú Prison to the loyal, trusted FOPE anti-terrorism police unit. The Paraguayan police chief agreed to option number two. I slept well that night knowing FOPE was in charge of securing Mr. Fourie.

In early June 1998, U.S. Deputy Marshals Darren Sartin and Craig Slack arrived in Asunción, via commercial air carrier, to escort William Fourie back to Austin. Due to airline regulations, returning William Fourie to Texas on a commercial airline was not an option. This circumstance left only one choice: a U.S. government aircraft would be needed for this human cargo.

Instead of having the U.S. Marshals charter an expensive aircraft to fly to Paraguay, an idea came to mind. During the terrorist crisis I had encountered in Paraguay with Marwan al-Safadi, prisoner transportation had been accomplished using a U.S. Department of Defense aircraft. A check with the embassy's U.S. Military Liaison Office revealed that a U.S. military flight was scheduled to arrive the following day.

Voila, problem solved.

As a result of so-called "career self-preservation," bureaucrats sometimes concoct reasons and justifications of why and how to not accomplish risky, "rock the boat" solutions. It would have been simple for the U.S. Defense Department to deny our prisoner transport request. But they did not. I continually marvel at the U.S. military's "improvise, adapt, and overcome" attitude. America's military really knows how to *Git-R-Done!*

On June 5, 1998, D-Day's anniversary eve, the Paraguayan police paddy wagon carrying our prized, flea-bitten prisoner arrived at the circus type atmosphere at the Silvio Pettirossi International Airport.

Judge Carlos Ortiz Barrios (center left) and Minister of Interior, Walter Bower (center), coordinate William Fourie's (center right) extradition to the United States at the airport.

Heavily armed FOPE police officers escort William Fourie to U.S. military aircraft.

Paraguayan Judge Carlos Ortiz Barrios established a makeshift judicial bench at the airport, insisting that the Paraguayan constitution be followed to the letter. To achieve Mr. Fourie's legal extradition, Judge Ortiz required dozens of Paraguayan officials to sign the prisoner's removal order. U.S. Deputy Marshals Darren Sartin, Craig Slack, and I were amazed at the chaos and pandemonium that broke out at the airport as Paraguayan officials clawed their way toward the front of the room to place their signatures on this historic first extradition order under the newly established Paraguayan government. However strange this process might have seemed, I remain grateful to the Paraguayans' willingness and ability to accomplish seemingly impossible feats, especially those that benefited the United States.

Minister of Interior Walter Bower admitted that he was fascinated by U.S. law enforcement. He asked to be present when Deputy Marshals Darren Sartin and Craig Slack took custody of the prisoner. The excited Interior Minister, Mr. Fourie, two U.S. Deputy Marshals, and I retreated to a private room, where Mr. Fourie was frisked and secured with hand- and leg-irons, all within Paraguay's Foreign Minister's watchful gaze.

Shackled like an escape-prone wild animal, William Fourie pleaded with the Deputy Marshals to remove the chains due to embarrassment from his eventual "perp walk." His face-saving pleas fell on deaf ears. Resembling a broken-spirited oaf, Mr. Fourie was loaded into a police

Paraguay officials verify nemesis criminal William Fourie's departure.

van and transported to the waiting U.S. Air Force C-141 aircraft. I was relieved as I watched Mr. Fourie waddle up the aircraft stairs.

Making direct eye contact with me, Pedro Martinez sported a well-deserved, national pride grin on his face.

Fortunately, this seventeen-hour military "fugitive" transport flight would be all but comfortable. Fourie would ride on web-seats via Brazil and South Carolina until reaching his final destination of Austin, Texas.

As he returned to Texas, the woman and the bail bondsman who had put up Fourie's bond argued unsuccessfully for their forfeited monies to be returned. Sadly, Fourie's ex-wife and his fiancé's parents lost their homes in order to repay the forfeited bail bond.

On November 10, 1999, U.S. Federal District Judge Sam Sparks sentenced William Fourie to 18 years in the federal penitentiary for conspiracy to commit wire fraud, money laundering, fraud, and misuse of a visa.[22] Judge Sparks pronounced Fourie as a "unique, extraordinary" person who "could probably take a lie detector test and pass... Maybe he's one of those types of persons who says something and later believes it... He's not accepted responsibility even as he sits here."

On April 29, 2014, William Fourie again walked out of prison gates, but this time he had fulfilled his court-ordered obligations to society.[23]

CHAPTER 7

A QUEASY TERRORIST

What was this suspected Hezbollah terrorist's
motive for being in Paraguay?

I n 1989, the German prison guard paused a moment from completing his administrative paperwork. With a puzzled look on his face, at first the guard could not place the strange back and forth pulsating sound that echoed through the prison cell blocks. Finally identifying the precise cell, the guard discovered the 21-year-old prisoner had sawed through one-third of the cell bars by using a prison-issued food knife.

The suspected Hezbollah terrorist had been sentenced to a two-year prison term for planning terrorist attacks against American and

Technical University in Darmstadt, Germany

Israeli targets. As punishment for an escape attempt, he was escorted to the prison wing used for solitary confinement.[24]

Prison time is slow time. During his "alone time" in solitary confinement, the young Lebanese prisoner, fluent in German, likely recalled the days leading to his prison incarceration. Soon after Hezbollah was formally recognized as a terrorist organization by the United States in the early 1980s, the prisoner had traveled to Germany.

This Lebanese man initially applied for political asylum in Germany, but on learning that he could not attend university in an asylum status, he withdrew his claim and returned to Lebanon. With the assistance of a church group, the prisoner returned to Germany, and by 1988, he enrolled in the Technical University in Darmstadt to study physics.

Darmstadt, located in southwestern Germany near Frankfurt, is in close proximity to numerous American military bases, and provided an opportune cover location for this young man, full of hate against the State of Israel and the United States of America.[25]

Forgoing his university studies, he engaged in significant amounts of time reconnoitering potential American military and Israeli targets for attack.

U.S. Consulate, Munich, Germany.

In his youthful cockiness, the young prisoner had not learned from history. Through many years and several wars, Germans have perfected the art and science of gathering intelligence. On September 23, 1988, German security services intercepted a package sent by the prisoner—destined for Lebanon—containing an atlas of the Rhine-Main area, a region dotted with American military bases. The package also included color photographs of several Israeli targets in Munich, including the Israeli Religious Community Building, Israel's El Al Israel Airlines office, and the Israeli Trade Representative's office.

The Germans also intercepted a list of twenty American targets transmitted to Lebanon, indicating that the prisoner was ready to engage in attacks as soon as he had the necessary weapons and explosives. Included in the German court documents, the American targets included military installations, restaurants, and bars attended by Americans.

The young man likely replayed in his mind his German arrest on June 22, 1989, that landed him in prison. Where did he go wrong? Subsequent to his arrest, the Germans had discovered him carrying a letter identifying all of the proposed attack targets. Also found in his apartment were instructions on how to use explosives and codebooks hidden in luggage and behind a picture frame.

Believing his cypher codes were unbreakable, the terrorist identified his targets by using automobile brand names. American targets were identified as Mercedes while Jewish targets were identified as BMWs. He further detailed his automobile codes through listings of various models. For example, he referred to a "Mercedes 200" to communicate bombing damage could be done to American property. "Mercedes 220" meant humans, including Americans, could be injured or killed in a bombing attack. "Mercedes 230.4" meant Americans could be harmed without injuring Germans. The term, "I have found a car in good condition," meant a suitable bombing target had been identified. Most chilling was when he wrote a letter informing that he was enthusiastically wanting to "buy" (bomb) several of the top-of-the-line Mercedes models, meaning attacks that would hurt or kill Americans but not Germans.

Other warning codes included, "Your brother-in-law sends his greetings," which announced the message "Leave the country; you are in danger." The phrase "Your mother sends greetings," communicated "Be careful, you are being watched." The word "mark" referred to dynamite charge, and "franc" meant other types of explosives. Of course the sophisticated German intelligence officers must have scoffed at the ease of deciphering the young man's codes that had likely been developed in Beirut.

Publicly espousing his hatred of America, Israel, and Jewish people during his German court hearings, this young terrorist was sentenced to a two-year prison term for crimes pertaining to his terrorist activities involving the planned bombing attacks.[26] Now on the European grid, the young terrorist knew he would need to operate in a very low profile for at least a decade before risking his freedom and Hezbollah's covert activities of advancing their anti-American and anti-Israeli ideology.

WHEN WORKING OVERSEAS, every day holds a new and interesting adventure. An RSO might deal with a terrorist crisis one day, a political crisis the next, and criminal investigations the following day, all the while protecting against espionage intrusions and harm to the American diplomatic community.

On September 15, 1998, a knock on my office door at the embassy in Asunción announced Charlie, a fellow Texan and ranking U.S. consular officer, wearing a Cheshire cat grin. His visit was to inform me of a telephone call he had just received from the Consulate General of Brazil in Asunción, Paraguay, notifying that U.S. passport holder Mohamad Gharib Makki, was requesting a Brazilian visa.

On this day, the Brazilian consulate in Asunción had become suspicious when an individual requested a Brazilian visa in a U.S.

passport (number Z7189091) issued in Damascus, Syria. Suspicion was aroused on learning that the passport had been issued as a replacement passport, the passport holder's signature line was left blank, and the passport had not been previously used for travel prior to the suspect's trip from Lebanon to Paraguay.

As a matter of routine, the U.S. consular officer also shared this information with the embassy's counterterrorism division chief. Criminal record checks for the name on the passport revealed that Mohamad Gharib Makki was suspected of being a former leader of the New York City Hezbollah cell, and had become a fugitive since his 195-count indictment on federal charges of mail and wire fraud in Brooklyn, New York. A naturalized U.S. citizen, Mohamad Gharib Makki had surrendered his passport to the court as a condition of his release on bond before fleeing the United States, purportedly to his home in Lebanon, where he was suspected of serving as a senior lieutenant with Hezbollah, reporting directly to Secretary-General Hassan Nasrallah.

This discovery of a fugitive Hezbollah lieutenant terrorist surfacing in Paraguay set off alarms throughout the entire U.S. intelligence and counterterrorism communities.

The embassy's counterterrorism officer emphatically told me that based on the outstanding U.S. federal arrest warrants, this investigative matter belonged exclusively to the Department of Justice and that the Diplomatic Security Service (DSS) had no role in this particular matter. Just like a football defensive back, I had been stiff-armed by the embassy's counterterrorism officer.

It is well known that the FBI retains primary jurisdiction for terrorism investigations. However, because the DSS has the primary responsibility for protecting diplomatic personnel and facilities, DSS retains primary jurisdiction for protective intelligence related to threats. DSS also specializes in passport and visa fraud investigations.

Because the Joint Terrorism Task Force (JTTF) in New York already possessed an arrest warrant for Mohamad Gharib Makki, I opted to not involve the U.S. ambassador in a potential bureaucratic turf squabble of which law enforcement agency should be appointed the lead agency in Paraguay, the FBI or DSS.

With the Marwan al-Safadi investigation, I had been down this road before with the embassy's counterterrorism office. The safety and well-being of U.S. diplomats and their dependents rested on my shoulders. I felt it imperative to participate, behind the scenes if necessary, in order to ensure there was no imminent threat against the U.S. Mission in Paraguay.

Using his polished consular officer's diplomatic demeanor, Charlie convinced the Brazilian Consulate General in Asunción to delay issuance of a Brazilian visa for the traveler posing as Mohamad Gharib Makki. On September 18, 1998, the suspected fugitive traveled to Ciudad del Este, Paraguay, located within the lawless confines of the tri-border area (TBA) of Paraguay, Argentina, and Brazil, anxious to obtain a Brazilian tourist visa.

The following morning at 8:30 a.m., a Brazilian consulate employee in Asunción notified the Brazilian consulate in Ciudad del Este of the American government's interest in the purported fugitive. However, the Brazilian consular officer in Ciudad del Este informed his counterpart that the suspect was already inside the consulate, making his visa application. The suspect heard an American inside the consulate speaking English with a consular officer and became suspicious. The suspect demanded his passport back from the consular officer and quickly departed.

Awaiting the suspect outside of the Brazilian consulate was FOPE, the most effective counterterrorism unit in Paraguay. The FOPE unit took the suspected Hezbollah terrorist into custody on the spot. Within minutes of the FOPE unit's return from Ciudad del Este to Asunción with their captured prisoner in hand, the FOPE tactical commander, nicknamed "Lagarto" (Lizard), called me to report that the prisoner was secure at the airport.

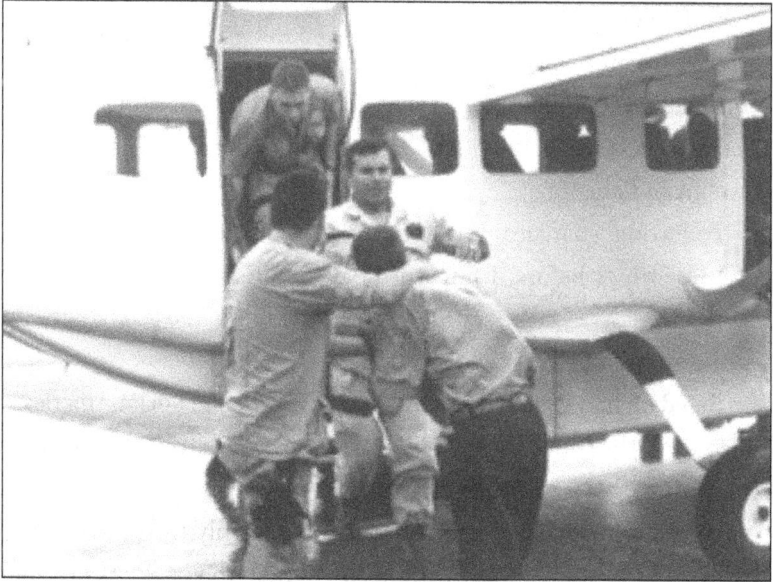

FOPE officers transport prisoner Makki from Ciudad del Este to Asunción.

I knew it would be important to interview the suspect as soon as possible, that is, while he was still confused by his capture. With my criminal investigative kit in hand, I quickly departed the embassy and drove to the airport to interview, fingerprint, photograph, and collect evidence from the suspected terrorist.

On my arrival, heavily armed FOPE officers escorted me to an internal airport office. The Hezbollah terrorist was a slender, clean-shaven young man wearing a light-blue, short-sleeved shirt and sporting a short, burr-type haircut. He could easily have blended into most situations in the United States and Latin America. His beady brown eyes revealed just how serious this predicament was to him.

As soon as the suspect saw me, "the American," the blood drained from his face like a child fearing the sight of a doctor's syringe destined for their arm. The man became physically ill, claiming he was dizzy, and he needed to lie down on a nearby couch. Perhaps it was images of waterboarding, or other thoughts of unspeakable tortures he himself had used on blameless victims that might now be used against him in the Paraguayan jungles. Now breeding reptiles of the mind, the terrorist began to dry-heave. When he regained his composure, he remained uncooperative, all the while claiming the identity of Mohamad Gharib Makki, the name listed on the U.S. passport he had used to travel from Lebanon.

Following standard investigative procedures I had conducted countless times before, I fingerprinted the prisoner and bagged his belongings for evidentiary purposes, including loose change, lip balm, and his address book.

Based on his physical reactions of rejecting the sight of an American, I deduced the suspect harbored deep-seated hatred and fear of Americans. This is the same type of deep-seated fear that is given safe refuge in the recessed crevices of one's mind, only to later manifest itself in the pit of the host's stomach. I knew then that FOPE had indeed captured a big fish.

What was this suspected Hezbollah terrorist's motive for being in Paraguay? Why was he eager to obtain a Brazilian tourist visa so quickly on his arrival? Why did he not sign his replacement American passport? Images of carnage and rubble clouded my memory: Hezbollah's 1983 bombings of the U.S. Embassy and Marine Barracks in Lebanon, and Hezbollah's bombing of the Israeli Embassy and Jewish cultural center in Buenos Aires, Argentina, that caused massive human loss.

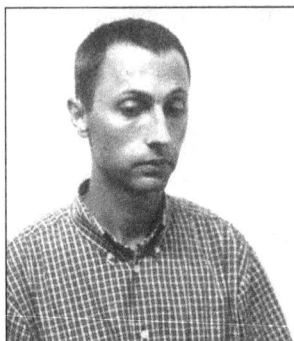

Mohamad Gharib Makki imposter.

On the same day, members of the JTTF New York loaded onto a U.S. government aircraft to travel to Asunción, Paraguay, in hopes of personally serving their arrest warrant based on the 195-count indictment of Mohamad Gharib Makki.

I questioned the logic of dispatching an FBI team to Paraguay without first confirming the prisoner's true identity. DSS excels in conducting identity theft investigations. Confirming identities of persons with criminal records is simply a matter of faxing enlarged individual fingerprint images (four-inches by four-inches) to the FBI fingerprint laboratory. The FBI typically responds quickly as to whether or not they have an identity match. Perhaps, given the prospect of taking custody of a captured "high-ranking" Hezbollah terrorist, the JTTF New York chose to not wait for a simple fingerprint comparison check. Instead, the JTTF New York chartered the Air Force plane to Paraguay at a steep and unnecessary cost to U.S. taxpayers. The next day, the aircraft and JTTF New York arrived in Paraguay.

The same embassy counterterrorism division chief who had earlier inferred I "butt out" of this case told me that he had asked the JTTF New York to delay its travel plans until the embassy had an opportunity to prove or refute Mohamad Gharib Makki's identity. Perhaps out of zeal to serve their warrant while garnishing headlines, the JTTF New York did not delay their flight.

When the task force arrived at Asunción's airport the following day on September 19, 1998, I was still operating in a limited role. Working with the Paraguayan police, I organized transportation for members of the JTTF New York to travel from the aircraft to the terminal. I drove an airport van to meet the C-141 aircraft, now parked on the tarmac, and picked up NYPD detective Wayne T. Parola, FBI special agent John G. Sorge, an FBI supervisor, and an FBI fingerprint specialist and transported them to the airport's main terminal.

After briefing the JTTF New York personnel and passing along the fingerprint cards I had taken of the suspect to the FBI fingerprint specialist, the JTTF team members were escorted to the room that held the person purporting to be Mohamad Gharib Makki.

At the conclusion of the subject interview conducted by the JTTF New York, NYPD detective Parola appeared disappointed and declared the suspect to be an imposter. This was not their Hezbollah fugitive, a conclusion supported by a fingerprint comparison. Detective Parola informed us that our prisoner changed his story, and was now claiming his identity was Hassan Mohamad Makki, cousin of fugitive Mohamad

Gharib Makki. Just like the young terrorist in the German prison years earlier was desperate to escape, our skinny prisoner was desperate to conceal his true identity.

Until now, embassy staff felt confident that the JTTF New York would remove the suspect from Paraguay. From the corner of my eye, I noticed the embassy's counterterrorism division chief in a spirited discussion with an FBI supervisor assigned to the JTTF New York. According to the FBI supervisor, a decision had been made in Washington, D.C., to depart Asunción without the suspect.

I was stunned at this decision.

The Paraguayan officials, including the President of the Republic of Paraguay, had extended tremendous support to the U.S. government by ordering the suspected terrorist deported to the United States versus requiring potentially lengthy extradition proceedings. If this unidentified imposter were to be left behind by the JTTF crew, concerns arose among embassy staff of potential irreparable damage to foreign relations with the Paraguayan police, immigration, and judicial authorities.

The embassy's counterterrorism chief and I pleaded with the JTTF supervisor to delay their team's departure to allow higher-ranking government agency executives to attempt to override the empty-handed departure decision. But the JTTF supervisor claimed that there was a miscommunication with their Air Force flight crew. According to the supervisor, the aircraft was prematurely refueled, resulting in its fuel tanks leaking while waiting on the tarmac. The JTTF New York members claimed an immediate departure was necessary and they quickly boarded the aircraft and departed Paraguay.

Dumbfounded, the embassy's counterterrorism division chief and I stood shoulder to shoulder. While peering out of an airport's large plate-glass window, we watched as the olive drab military plane slowly lifted off the runway to return home without John Doe, who still sat handcuffed inside the airport terminal. The U.S. Embassy staff was left to deal with the situation in which the host government accused the U.S. government of ramping up terrorism concerns and eventually reneging on its agreement to remove the purported terrorist.

Through high-level negotiations by the U.S. ambassador, Deputy Chief of Mission, and me, a Paraguayan judge granted the U.S. government 24 hours to obtain an arrest warrant and remove the prisoner. If not, the Paraguayan police were ordered to set him free.

Vital foreign relations and the continued detention of the suspect were at stake.

I was faced with the unprecedented challenge of establishing a criminal passport fraud case against our suspect—for a U.S. court—based on events that had taken place entirely in a foreign country. Complicating the matter was the ticking clock from the Paraguayan timekeepers.

In the movie *The Matrix*,[27] the character Trinity laments about accomplishing an act by means of a solution that has never before been attempted. Keanu Reeves' character, Neo, replies that is precisely why the solution will work.

If a solution existed, my DSS brethren and I would find it. It was finding solutions to conundrums like this that allowed the DSS to excel in its global law enforcement and security responsibilities. While still standing next to the embassy's counterterrorism officer at the airport, I phoned the DSS Washington field office. It was a number I remembered easily, as I had been assigned to the field office prior to my arrival in Paraguay.

Given the late hour at the onset of the weekend, I assumed this phone call was merely perfunctory. Surprisingly, a DSS special agent picked up the phone on the second ring. I quickly explained my situation to the agent and the need to "think outside the box." In short, I said I needed, "paper, any paper,"—even an arrest warrant for jaywalking—to salvage our local Paraguayan relationships.

As a former Regional Security Officer, the DSS special agent on the other end of the phone line easily grasped our predicament and immediately contacted the Assistant United States Attorney (AUSA) duty officer in Washington, D.C., to request a "John Doe" arrest warrant. Presented with an intriguing international investigation, the U.S. Attorney's Office accepted the case for prosecution. I was instructed to draft a comprehensive affidavit for an arrest warrant that would be presented to a federal magistrate judge the following day (Saturday).

To achieve an arrest warrant based on probable cause, and unsure of the legal standing for U.S. passport crimes committed in a foreign country, I knew the U.S. Attorney's Office and team-DSS had our work cut out in order to "pull a legal rabbit out of a hat." I returned to the embassy and worked through the night, meticulously drafting an affidavit for an arrest warrant. In the morning, operating with three hours sleep, I packed my travel bags and went directly to the airport, hoping for approval to escort the prisoner to the United States.

At the airport, I phoned the DSS special agent in Washington, D.C., and the Assistant U.S. Attorney, who were both at the federal judge's residence awaiting his decision on issuing an arrest warrant based on my affidavit.

Concern that judicial precedence had not been established for the issuance of an arrest warrant for U.S. passport fraud committed in a foreign country continued to niggle at me.

American Airlines was the only United States flagged air carrier that provided service between Asunción and Miami. At its departure gate, the Paraguayan-based American Airlines security officer informed me that the plane was 10 minutes overdue from its scheduled departure. He plainly stated that I had to decide now, this very moment, whether or not the prisoner was to be loaded onto the plane. With or without our prisoner, the aircraft was about to depart.

Given all of the hoopla generated by the JTTF New York's trip to Paraguay based on their mistaken belief that Hezbollah terrorist fugitive Mohamad Gharib Makki had been captured, the Paraguayan government was upset that the Americans did not follow through by removing the suspect from Paraguay. Sandwiched between the

American Airlines security officer and a high-ranking Paraguayan police officer, the tension mounted when the police officer advised that if the American Airlines plane departed without the suspect (whose true identity was still unknown at this time), he would be released from police custody.

Frankly, in light of not knowing our subject's identity, salvaging foreign relations with Paraguay was paramount. Offices and agencies within the U.S. Embassy were depending on me and team-DSS to salvage our foreign relations and get a bad guy off the streets.

Bridging this back-and-forth telephone call was the DSS Assistant Special Agent-in-Charge (ASAC), Washington field office, on a separate line with the DSS case agent, and the AUSA at the judge's residence. I told the DSS ASAC that I had to know at that moment whether or not the judge would issue an arrest warrant. Without it, we would for sure lose our prisoner.

With the cinematic suspense of a Hitchcock movie, seconds felt like hours. Finally, verbal instructions were relayed from Washington to Asunción. The U.S. magistrate judge approved the DSS application for an arrest warrant for passport fraud for our John Doe suspect.

Hallelujah! Let's take our man into the wild blue yonder.

CHAPTER 8

STRANDED WITH HEZBOLLAH

*...without a formal extradition order, technically,
I could be detained for kidnapping.*

iving the two thumbs-up to the Paraguayan police supervisor and airlines security officer, my FOPE friend, "Lagarto," and the police commander in charge of Paraguay's counterterrorism investigative division had arrived to accompany me in escorting the prisoner to Miami.

Silvio Pettirossi International Airport, Asuncion, Paraguay.

Wearing black ninja-like uniforms and carrying military-grade assault rifles tethered to their necks, a dozen FOPE officers escorted the prisoner down the passenger terminal walkway, stopped at the aircraft door, removed his handcuffs and ballistic vest, then re-cuffed him and concealed the cuffs with a sweater. The surprised, uninformed American Airlines flight attendants scrambled to close the First Class curtains in order to alleviate passenger fears about their new fellow travelers.

A helpful flight attendant escorted the prisoner, two Paraguayan police officers, and me to the last row in coach. I exhaled in relief. Finally, we were on our way to Miami, with a sole layover in São Paulo, Brazil.

En route to São Paulo, the flight attendant offered selections for the in-flight meal to the prisoner. The prisoner refused to select a specific meal. Perhaps feeling compassion for our John Doe traveler, the flight attendant set a steak meal on the prisoner's seat table. Generally subdued, the prisoner spoke up and emphatically scolded the flight attendant, saying that he refused to eat meat because he was a devout vegetarian. I winked at the flustered flight attendant and told her the food for the prisoner was fine.

São Paulo, Brazil.

The prisoner, still feeling his oats from his dietary diatribe, turned and defiantly told me it was time to pray. I answered that he may begin at any time. He then instructed me to throw down a blanket in the plane's service area to allow him to face Mecca. Maintaining professionalism, I politely declined his request.

Unbeknownst to me, a passenger made his way to the aircraft's cockpit to show the captain the front page headlines of a Paraguayan newspaper that prominently proclaimed that the FBI had arrested a Hezbollah terrorist with photographs of our John Doe and the chartered U.S. Air Force plane.

This wild ride was about to go into overdrive!

Nazi Herberts Cukurs, "Butcher of Riga."

As we flew over São Paulo's sprawling metropolis, I thought how this city was once home of Herberts Cukurs (*Butcher of Riga*), deceased member of the infamous Nazi's Arajs Kommando. Herberts Cukurs was accused of participating in the Holocaust by mass murdering more than 30,000 Latvian Jews.

After landing, our prisoner and team exited the aircraft last. My "Spidey" senses kicked in, and I felt something was terribly wrong. As we walked past the cockpit, I noted the captain's flushed face and knew he was upset. Leaving on the passenger transit terminal ramp, the captain stormed past us, with striking determination. At the departure gate, I learned from the local American Airlines security officer that the captain had rejected our group from his connecting flight to Miami based on an internal company policy disallowing the transportation of prisoners in excess of fourteen-hour trips.

Given the pressures of maintaining their flight schedule, and the confusion caused by our delay of departing Paraguay while waiting the judge's decision of issuing an arrest warrant, the American Airlines security officer had failed to notify the captain and flight crew of our prisoner escort to the United States. I could understand the captain's fury at being surprised by having transported a Hezbollah terrorist aboard his aircraft, even though the prisoner was not the terrorist sought by the JTTF New York.

In an effort to counter the captain's eviction order from this aircraft, I attempted to convince the airline security officer that our prisoner was actually a travel companion by instructing one of the Paraguayan police officers to quickly remove the suspect's handcuffs. Smiling, the security officer saw through my ploy and replied that it was too late. The handcuffs had alerted everyone within eyesight of our prisoner's escort situation.

I took a deep breath and reassessed the situation. I was not on Brazil's U.S. diplomatic immunity list; hence, without a formal extradition order, technically, I could be detained for kidnapping. The two Paraguayan police officers traveling with me had no authority in Brazil, therefore their police status was useless. We had a man in handcuffs whose true identity we did not know. And all I had to rely on was a verbal instruction from a DSS special agent that a U.S. federal judge had approved an application for an arrest warrant.

Now stranded with a purported Hezbollah terrorist, I found myself up a really bad Amazonian river without a paddle!

Needing an act of divine intervention, it was delivered! A stranger appeared from the crowded terminal and began calling my name. I waived my hand and caught his attention. I was relieved that instead of arresting me, as I had feared, he handed me a facsimile copy of the U.S. arrest warrant signed by the federal magistrate judge in Washington, D.C. Impressively, someone up the DSS chain-of-command ensured the arrest warrant was handed off to me at the airport. Not yet free from my predicament, at least I now had an international "get out of jail card."

The American Airlines security officer was a genuine gentleman. He re-booked the four of us on another foreign air carrier. The security officer strongly suggested I remove the suspect's handcuffs to avoid further unwanted scrutiny. Waiting in the airport terminal, the two Paraguayan police officers and I transitioned into a psychological operations tag team by each intensively explaining to the prisoner why it would not be in his best interest to attempt to escape when we removed the handcuffs. Three long hours later, we boarded the Varig Airlines flight to Miami. To ensure passenger safety, we drank coffee and propped our eyelids open with toothpicks to stay awake.

A cadre of DSS special agents from the DSS Miami field office met our plane on landing and took custody of our prisoner. The prisoner was arraigned in Miami under the name he had provided the JTTF New York, Hassan Mohamad Makki, and he was slated to be transferred to Washington, D.C., to stand trial.

On a side note, as an act of diplomacy, I was instructed to spend an entire week in Miami to allow the two Paraguayan police officers to experience a "good time," all expenses paid by the embassy's counterterrorism office. No arm-twisting would be required for this South Beach duty. As bad luck would have it, Hurricane George was bearing down toward Miami, so I had to cut our trip short after only two days in Miami.

Meanwhile, DSS agents in Miami faxed a copy of the suspect's photo to the DSS Regional Security Officer assigned to the U.S. Embassy in Beirut, Lebanon.

The DSS special agent assigned to the Regional Security Office at the U.S. Embassy who received Miami's investigative lead was none other than the legendary eighteen-year DSS veteran, Michael J. Hudspeth, who two years earlier, had assisted me in escorting the dangerous Islamic terrorist Marwan al-Safadi from Asunción, Paraguay, to the United States.

Map of Lebanon.

Now charged with the task of uncovering the true identity of our

John Doe prisoner—representing himself first as Mohamad Gharib Makki and secondly as Hassan Mohamad Makki—DSS Special Agent Hudspeth had developed a reliable network of sources within Lebanon, a dangerous Iranian-backed Hezbollah stronghold.

A meeting between Agent Hudspeth and his trusted confidential informant, with whom he had met on multiple occasions, had been arranged in a rural Lebanese town, away from prying eyes that consistently watched the U.S. Embassy in Beirut. Agent Hudspeth was keenly aware of the risk he was taking, and he knew that an official American captured in the rural confines of Lebanon would certainly result in a hostage situation at best, and at worst, torture.

Disregarding his personal safety for the greater cause of protecting U.S. national security, DSS Agent Hudspeth dismissed the Lebanese bodyguards who normally accompanied all official Americans in Lebanon and covertly drove himself to a secluded location in the rural countryside.

Given its political "tug-o'-war" struggles, dangers for American diplomats in Lebanon were real and the consequences of a wrong step—even a perceived wrong step—were lasting, even to death.

As Agent Hudspeth later shared in a court affidavit,[28, 29] "The face of the confidential informant clearly registered the emotions of surprise, fear, and anger on viewing the photograph."

Now clearly upset, the informant identified the man in the photograph of our John Doe as Bassam Gharib Makki from Maroun El-Ras, a small village in southern Lebanon. As fate would have it, Bassam Gharib Makki happened to be the same man who was arrested almost a decade earlier in Germany and sentenced to two years in Darmstadt, Germany, for planning bombing attacks against American facilities and Israeli targets. Hudspeth's informant shared that Bassam Gharib Makki was the brother of Mohamad Gharib Makki, the fugitive sought by the JTTF New York and cousin of Hassan Makki. The informant noted that Mohamad Gharib Makki fled the United States after his arrest in New York for what he believed were crimes related to funding Hezbollah activities.

In Lebanon, the land of cedars, the informant emphatically stated that all three Makkis were trusted senior lieutenants who directly reported to Hezbollah's Secretary-General Hassan Nasrallah. Bassam Gharib Makki was believed to be in charge of training of Hezbollah terrorists. What might that training have consisted of?

Similar to U.S. government agencies, seasoned terrorist organizations have comprehensive training manuals, oftentimes consisting of information derived from military warfare manuals.

Hezbollah Secretary-General Hassan Nasrallah.

Training to plan an attack generally incorporates sophisticated methods consisting of coordinated assets that follow three integrated and inseparable phases, including a reconnaissance stage, planning stage, and execution stage. DSS agents are responsible for detecting and disrupting planned terrorist attacks during any of these three phases.

Agent Hudspeth listened intently as the frightened confidential informant stated, "… whatever Bassam Gharib Makki's activities were in Paraguay, Bassam was sent to Paraguay at the express direction of [Hassan] Nasrallah and was executing specific functions for Hezbollah on behalf of Nasrallah."

As the butterflies of fear now swarmed within the informant's stomach, he cautioned Agent Hudspeth that any further inquiries about Bassam Makki would be considered by Hezbollah to be a direct attack against Secretary Nasrallah and the investigators would be immediately targeted for execution. Hudspeth had had uneventful meetings with this informant on other occasions.

However, wrapping up his sobering meeting, Agent Hudspeth noted that this was the first time he had seen this informant so frightened— and angry—his face reflected life-threatening anxiety to Hudspeth for exposing him to unwanted risk. The vulnerable informant pleaded with Agent Hudspeth that any slip-up that revealed his identity as an informant would surely result in his death at the hands of Hezbollah.

When Hudspeth later approached the informant to inquire further about Bassam Makki, the informant stated that too much information had been divulged and refused to provide any additional information.

In 1999, another informant discovered a computer business purportedly owned by Bassam Makki, located in a Beirut neighborhood under the control of Hezbollah's security. Due to the critical threat against official Americans, diplomats were only allowed to depart the embassy with local bodyguards using armored vehicles. Consequently, the bulk of street-level investigations were conducted by locally hired Lebanese investigators, who also operate under severe restrictions for their personal safety. A local Lebanese investigator had been recently kidnapped for sixteen hours by Hezbollah[30] (and purportedly tortured for continuing the investigation into Bassam Makki's activities). Jeopardizing his personal safety, Agent Hudspeth had discovered the true identity of a dangerous terrorist, now in U.S. custody.

Tina Sciocchetti, federal prosecutor in Washington, D.C., was assigned to prosecute Bassam Makki. During subsequent United States court hearings, our suspect (Bassam Makki) continued to present a false identity to the federal magistrate. However, in a Perry Mason-type moment, AUSA Sciocchetti shocked the court by announcing the prisoner's true identity, a suspected Hezbollah terrorist who had previously been convicted of planning bombing attacks against American, Israeli, and Jewish interests in Germany.

On December 16, 1998, Bassam Gharib Makki pled guilty in Washington's federal district court to passport violations. During Makki's sentencing hearing, U.S. Federal Judge Paul L. Friedman denied the defendant's motion to dismiss the indictment on the grounds that the United States lacked jurisdiction over Makki's conduct in Paraguay with the intention of traveling to Brazil. Judge Friedman explained that international law recognizes the right of the United States to punish conduct that undermines the integrity of the official documents of the United States. Judge Friedman's ruling established judicial precedence by allowing United States special agents and prosecutors jurisdiction for passport fraud committed in foreign countries.[31]

Bassam Gharib Makki told the U.S. probation officer that he had used the identity of Mohamad Gharib Makki (his brother) due to the great shame he felt and the potential problems that he would face in his country (Lebanon) due to his (German) conviction "[...] for terrorist activity (presumably his planned attacks against the United States and Israeli targets)."[32]

On March 7, 2000, Bassam Gharib Makki was deported from the United States and returned to Lebanon. The motive for why Bassam Gharib Makki had exposed himself by traveling on a false U.S. passport under his brother's identity may never be known. What is known is that Bassam Gharib Makki, a suspected high-ranking member of Hezbollah, told German court officials years earlier, that he hated America and Americans.

An informant in South America noted that Hezbollah's Abdallah clan, led by Mohamad Youssef Abdallah, aligned with Mohamad Hussein Fadlallah (now deceased), the spiritual leader of Hezbollah in Lebanon, and the contender for the control of the entire Hezbollah organization. The other competing Hezbollah faction in the tri-border is the Barakat clan, which is aligned with Hassan Nasrallah, the secretary-general of Hezbollah in Lebanon.

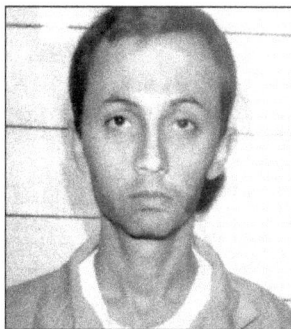

Bassam Gharib Makki.

Just as Fadlallah and Nasrallah compete for leadership in Lebanon, Abdallah and Barakat clans compete for Hezbollah's control in the tri-border and carry out a secret war for absolute control of the tri-border's Hezbollah contingent.[33]

Perhaps Bassam Makki traveled to the tri-border with the intent to meet with and convince leaders to mend relations between their two warring Hezbollah factions in an effort to focus terrorist operations against American, Israeli, and Jewish targets in Latin America, and Makki's own goal of infiltrating the United States.

The deputy chief of mission at the U.S. Embassy in Asunción stated that accomplishments by the DSS team and U.S. Justice Department resulted in Makki being the first Hezbollah terrorist arrested and prosecuted in the Unites States in the past 10 years.

Whatever Bassam Makki's reason for traveling to Paraguay and Brazil under a fraudulent passport, the quick and resourceful actions of the Paraguayan police, DSS and the U.S. Attorney's Office likely prevented and disrupted terrorist acts worldwide, while potentially saving lives.

CHAPTER 9

ASSASSINATION
OF A FLEDGLING NATION

With Argaña's death,
Lino Oviedo's "bloody street" prophecy
had just become reality.

P edro Martinez—his face pale—made his way into my office and sadly reported, "Robert, I just received word that Vice President Argaña has been assassinated." If Pedro's information about Vice President Luis María Argaña was confirmed, we both contemplated the consequences that would soon follow—a potential coup d'état followed by civil war.

Paraguayan Vice President Luis María Argaña.

Pedro Martinez was a seasoned embassy inves- tigator who was no stranger to assassinations in Paraguay. Years before Luis Argaña's assassination, on September 17, 1980, while working for the U.S. Embassy, Pedro had been dispatched to a different attack site along España Avenue in Asunción. Anastasio "Tachito" Somoza Debayle, the 54-year-old former Nicaraguan President exiled to Paraguay

Nicaraguan President Anastasio Somoza

under political asylum, was assassinated. A seven-member Sandinista hit squad killed him with a rocket-propelled grenade (RPG).

In order to improve my executive protection skills, on my arrival in Paraguay, I studied this attack site. Pedro and I stood at the area where pre-attack surveillance was conducted by an assassin posing as a street-side newspaper stand vendor. From this newspaper stand, a line-of-site signal was passed to the attack team located in a multi-story building several hundred yards from the stand.

I paused, knowing the importance for executive protection security agents to remain ultra-observant, even to the point of noticing a slight, but suspicious hand or eye movement leading to a potential attack. Unfortunately, the surveillance and attack signals were missed, and a rocket-propelled grenade smashed into and exploded on impact with the sedan carrying President Somoza. Pedro pointed out the

Sedan that carried Nicaraguan President Anastasio Somoza during his assassination in Asunción, Paraguay.

President Francisco Solano López (L), President Andres Rodriguez (C), President Alfredo Stroessner (R).

precise location he had found President Somoza's Rolex wrist watch on the ground after the fatal attack.

For more than a century, Paraguay had been beleaguered with a history of power-thirsty dictators President (Mariscal) Francisco Solano López, considered a national hero by many (1862–1870); dictator Alfredo Stroessner (1954–1989); General Andrés Rodriguez (1989–1993).

Governing under a new and fragile constitution, it was only a matter of time before another dictator-in-waiting stepped forward to take his place of leadership, forced on his nation.

In 1989, Lino César Oviedo, a former Paraguayan military general, purportedly assisted General Rodriguez to overthrow

Paraguayan General Lino Oviedo.

President Stroessner. Bullet holes at the Presidential Guard headquarters building in Asunción are a visual reminder of the dangers that unfolded during the 1989 coup d'état.

Lino Oviedo was also suspected of rigging the 1993 presidential elections, resulting in Juan Carlos Wasmosy wresting the presidency from his political competitor, Luis María Argaña. Paraguay's coup d'état cauldron once again began to simmer in April 1996 when Lino Oviedo was denied after he attempted to overthrow President Wasmosy.[34]

Bullet riddled SUV used by Argana during his assassination.

Lino Oviedo, suspected of having protected international drug cartels, was now banned by the Paraguayan courts from holding presidential office for the rest of his life. Aspirations of power continued to fuel Lino Oviedo to rebel against the court ruling by campaigning for presidency. If prevented from acquiring the position of President, Oviedo purportedly declared, "The streets will flow with blood."

Just a few blocks from my residence, I dispatched Pedro Martinez to prove or refute the information about the assassination he had just received. Twenty minutes later, Pedro called with the dreaded news. The vice president had indeed been assassinated. According to witnesses, Vice President Argaña's red Nissan Patrol SUV had been blocked by one vehicle while weapon-wielding thugs from a second vehicle to the rear exited and murdered the high-ranking politician by riddling his body with bullets, allegedly by supporters of retired General Lino Oviedo.[35]

Pedro Martinez's anxious facial expression reflected the pain of his nation's history of turbulence and political strife.

With Argaña's death, Lino Oviedo's "bloody street" prophecy had just become reality. I quickly made my way to the embassy's executive office and interrupted a meeting hosted by Ambassador Maura Harty.

FOPE bomb unit removes explosive device.

I asked the Deputy Chief of Mission Stephen McFarland to step outside. After I explained the situation to the seasoned U.S. Foreign Service officer, the DCM calmly and methodically reviewed the situation step by step before briefing Ambassador Harty. The Ambassador quickly assembled the embassy's emergency action committee to begin making preparations for worst-case scenarios. Paraguay was a nation on edge leading up to what was to be a violent coup d'état.

Shortly afterward, while reviewing our emergency action plans, I was interrupted by a telephone call. The voice on the other end of the line seemed overly excited.

"Mr. Starnes, this is Lezcono from FOPE."

Lezcono had attended the challenging six-month DS/ATA–sponsored explosive ordnance device (EOD) training course administered in Baton Rouge, Louisiana. In addition to his state-of-the-art training, DS/ATA had provided him with an explosive-detection German shepherd, tools, an X-ray unit, and a bomb-disrupting water cannon. This young FOPE officer was extremely loyal to the United States and even offered to enlist in the U.S. Marine Corps.

"I have something to show you. Please come to my office today," said Lezcono.

I hung up the telephone; the suspense was overwhelming. Given the degenerating security environment in the capital city, my security preparations would have to wait a few hours. I made the 20-minute drive to FOPE's headquarters to discover his guarded surprise.

He escorted me into a back room where I observed a conference room table littered with shreds of paper and plastic.

"I see you have neglected house cleaning," I said, while pointing at the trash heap that lay before me.

Like a child excited by an extraordinary accomplishment, a huge smile appeared on his face. He explained how that morning, he was dispatched to check out a suspicious package in the heart of the city's financial district. Following bomb technician protocol, Lezcono's EOD-trained canine alerted him to the suspicious package and its potentially dangerous contents. Speaking quickly, he described how he had X-rayed the package, assembled and activated the water cannon, and destroyed the package and its unknown contents.

On further analysis, Lezcono discovered the package he had just disrupted was a bomb consisting of 40 sticks of dynamite. Momentarily silent, I imagined the potential human carnage that would have manifested if this bomb had detonated in Asunción's busily-traveled financial district. People who would have filled the sidewalks, making their way to work (attorneys, bankers, secretaries, students, and vendors), all simply trying to live their lives in the midst of those intent on seizing political power and control.

Still sporting a grin, this FOPE bomb technician broke the temporary silence and humbly thanked me for the DS/ATA support provided to him to protect his citizenry. Still stunned at his revelation, I simply told him, "Well done, Lezcono."

During the 1998 campaign, Lino Oviedo chose Raúl Cubas Grau as his political party running mate. A few months prior to the elections, Lino Oviedo was disqualified and sentenced to 10 years in prison for his role during the 1996 attempted coup. Grau took Oviedo's place on the ballot and was elected president under the slogan, "Cubas in Government, Oviedo in Power." In an attempt

Paraguayan President Raul Cubas

to minimize Oviedo's puppetry power, the Paraguayan Congress passed a law constraining presidential pardon powers. In order for the political

party to retain its political control, Luis Argaña, who had been leading the anti-Oviedo bloc, was named as Cubas' vice-presidential running mate.

Days after his presidential inauguration, Cubas authorized Lino Oviedo's release from prison based on time served. Cubas refused a Paraguayan Supreme Court order to re-jail Oviedo. Shortly afterward, the Paraguayan Congress charged President Cubas with abuse of power, but came up two votes short of impeachment. As chaos within the government took hold, freedom-minded students supporting the rule of law amassed and demanded the newly appointed President Raúl Cubas Grau to resign. It had become painfully clear that Oviedo's apparent plan was to eventually wrest control from the country's constitu-

Paraguayan President Juan Carlos Wasmosy

tionally elected leadership. Lino Oviedo's grip on power was not to be underestimated. His minions included the Police Commissioner, many of the military's top brass, an array of Congressional politicians, and a host of henchmen and thugs from the hinterlands.

I knew many of the Paraguayan military officers and enlisted soldiers involved in supporting Lino Oviedo. Even more disconcerting, I may have unknowingly enabled some of these soldiers to topple their own government, if such an order were to be delivered.

A year earlier, Paraguayan President Juan Carlos Wasmosy requested U.S. security assistance from U.S. Ambassador Robert Service to provide executive protection training for the Paraguayan military in preparations for the Rio Group Conference, including 10 visiting heads-of-state.

Ambassador Service had agreed to the Paraguayan president's request and directly instructed me to ensure this task was met in a timely manner. To my knowledge, the Paraguayan military had never provided civilian executive protective services, and due to the short notice of the president's security assistance request, U.S. Department of State headquarters training assets were unavailable.

Police confront demonstrator after Argaña's assassination.

In order to improvise, I was given operational command of a visiting elite U.S. military team. I developed a three-day Spanish language training curriculum, including attack recognition, walking formations, motorcades, and attack responses. In typical fashion, the U.S. military team performed admirably and provided real-life motorcade attack scenarios using actual explosives. The training was a success and the Rio Group Conference ended without incident. The Presidential Guard Commander commended the entire U.S.-led security training team for quickly preparing his troops to react against threats that could have resulted in international incidents.

As tension mounted after Vice President Argaña's assassination, gunshots rang out from Asunción's downtown rooftop positions by snipers purportedly loyal to Lino Oviedo. A call from the on-duty U.S. Marine Security Guard summoned me to the embassy's visitor area where I greeted Lincoln Alfieri, chief security officer for Paraguayan Senator Luis Ángel González Macchi.

Mr. Lincoln Alfieri appeared shaken and was anxious to meet outside of public view. Moving to the safe confines of an internal conference room, the Paraguayan security officer went into detail how he and Senator González Macchi had come under sniper fire at the downtown congressional building earlier that day. Based on the Paraguayan constitution, Senator González Macchi was next in line for presidential succession. Grasping the full gravity of the security officer's plight, and the importance of keeping the senator alive, I donated ballistic vests to Mr. Lincoln Alfieri and to Senator González Macchi.

As the nation spiraled further into chaos, embassy staff learned that Lino Oviedo supporters throughout rural Paraguay were planning to converge in the capital city to squash the protesters with overwhelming force. We received intelligence that, after eliminating the pesky downtown protesters, Lino Oviedo's band of henchmen would then turn their sights against the Americans by storming the U.S. Embassy compound, including the Chancery building, ambassador's residence, and the Marine Security Guard residence.

Fortunately, during the early stages of the coup, dependents of U.S. diplomats had been encouraged to stock up on provisions and lock themselves inside their embassy-leased residences that were scattered throughout the city to weather the political storm or to await evacuation orders.

During the height of the violence, my wife Pam was stalwart for our children—and a multitude of American missionary families—by providing safe refuge, comfort, and food inside our fortified home. Pam had previously attended the DSS counterterrorism training course for Foreign Service officers and dependents. Not surprisingly, Pam had achieved the highest marksmanship score when shooting an Uzi submachine gun, competing against both men and women. From pioneer stock, Pam exemplified a Texan's bravery and ability to use firearms.

During an embassy crisis management meeting, in order to control anxieties, I encouraged Ambassador Harty to provide daily situation updates to the dependents and American citizens via the embassy's

Paraguayan police aim pistols at rioting demonstrators.

radio system. Similar to President Franklin D. Roosevelt's WWII fireside chats, specific times were established for the ambassador to broadcast security updates to the worried dependents.

I reached out to FOPE to request protective assistance from this trusted and highly trained police unit. I had a bittersweet disappointment of learning that the corrupt Paraguayan police commissioner had locked down FOPE, restricting them to their barracks.

Demonstrators help an injured friend following assassination of vice President Luis Argana.

The relationship that had been forged between FOPE and the U.S. Embassy, and their advanced police commando-type capabilities acquired primarily through DS/ATA training, left doubt in the pro-Oviedo police commissioner's mind when it came to obeying his illegal commands.

While making final security preparations for the U.S. Embassy, I watched

Military deployed at the Presidential Palace.

a news story broadcast live by a local television station. My stomach turned when the cameras recorded a civilian shooting a rifle into the crowd of protesters while standing shoulder-to-shoulder with uniformed police officers. Like shooting fish in a barrel, armed pro-Oviedo and pro-Cubas police and civilian supporters killed seven student demonstrators and injured at least one hundred other protesters.[36] I took note of these murders and thought if Lino Oviedo's supporters had such blatant disregard for life, their purported planned assault against our embassy would become a siege for the ages.

Unable to secure the services of FOPE, I received cabled permission from DSS headquarters to double the size of our U.S. Marine Security Guard detachment. Now, without armed support from the Paraguayan police on our exterior perimeter, I knew that several hundred Oviedo attackers would require us to use the embassy building as a safe haven while awaiting U.S. military support units that may or may not arrive in time to rescue the embassy staff.

Ironically, the embassy's radio call signal was "Alamo." To this Texan, the name Alamo invoked historical acts of bravery and heroism. However, it also bestows an order of "no quarter" for those choosing to take a stand. Given Oviedo's supporters' displeasure with America's obstacle of supporting democracy and rule of law, I believe a siege of the embassy may have likely resembled Santa Anna's no quarter order.

During the height of the violence downtown, two American missionaries based in Asunción accompanied a group of young Vineyard Church members to the government plaza that served as the protesters' epicenter.

Pleas and chants for justice shouted in Spanish were shattered when shots from pro-Oviedo snipers rang out, resulting in chaos and killings. In a display of bravery and national patriotism, young Vineyard Church members formed a tight "human shield" circle around the two American missionaries and escorted them several blocks from the dangerous government plaza area to a taxi cab.

Before stuffing the two missionaries into the taxi, a young Paraguayan church member said, "If blood needs to be shed for this nation, it should be ours, not yours. It will only complicate things if an American is killed here tonight." As the taxi cab drove them to safety, the two missionaries were amazed as they contemplated the courage exhibited by their young congregation members.

Although I was moved by the Vineyard Church members' sense of nationalism, I knew the United States Embassy would play an important role in assisting Paraguay in reestablishing constitutional democracy.

Lino Oviedo allegedly passed instructions to his crony police and military commanders and civilian supporters to open fire on the protesters. Government forces attacked the parliament building with tanks and seized radio stations, calling for the government's overthrow.

I snatched the opportunity to again request FOPE's assistance. Like an attack dog waiting to be unleashed, FOPE quickly disobeyed the illegal instructions issued by their corrupt police chief. FOPE deployed heavily armed officers around the U.S. Embassy and supplemented Ambassador Harty's executive protective detail. Momentum began to shift and all knew that leadership control must be quickly seized to end the madness that gripped this South American nation.

Night had fallen. U.S. Marines, dressed in combat fatigues, had retired the Colors (American flag) for the day. It was an exceptionally hot, muggy, and windless night. Locked and loaded, the U.S. Marines and I awaited the thugs that were planning to scale our compound walls and lay siege to our Chancery. While the detachment commander and I reviewed the Marine positions, Ambassador Harty summoned me to her office and informed me that Senator Luis Ángel González Macchi and his advisor had been invited and were en route to the U.S. Embassy compound.

Ambassador Harty emphatically repeated, "Make sure our guests get inside the compound safely."

I replied, "Yes, ma'am."

Lagarto, FOPE's tactical commander, and I quickly made our way to the designated vehicular access gate, using shrubs to conceal our trek in the event rogue pro-Oviedo snipers might be conducting reconnaissance leading to their planned embassy siege. After a few uncomfortable minutes had passed, the headlights of a convoy approached the embassy compound. Lagarto provided invaluable assistance by visually identifying Senator González Macchi, who was subsequently whisked into the embassy and to the ambassador's second-story office suite.

Senator González Macchi must have suspected his visit to the U.S. Embassy that night would last well into the early morning hours and possibly manifest into an overnight refuge, if needed, during the apex of chaos that unfolded downtown. Of course, precedence of providing overnight refuge for Paraguay's leader had been previously established when in 1996, Ambassador Service allowed President Wasmosy to stay overnight within the U.S. Embassy compound during Lino Oviedo's planned coup d'état.[37]

Unknown to Senator González Macchi, embassy personnel had also invited other trusted, high-ranking Paraguayan government officials and politicians to the U.S. Embassy, including military and police personnel. On their arrival, the U.S. Embassy became a beehive of activity. Breakout meetings ensued, papers shuffled, embassy division chiefs discussed options with their direct counterparts, and occasional calls were made to Washington to provide situational updates.

Of course, with any power structure, the entity possessing the strongest armed force elements usually retains power and control. At this very moment, the most

Paraguayan President Ángel González Macchi.

pivotal person in regaining constitutional control was General Torres Heyn, Paraguay's senior military officer. Oddly, General Heyn occupied a position with limited command authority. Although American-trained, Paraguay's Defense Deputy Chief of Staff opted to support Lino Oviedo.

During the moments leading to the coup, the Paraguayan military was fractured. In general, the army cavalry staff supported Lino Oviedo. The U.S.-trained Presidential Guard Regiment was loyal to constitutional rule. The Paraguayan Air Force evacuated their aircraft to airstrips outside of Asunción. The Paraguayan Naval Marines were neutral, remained at their barracks, and guarded their headquarters during the coup. The Navy, Air Force, and Presidential Guard Regiment were temporarily aligned in neutrality. Paraguay's sole naval helicopter provided the Air Force and Presidential Guard Regiment components with communication relay, support, and aerial reconnaissance.

Within the next few hours, the entire Paraguayan leadership structure would be reestablished inside of the ambassador's office and nearby conference room. I was amazed how seemingly simple this exercise had become. Standing about six feet in stature, Senator Luis Ángel González Macchi seemed overwhelmed and unsure how to best proceed in this surreal leadership moment. After embassy staff had provided coordination suggestions, Senator Macchi literally pointed to individuals in his trusted circle and declared each person's new position, including the military commander, chief of police, minister of interior, and so on.

Although Paraguayan citizens had been killed by government forces, the number of protesters increased. In this moment of divine intervention, Lino Oviedo realized that his grip on power was beginning to unravel. He had lost the support of the majority of the Paraguayan citizens. In shame, while purportedly carrying suitcases full of U.S. currency, Lino Oviedo fled Paraguay in exile to Argentina.

Senator González Macchi was obviously shaken at the violence that had unfolded against his citizenry. Naturally, in light of Vice President Argaña's assassination, and the snipers that purportedly caused chaos in Asuncion, the Senator feared for his safety. It was then that the five-foot, one-inch tall U.S. Ambassador Maura Harty squared up to the much taller politician and exhorted Senator González Macchi to embrace his historical destiny to reclaim his nation that had been plagued by power-thirsty dictators, by accepting Paraguay's next presidency.

I have never been more proud of a United States ambassador as I was of Maura Harty's display of exceptional leadership during the height of this violent crisis. After securing positions for a new government as quickly as the convoys had reached the U.S. Embassy, they departed for the Mburuvichá Roga, Paraguay's Presidential residence, located near the embassy. It was here, at the forty-acre residential compound consisting of a stately residence and manicured gardens, where Raúl Cubas Grau submitted his resignation as Paraguay's president, making it possible for Senator Macchi's ascension to the office of president.

While standing in front of his peers, Senator González Macchi, still wearing the ballistic vest I had given him, raised his hand and was sworn in as Paraguay's democratically elected president.

Democracy survived and rule of law was once again in place.

In the aftermath of the coup d'état, the Paraguayan police chief asked my office to assist his country in restructuring their executive protective division by developing a new command structure and training schedule. The plan was wholeheartedly received and rapidly implemented to protect Paraguayan officials, diplomatic facilities, and visiting foreign dignitaries.

Deservingly, during a joint session of the Paraguayan congress, USMC General William E. Wilhelm, Commander, U.S. Southern Command, awarded the U.S. Medal of Merit to Paraguayan General Torres Heyn for his contributions with supporting democracy.

The entire U.S. Embassy team was awarded a U.S. Department of State Superior Honor Award. The citation stated:

> *Presented for sustained effort in 1998 and 1999 to advance United States interest by strengthening and protecting Paraguay's democratic institution. Post's skillful use of assistance programs, its well-coordinated reporting and analysis, and its continual emphasis that the international community would not tolerate anti-democratic actions helped ensure the continuation of Paraguayan democracy.*

Showing their appreciation for DSS' continued training and resources support, FOPE hosted my farewell ceremony. During this event, I was moved when Lagarto, the FOPE commander who had accompanied me to Miami with the Hezbollah terrorist and stood shoulder to shoulder with me during the height of the coup d'état, inducted me into FOPE as an honorary member and presented me with an authentic FOPE black beret. I humbly accepted brotherhood with these exceptional men and women and will always cherish our time spent together during times of crisis.

During a separate farewell award ceremony hosted by the Paraguayan government for Ambassador Maura Harty, several of the student protesters who had been wounded during the coup d'état by government forces were present to share their appreciation. Some were still aided by crutches, and stood to show their support to Ambassador Maura Harty, U.S. Embassy staff, and the United States government for supporting their fledgling nation of Paraguay.

IN THE
TEETH OF A
CIVIL WAR

CHAPTER 10

LET'S GET OUR MAN!

"Well, let's see what a colonel is worth"

U.S. Ambassador John Gordon Mein.

The air conditioner blew much welcomed cool air to counter Guatemala's summer heat from the midday sunshine on August 28, 1968. The chauffer-driven limousine carrying U.S. Ambassador John Gordon Mein weaved its way through the busy streets of Guatemala City, the capital and largest city of the Republic of Guatemala. Built a mile above sea level, this picturesque city was a colorful jewel to the developing nation that had once been occupied by Mayans.

Unbeknownst to Ambassador Mein, two vehicles occupied by pro-Cuban Marxist Fuerzas Armadas Rebeldes (FAR) guerrillas covertly positioned their vehicles for an attack.

Due to successes by the Guatemalan security forces, supported by the United States, of countering this pro-communist organization, FAR had previously targeted Americans in Guatemala, including planning a series of bombings during President Lyndon B. Johnson's visit to Guatemala. Just seven months earlier, FAR assassinated the U.S. military group commander and chief of the U.S. naval section, and wounded two other U.S. mission employees, purportedly in retaliation for the killing and mutilation by Guatemalan security forces of the beauty queen who was a lover of a FAR member.[38]

The Buick sedan and red pickup truck orchestrated an abrupt stop, boxing in the senior diplomat's Cadillac. Donning green military-style fatigues, the heavily-armed FAR terrorists quickly exited their vehicles and ordered Ambassador Mein to exit the limousine.

Ambassador Mein, now on his third year as U.S. President Johnson's representative to this war-ravaged Central American nation, refused to be taken hostage by this anti-American communist group. This brave ambassador took a calculated risk when he ran from his attackers to evade capture. The terrorists opened fire, killing the unarmed diplomat. Up until that date, Ambassador Mein's murder was the first such assassination of a U.S. ambassador serving abroad in American history.

Due to the real and present danger since Ambassador Mein's murder, all U.S. ambassadors serving in Guatemala were assigned robust protective details comprised of DSS special agents and local Guatemalan police officers on stipend.

⁎⁎⁎

During the 19th century, through immense wealth, the American banana company, United Fruit Company, had developed the political and economic landscapes in Guatemala to maintain market dominance through bribery and worker exploitation. Many North American nations—viewed as controlled by the United Fruit Company through corrupt dictators—became known as "Banana Republics."

In 1989, in a rather uncivil way, Guatemala was struggling with its civil war. To the south, war raged between the Contras and Sandinistas in Nicaragua, Honduras, and El Salvador. To the north, Chiapas rebels from southern Mexico consistently attacked strategic sites within the

View of Volcán de Agua from Antigua, Guatemala.

Guatemalan double-canopy jungles in the Petén District. Communist-backed rebels attempted to wreak havoc within Guatemala in their effort to overthrow the military-dominated government.

Guatemala possesses stunning, natural, and diverse beauty. The hue of orange lava streams gushing from active volcano eruptions, brown clay tile roof-laden villages, the white sands of the Caribbean Sea, and the black sands of the Pacific Ocean make Guatemala a picturesque and marvelous place to live. The grass-covered rolling hills, sugar cane fields, deep blue natural lakes, Mayan ruins towering above double-canopy jungles, abundant wildlife, year-around flowers in color-ful bloom, and historical remnants of Spanish conquistadors are all contradicted by a violent culture and endless wars. Guatemala is a dichotomy of paradise and danger.

In the late 1980s, civil war had become a way of life in Guatemala. Periodic sounds of propaganda bombs, designed to spread pro-communist leaflets, could be heard nightly.

Rated as a high crime post by DSS crime analysis, danger from street crimes equaled dangers from the communist-backed guerrillas. In Guatemala, mayhem accompanied death and indiscriminately came to people by muggers or insurgents intent on wrestling power from the government. U.S. diplomats were cautioned to discourage car robberies by discarding new, expensive vehicles for old clunkers. Diplomats were only allowed to live in selected parts of the city. Their barred windows and doors resembled prisons more than homes. For some, the tradeoff of protection from home invaders was tempered by fear of not being able to escape the heavily-fortified concrete constructed houses during Guatemala's frequent earthquakes. The diplomats' children were transported to school by embassy vans with heavily armed guards.

During the heat of midsummer, Guatemala was on edge after a Guatemalan woman, driving a Mercedes, was pulled from her vehicle at gunpoint while stopped at a traffic light. The woman driver was shot in the chest and died while trying to retrieve her infant who was strapped into a car seat. Oblivious to the threat, a spouse of a U.S. Agency for International Development (USAID) official imported a new, shiny Isuzu SUV. She was also carjacked at gunpoint with her child secured by a seat belt. Fortunately for her, the armed robber had a heart and allowed her to collect her child before driving away. A glutton for punishment, instead of learning from this life-threatening experience, the spouse imported another new Isuzu.

On my family's arrival to Guatemala City, with luggage loaded, the embassy vehicle departed the airport and drove my family and me through the crowded capital city traffic to the Hotel Camino Real. Located on 14th Street, the Hotel Camino Real was in close proximity to where U.S. Ambassador Mein was assassinated.

I recall the first night my wife, infant son Jacob, and I arrived in this fascinating mile-high city in 1989. In their effort to overthrow the Guatemalan government, the communist-backed insurgents had bombed a local power plant earlier in the day, knocking out the electric grid to our temporary hotel residence. Eerily on August 28th, my son Jacob's first birthday, I peered out of the hotel window toward the location

Damage from a grenade blast at Guatemala City's Hotel Camino Real.

where U.S. Ambassador John Gordon Mein had been assassinated, 21-years earlier to the day.

On our first assignment abroad with the U.S. Department of State, now sitting in total darkness in our hotel room, I was unsure how my wife Pam would react to the temporary discomforts afforded us by the insurgents. Acting on unmovable character, my wife quipped that the bombing offered us an opportunity for a candlelight dinner. Possessing a true Texan woman's pioneer spirit, my wife literally put into practice Eleanor Roosevelt's echoed conviction: "It is better to light a candle than curse the darkness."

A few days later, while sitting inside our hotel room, the communist guerillas announced their presence by throwing a grenade at the hotel. The explosion occurred a few yards from our window, causing significant damage to the hotel landscape. A DSS agent residing in an apartment building across the street recalled stepping out on his balcony after hearing the grenade explosion. At that moment, the DSS agent saw a blast of fire belch from the apartment building's ground floor. We later learned that the rebels had detonated a satchel (suitcase) bomb inside the apartment building's lobby. Our first few days in Guatemala were interesting, to say the least. Like Molly Brown, Pam remained unsinkable and unshakable. What a woman!

On reporting to duty at the U.S. Embassy, I was assigned to the U.S. ambassador's protective detail. This unit consisted of four DSS special agents and a large and very capable contingency of Guatemalan police officers trained by the DSS. I have fond memories during my time spent in Guatemala and experienced some of the greatest adventures of my life, especially while serving under Ambassador Thomas Stroock.

Thomas Stroock was an Ivy League-educated man who had been taken away from a life of mischievous adolescence, leading to street gangs of New York City. He became a self-made man in Wyoming's oil fields and served prominently in the Wyoming State legislature. The unique blend of street-wisdom, prestigious university education, and military service with the U.S. Marine Corps during World War II, tempered by Wyoming's wild outdoors, manifested into the persona of the U.S. ambassador in an exceptionally difficult assignment.

During an interview, when explaining his path in life, Tom Stroock said, "…in 1943 after my freshman year, I went into the Marines, and I went to Paris Island in June of that year. And then I was in the 10th

President George H. W. Bush (R); Amb. Thomas Stroock (C); and Marta Stroock (L) during White House meeting.

Marine Artillery Regiment of the Second Marine Division and joined them on the West Coast. We went to Auckland, New Zealand, where we staged for Guam. Then we were in Guam, Saipan and Tinian. And then my name, with about 4,000 others, dropped out of the old IBM card record files as having an IQ of x, whatever x was, and one year of college. And they shipped us back to the United States to go to Platoon Leaders Class in preparation for the attack on the Japanese home islands which, thank God, never occurred, or I probably wouldn't be here..."[39]

In Guatemala, Thomas Stroock enjoyed support from President George H. W. Bush, the U.S. Commander-in-Chief, whom he had befriended and was a fellow teammate on Yale University's baseball team.

Ambassador Stroock arrived in Guatemala during a violent civil war between the corrupt Guatemalan military command and communist-backed insurgents. Since the 1968 assassination of Ambassador Mein, U.S. Ambassadors assigned to Guatemala rated a full protective detail.

During my assignment to the embassy in Guatemala, concerns were aroused by the alleged rape of American citizen Dianna Ortiz, a Catholic nun, and the murder of Michael DeVine, an American who had owned a farm and hostel in Guatemala. Both individuals were allegedly victimized at the hands of suspected CIA-backed Guatemalan military. Intelligence units within the Guatemalan military were also suspected of committing mass genocide against rural indigenous people. These potential human rights violations led to demands for the release of U.S. classified documents.[40]

Concerns of prohibited CIA support were validated when President Bill Clinton declassified CIA documents that proved the intelligence agency had improperly supported the Guatemalan military that had been prohibited by the U.S. Congress. This revelation confirmed that for decades, the United States had supported Guatemala's genocide efforts of its rural indigenous peoples. The CIA-funded program was shut down by Congress.

Almost comically, in a corporate marketing-style attempt to rebrand its tarnished image from a genocide hit squad unit, the powerful Naziesque Guatemalan military intelligence changed its name from D-2 to G-2.

Millions of U.S. Congressional-approved dollars earmarked for Guatemalan military aid were sporadically extended and retracted during the precarious ebb and flow, roller coaster relationship between the U.S. Embassy and Guatemalan military over human rights violations.

Once, the Guatemalan Minister of Defense visited Ambassador Stroock at his official residence. I escorted two Guatemalan military officers to the library during the high-level meeting. One of the arrogant military officers sat down, looked me straight in the eyes and asked, "What happened to your country during the Vietnam War?"

The Texan spirit inside wanted to respond by asking the military officer, "What happened to YOUR country during the war with Belize (formerly British Honduras)?" Belize is a sore subject for many Guatemalans, especially the military elite. To this day, most Guatemalan maps indicate Belize as still part of Guatemala proper. Mustering every ounce of diplomacy, I bit my tongue and refused to verbally retaliate against the smug Guatemalan military officer.

I had enough savvy to know that confronting the corrupt foreign military was the job of an ambassador—through checkbook diplomacy or military intervention.

Tom Tonkin, an embassy political officer, best summed up Ambassador Stroock's foreign affairs strategy during a journalist's interview when he stated,

"... Finding the killer of American citizen Michael DeVine, who was beheaded in Guatemala in 1990, epitomizes how many know former Wyoming senator and U.S. Ambassador of Guatemala Thomas (Tom) Stroock: determined, tough and confident. Stroock knew the atrocity likely was committed by the country's military—already known for its gross human rights violations. Tom wanted it investigated and the guilty punished. He wasn't going to put up with any smokescreens."[41]

A few weeks after the incident, when nothing had been resolved, Stroock said to Tonkin, "...Well, let's see what a colonel is worth."

By this time, the U.S. Embassy had learned a Guatemalan colonel was linked to DeVine's death. Tonkin said in amazement, "So he just cut off military aid. I didn't know you could do things like that."

But Stroock did more than that. His strong-arm tactics went as far as withholding checks to the Guatemalan government. Tonkin, who had spent decades working at U.S. embassies around the world, never had seen an ambassador do something so bold. Tonkin related, "… A check would come across Tom's [Stroock] desk, and he would look at it, he would sniff, then he would open his bottom safe drawer and toss the check in there. I said when I first saw this, 'What are you doing?'

"He [Stroock] said, 'I'm not going to give them this.' I said, 'Tom, some of this is really theirs. Are we holding back everything?'

"He said, 'Yes. We've got to get their attention.' I'm thinking to myself, 'This may not even be legal, but this is great!'"

Stroock assured Tonkin, "I'm not worried. I'm not bucking for a promotion. I'm doing my job."

"So he did. And he kept tossing (the checks) in there [safe]," Tonkin laughed.

"In the end, the colonel was worth about $2 million when the Guatemalan military finally decided to prosecute," Tonkin said with a laugh. Colonel Julio Roberto Alpirez was sentenced to 25 years in prison.[42]

A man of his convictions, during the peak of withholding U.S. military aid, Ambassador Stroock was recalled to Washington, D.C. In a meeting at the State Department headquarters, Ambassador Stroock was instructed by an assistant secretary to release the funds to the Guatemalan military. Ambassador Stroock refused and insisted on a meeting with Secretary of State James Baker to further discuss the matter. Secretary Baker supported Ambassador Stroock's decision. Time would eventually prove Ambassador Stroock's decision to be correct, as the Guatemalan military eventually acquiesced under the financial pressure.

In threatening environments, a unique bond generally forms between executive protective detail agents and protectees. Given

Ambassador Stroock's genuine personality, camaraderie quickly developed between Ambassador Stroock and DSS special agents. In fact, there was not a security specialist, American or Guatemalan, who would not have walked through fire to protect the embassy's leader, and vice versa. With Ambassador Stroock, one never really knew what to expect day to day. I suppose the adventures that awaited us with the "old man" each day were what kept us on our toes.

Unfortunately for the U.S. security team, possibly because of the pressure the embassy was putting on the Guatemalan officials pertaining to the Ortiz and DeVine investigations, the diplomatic relationship was at an all-time low.

Ambassador Stroock, DSS and FBI special agents, and Guatemalan police filled the eight-car motorcade while waiting on the hot tarmac at the La Aurora International Airport in Guatemala City. The line of armored vehicles resembled a heavily armed snake. Multiple aircraft landing lights pierced the clear blue sky during their final landing approach in this mile-high, fertile, floral-laden capital city nestled in picturesque Central America.

Heads-of-state and foreign dignitaries flooded the skies on their way to attend the newly elected Guatemalan president's inauguration. The ominous Agua Volcano served as a backdrop to the oncoming jets. This extinct volcano separated Guatemala City from the quaint village of Antigua, with its cobblestone streets, mountainous coffee fields, and Mayan descendants adorned in their colorful tribal dress.

Tensions were running higher than normal this day. The United States had recently declared war against Iraq and Saddam Hussein. Now elevated to a high-threat security environment, the newly declared Gulf War informally elevated the security threat to critical-high. For the DSS protective detail, memories of that infamous day of U.S. Ambassador Gordon Mein's assassination loomed heavily.

As a symbol of diplomacy, it is customary for heads-of-state to attend other heads-of-state's inaugurations. Due to the U.S. focus and priority for the Gulf War, U.S. Attorney General Richard L. "Dick"

La Aurora International Airport, Guatemala

Thornburgh was the highest-ranking official from President George H. W. Bush's administration available to attend the Guatemalan presidential inauguration.

Word was received from the air traffic control tower and quickly passed to Ambassador Stroock of the U.S. Air Force jet's final approach and imminent arrival carrying his friend and fellow Yale alumni, U.S. Attorney General Thornburgh.

A final check of the security team was conducted; all was ready for the 20-block ride to the ambassadorial residence. As the U.S. Air Force passenger jet began its final taxi toward the civilian side of the airport's shared runway, the Guatemalan military control tower overrode the civilian air controller and instructed the jet to taxi and park on the military side of the airport, directly across the active runway from where our motorcade was staged.

This was obviously an intentional message delivered from the host government's military leadership of their displeasure of again being accused of human rights violations, the Ortiz and DeVine investigations, and more importantly, Ambassador Stroock withholding U.S. military aid funds in the latest 'tit-for-tat' diplomatic relationship with the U.S. government.

Like a battlefield commander, Ambassador Stroock sprang out of his armored limo to survey the situation.

Over the noise of jet engines, I yelled to the ambassador, "Sir, do you want us to drive around the airport to the military side of the runway?"

"Hell, no!" retorted Ambassador Stroock.

Resembling something out of a Hollywood war movie, the five-foot, eight-inch, square-jawed, former Marine made his decision, circled his arm, pointed his index finger across the runway toward the parked U.S. jet and said, "Load up, boys. Let's get our man!"

A U.S. Army sergeant from the U.S. military attaché's office responded, "But sir, this is an active runway."

Following the military code of honor, "leave no man behind," with unrelenting determination, Ambassador Stroock said, "I don't care. We're going to get our man!"

Adrenaline pumping, I muttered, "Yes, sir," and instructed the motorcade to cross the active runway.

I can only imagine the incoming pilots' surprise at seeing a string of eight vehicles creep across the active runway where they were preparing to land. Sparks spewed from the ambassador's armored limo's undercarriage as it scraped against the airport's elevated concrete runway.

We positioned the motorcade next to the stopped U.S. Air Force aircraft. The composed chief of mission exited the limo and greeted Attorney General Thornburgh, who was oblivious to the high-stake chess match now underway.

With Attorney General Thornburgh in the limousine, the U.S. Army sergeant asked the ambassador if he wanted him to seek permission from the Guatemalan base commander to use their vehicle gate to exit.

Ambassador Stroock responded, "Hell, no! We are going back across to the other side."

Guatemalan President Jorge Antonio Serrano Elías.

Locked and loaded, the motorcade snaked its way back across the active runway and exited the airport from the civilian side. I imagine our actions must have caused ulcers for the air traffic controllers and incoming pilots.

The historic 1952 Central Intelligence Agency plan—backed by the United Fruit Company and approved by President Truman—to overthrow Guatemalan President Jacobo Árbenz might still temper Guatemalan officials now intent on harming American diplomats.

Queen takes their knight! It was the Guatemalan military's next move.

Resembling a movie mobster from the U.S. prohibition era, I stared at the teardrop sunglasses of an arrogant Guatemalan military colonel attached to the Guatemalan G-2 (military intelligence). The colonel assessed the approaching U.S. executive protection security team. Attorney General Thornburgh was transported to view newly elected Jorge Antonio Serrano Elías' presidential inauguration at Guatemala's National Stadium.

The foreign diplomats and visitors seeking entrance into the stadium's confused and poorly organized bottleneck security check-point resembled a crowded New York subway car. The entire security team elbowed its way through the impatient crowd. We reached the stadium's security checkpoint. With Attorney General Thornburgh standing behind me, the Guatemalan colonel raised his arm to my chest, abruptly halting the entire American team at the stadium's entrance.

I quickly inquired as to the nature of our access denial. Pointing at our event identification cards, the Guatemalan colonel responded that the brown-colored background on the Guatemalan military-issued access cards were not the proper shade of brown, thus he deemed the ID cards as illegitimate.

An FBI advance agent and former Navy Seal who had worked alongside me for the week leading up to Thornburgh's visit removed his badge and held it close to the colonel's face, pointing out that his boss, the commander of the Guatemalan Estado Mayor, personally signed our identification cards. It was obvious that the Guatemalan military was making a statement about their displeasure with America withholding military aid, or Ambassador Stroock's trump play that had transpired earlier at the airport. Either way, this slimy colonel was Guatemala's point hatchet man.

The colonel instructed me to move aside and clear the metal detector access path for the other diplomats. When I and the entire American contingent refused the colonel's order, he positioned himself inches from my face, nose to nose, and began yelling, "No que!, no que!" (no what!, no what!)

Reacting to their commanding officer's agitated state, I assessed the dozen or so young, gung-ho Guatemalan soldiers, unschooled in political savviness and visibly displeased with their "jefe's" emotional outburst. These peach fuzz-faced soldiers were capable of opening fire against the unwelcome gringos at any time. With fingers on triggers, the unpredictable soldiers, eager to please their commander, fanned out and positioned themselves across the stadium fence directly opposite the U.S. security team. The louder the colonel yelled in my face, the more agitated his soldiers became.

Things were getting real bad, real fast, and Attorney General Thornburgh's safety was in real jeopardy in this Mexican-style standoff. Obviously sensing something was awry, Attorney General Thornburgh, who was standing directly behind me, inquired as to the conundrum that was unfolding before his eyes. I responded that everything was under control and asked him to remain patient.

Our strategy of clogging the only entrance and exit designated for the visiting dignitaries appeared to work as the pressure of jeers from the unhappy crowd of diplomats caused the colonel to blink.

The G-2 intelligence colonel said he would only allow the Attorney General to pass and enter the stadium. I acquiesced, stepped aside, and allowed the Attorney General and his FBI agent-in-charge to pass. Another plainclothes military thug grabbed the FBI's agent-in-charge as he passed through the metal detector. The FBI agent aggressively pulled away from the soldier and continued with the Attorney General.

The remaining U.S. security team back-filled the void left by the Attorney General and demanded the colonel allow us entrance before we would move. Having succeeded in countering our airport arrival response, the colonel agreed. The beads of sweat that now dripped from the colonel's forehead telegraphed his concern at how things had quickly spun out of control and how close we came to an armed conflict and international incident involving the U.S. Attorney General.

U.S. Attorney General Richard "Dick" Thornburgh.

No one really knows why the Guatemalan colonel acquiesced to the Americans. Perhaps the Guatemalan colonel backed down from fears of reprisal and retribution against him based on stories shared by his grandfather or father about the former influential and suspected CIA-backed United Fruit Company.

Regardless of the colonel's reason for retreating, the FBI and DSS stood our ground and successfully protected the Attorney General.

CHAPTER 11

TRUE GRIT

I began to wonder if my chances of survival
would improve if I were on the ground,
even if it meant engaging the enemy.

On a crisp and colorful spring morning in Guatemala City, I pondered, filling my lungs with fresh air, and decided to walk the 10 city blocks from my fortress-style residence to the U.S. Embassy. I planned to meet with and transport the motorcade to the ambassador's residence.

One block from the embassy, I crossed the lightly-traveled public street. A convenience store adjoined modest residences to the backside of the U.S. Embassy building. Using a cruel form of advertisement, this store had a leashed spider monkey, nicknamed Chilo. He was tied to a wire that strung the distance of the front yard closest to the public sidewalk. People passing by would oftentimes taunt Chilo by throwing trash or flicking cigarettes at him in order to evoke a primate response. To cope with captivity and harassment, through years of this interactive zoo-like atmosphere, Chilo developed a mischievous attitude.

While standing in Chilo's territory, very near one of the two rear gates at the U.S. Embassy, I was approached by a young, attractive woman. Speaking fluent Spanish, the woman identified herself as a flight attendant for a Central American airline. Her request mirrored the hundreds of similar requests made to American diplomats worldwide: she needed assistance to acquire a U.S. visa.

The human brain is an amazing organ that can process information in nanoseconds. As soon as this woman mentioned her country of origin, my mind raced ahead to the Contact Reporting Form required by U.S. government employees possessing a Top Secret security clearance, which required reporting any contacts with certain foreign nationals from countries deemed hostile to U.S. national security. Although the reporting list is classified, all contact between U.S. diplomats and nationals from this woman's country of citizenship were required to report, track, and control potential attempts of espionage. The day had not yet begun, and I was a bureaucratic victim of the morning's circumstances. At the precise moment my mind was calculating how quickly I could complete the Contact Reporting Form before I assumed my day's assignment of riding in the ambassador's armored limo, she suddenly began screaming hysterically.

Again, quantum physics engaged as my synaptic response now transitioned to constructing a defense to the woman's potential accusations that might be hurled in my direction. In her desire to flee her nation that was at war, would this desperate flight attendant resort to extortion by concocting an allegation of an improper touch in exchange for that all-important travel document known as a visa? I wondered if the embassy CCTV cameras and nearby witnesses would exonerate any false accusations levied against me.

Just as I was mentally preparing to hire attorney Perry Mason, the woman turned sideways, revealing the mischievous spider monkey attached to the back of her scalp, grasping all digits deeply into her thick, long black hair, similar to a reverse hold of the creature on the astronaut's face in the 1979 movie *Alien*.

A trained specialist in crisis management, I quickly summoned a man walking nearby. Like peeling a banana, the man and I attempted to dislodge Chilo's grip from the woman's head.

However, this street-wise monkey owned the day. Through the tactical element of surprise, Chilo had captured and controlled the high ground. Spanking this monkey and putting him to bed would only be accomplished on Chilo's terms. Chilo was a bad, bad monkey intent on venting years of pent-up frustrations.

Just a week earlier, I had read an article presuming that the Ebola virus was believed to have spread to humans through a monkey bite. Cautious of the infectious ramifications, each time the good Samaritan and I lifted Chilo's arms and legs, a snap of Chilo's teeth closely missed our exposed skin, resulting in our rapid retreat and release of his tense limbs.

A few minutes must have seemed like hours to the helpless flight attendant. Chilo soon became disenchanted and decided to "undock" and retreat to his lair. Unfortunately for the young flight attendant, who was now scratching the newly-introduced monkey mites, she left humiliated, dejected and without a U.S. visa as a result of an ill-timed jump from the naughty primate.

To my dismay, I looked up and found the protective detail agents laughing at my morning's *Wild Kingdom* encounter, an omen that not all was right in Guatemala City. The detail agents and I completed our early morning security checklist before making our way to pick up Ambassador Thomas Stroock at the official residence.

On arriving at the official residence, Ambassador Stroock stepped out of the U.S.-owned mansion into the bright sunlight. The 10-acre fort-like residential compound was surrounded by a high concrete wall supporting concertina wire and armed guard–filled towers. A Wyomingite, Ambassador Stroock proudly flew the Wyoming state flag below the American flag at the official residence.

Lifting his arms in the fresh mile-high air, the ambassador proclaimed, "God, what a beautiful morning. Fellas, I am going to walk into work this morning."

I quickly retorted that a French diplomat had reportedly been assassinated the previous night near the U.S. ambassador's official residence, about 10 city blocks from the U.S. Embassy, the precise route Ambassador Stroock desired to walk. For the most highly visible diplomat in this Central American country to walk fifteen blocks from his residence to the embassy was simply out of the question.

The ambassador smiled and responded to my protest by asking, "Who is in charge of this mission?"

To which I responded, "You, sir."

"Well then, we will walk to the embassy this morning."

A four-star equivalent diplomat easily outranks a low-ranking DSS special agent. End of discussion.

Not wishing to spar with an ambassador, we quickly arranged for motorcade shadowing moves and began our long trek through precarious urban terrain.

Ambassador Stroock always insisted on excellence in performance for the entire U.S. mission staff. In addition, the Ambassador possessed a unique sense of humor that put those around him at ease.

During his morning walk, about seven blocks from the embassy, the ambassador stopped to admire a plethora of colorful flowers in full bloom hanging from a large residential wall. After absorbing the beauty that lay before him, Ambassador Stroock lifted both hands to the sky, looked to the heavens, and proclaimed, "God, this is a beautiful country!"

At that precise moment, a bird perched in a tree branch directly above the ambassador defecated in his right hand.

An awkward pause ensued as seconds seemed like minutes. Responding with his quick-witted humor, the ambassador displayed the wet, white spot now in the middle of his palm and said, "I finally compliment this country and look what happens—I get crapped on."

The Ambassador then looked to me and the other DSS agent and asked why we had not stopped the bird from relieving itself at the expense of an ambassador's dignity. The other DSS agent jokingly responded that we would have had to shoot the bird, which would have aroused too much commotion.

Ambassador Stroock smiled, put his head down and trudged the remaining distance to the embassy's rear entrance. On arriving at the embassy, the ambassador was met by Phil Taylor, Deputy Chief of Mission (DCM), who extended his right hand for a morning greeting. The ambassador paused for a moment and thought about this once-in-a-lifetime opportunity, laughed, and told the DCM that this was not a good time for a handshake.

Ambassador Stroock required all employees to think quickly and remain nimble of foot and mind. He enjoyed a friendly bantering session and gave random quizzes to the DSS agents.

The protective detail utilized a fully armored limo, a lightly armored lead Chevrolet Suburban SUV and trail Suburban, commonly referred to as the follow or chase vehicle, staffed by a contingent of seasoned Guatemalan police officers assigned to the U.S. mission. Each day, one DSS agent served as the Agent-in-Charge, seated in the right front of the limo, while the other DSS agent served as the detail Shift Leader (tactical commander) seated in the follow vehicle.

During a trip to the Presidential Palace, Ambassador Stroock asked the DSS Agent-in-Charge what the agent would do at that precise moment if the limo came under gunfire. The agent (a former New York comedian) quipped, "I don't know about you, sir, but I would duck." The Ambassador chuckled at the agent's "touché" response.

The ambassador enjoyed smoking Cuban stogies, especially inside the limo. Unfortunately, the windows in the fully armored limo were permanently disabled in the up position. With each puff, cigar smoke filled the limo thicker than a San Francisco fog-out. Marta, his spouse, tried but was unsuccessful with curbing this unwanted behavior while the DSS agents tried not to cough, or worse, become asphyxiated.

One morning, a DSS agent devised a silent protest. While serving as the agent-in-charge in the limo, the DSS agent hid a gas mask at

Guatemalan military outpost situated on top of unexcavated Mayan temple along the Mexican border.

his feet. Like clockwork, Ambassador Stroock fired up a Cuban while en route to a downtown meeting. When the ambassador inquired as to the estimated drive-time, the agent bent forward, donned the gas mask, and turned to the ambassador to provide an answer. Ambassador Stoock smiled and retorted that he got the message and never again lit a cigar inside the limo.

Once, while walking to a gymnasium across the street from the official residence, Ambassador Stroock asked me and another DSS agent what we would do at that moment if we were attacked by guerrillas.

The accompanying agent quickly responded, "Sir, please understand, we don't need to outrun the guerrillas; we only need to outrun you."

Ambassador Stroock smiled but had a quizzical look on his face, probably from not having thought about that potential scenario.

Of course, in reality, the entire detail respected Ambassador Stroock. I firmly believe that most leaders possess an ability to manage people and programs. However, I am convinced that very few managers are true leaders. Ambassador Stroock was an outstanding manager of U.S. Embassy personnel and assets, but more importantly, he earned the respect of all through his uncompromising leadership. Ambassador Stroock possessed an innate ability to liaise with the highest-ranking world figures while maintaining a personable outreach to employees on the lowest-ranking echelon.

Not a month goes by when I don't access my memory banks to retrieve an event or life experience involving Ambassador Stroock when searching for a proper character trait to assist me while coping with an issue or problem. For me, Ambassador Stroock set the gold standard of leadership and management.

During my Guatemalan tour, I once accompanied the ambassador on a fishing trip to El Naranjo, located on the Petén's far western side, near the border with Mexico. Our intelligence placed the last known location of the insurgents at about 70 kilometers from the lodge where we planned to stay.

Prior to departing for this trip, I conducted a thorough research of the dangers that could harm us in that area. In addition to insurgents, the area was a habitat for poisonous spiders, scorpions, alligators, and a very venomous snake called *barba amarilla* or "Yellow Beard" due to the small yellow spot under the snake's head. This snake's venom consisted of neurotoxins, and without anti-venom, victims had but a few hours to live. I requested vials of anti-venom from the Department of State's Regional Medical Doctor, but was denied, as in his words, I was deemed medically unqualified to administer medication.

The ambassador, his wife Marta, another DSS agent, and I flew on a small twin-engine Cessna from Guatemala City to a remote grass airstrip in El Naranjo. Before landing the aircraft, the pilot had to make several passes to allow a man to clear the airstrip of cattle and horses. Several dirt mounds of unexcavated Mayan ruins served as .50-caliber machine-gun emplacements for Guatemalan soldiers. The soldiers were assigned to a small military outpost responsible for counterinsurgency patrols and to combat narcotic traffickers. We made our way to the rustic grass-thatched huts which made up the lodge. At Ambassador Stroock's request, a Belizean tour guide we had met previously on our trips to the Tikal Mayan ruins accompanied us as a guide and cook.

The other DSS agent had grown up in Philadelphia and despised the primitive living conditions, biting bugs, and the notion of having to start the water well-pump motor in order to take a cold morning shower. The security agent and I shared a room which consisted of two beds made from logs cut from the surrounding jungle. Each bed was draped with mosquito nets. One night we experienced a torrential tropical downpour. The grass roof held for several hours but eventually sprang a leak directly over the other agent's head, pouring water into his face. The DSS agent awoke grumbling about the hardships. While dragging his heavy bed to a dryer location, I reminded him about the dangers of walking barefooted due to the large black scorpions.

During the ambassador's fishing outings, the DSS agent and I shared a follow boat. The river was pristine and several troops of monkeys walked among the tree limbs. As we approached the lodge in the late evening, I noticed several men dressed in green clothing standing on the lodge's dock. We thought these men may have been insurgents but were not sure. As we approached the dock, we were relieved to discover the men were soldiers from the nearby outpost who wanted to welcome our ambassador to their remote outpost.

The lodge owner's son had an unsettling sense of humor, extending his hand to shake mine. After shaking his hand, he showed me a large black scorpion he was holding in the same hand that shook mine. Fortunately for me, he had removed the scorpion's stinger. I found no humor in his joke.

On the last night of our visit, the owner's son asked the ambassador if he wanted to accompany him for a nighttime fishing venture. Ambassador Stroock graciously declined his tempting offer. During the following day, just prior to departing the lodge for the grassy runway, the owner's son presented Ambassador Stroock with a small alligator he had killed the previous night. Not wanting to hurt the son's feelings, the ambassador diplomatically accepted the gift. On returning to Guatemala, the ambassador had the small alligator mounted by a taxidermist.

During the rest of Ambassador Stroock's tenure in Guatemala, at the conclusion of each weekly country team meeting attended by all embassy section heads, the ambassador presented the person who provided the worst briefing the "croc award." That person was required to keep the stuffed croc for a week. Ambassador Stroock's brilliant and humorous managerial technique inspired all section chiefs to do their homework in order to avoid earning the dreaded "croc award."

In addition to Amabassador Stroock's humor, we did share some tense moments.

Petén, Guatemala's largest state, is located at the northern-most part of the country. Petén consists mostly of double-canopy jungles with many unexcavated ruins. Tikal is the largest excavated Mayan city in Petén. During the late 1980s and early 1990s, Petén was known for lawlessness. Guatemalan oil fields in Petén were frequent bombing targets by the communist guerrillas based in southern Mexico's Chiapas district.

I accompanied the ambassador to a remote Mayan clear-water lake excavation site called Blue Lake. We flew into the airport in Flores and drove about an hour on a gravel road, traversed a portion of national parkland, then drove down a long dirt road before arriving at a rustic lakeside lodge.

Acting as the embassy's control officer, a female employee with the U.S. Agency for International Development (USAID) accompanied us on this trip. While passing through the park entrance, we all noticed several mounds of dirt with a sign posted atop declaring it was illegal to remove the dirt. Exercising complete disregard, a dump truck was parked next to the mound with several men shoveling dirt into the truck.

A few minutes after driving through the thick double canopy jungle, we arrived at a rustic cabin situated along the lakeside. Ambassador Stroock, the other DSS agent, and I were invited to board two canoes where we boated to the rarely seen Mayan ruins. Unknown to me and the other DSS agent, the USAID employee returned to the dirt mounds and confronted the men loading the dirt. Obviously shaken, the USAID employee returned to the lodge and informed us that the "jefe" brandished a handgun and ordered her to leave, or else. We instructed the USAID employee not to confront the men on our departure, as we did not want to provoke danger for the ambassador during our trip.

Lo and behold, when we departed the lodge, the USAID employee who was driving the vehicle with the ambassador and DSS agent stopped and again confronted the men, demanding they cease stealing dirt. I was sitting in the security follow vehicle and noticed the men atop the dump truck become agitated, looking at their "jefe" for instructions. Not wanting the situation to escalate, I raised my Uzi machine gun to visually communicate that it would not be in these men's best interest to un-holster their handgun. In the event that things broke bad, I was prepared to neutralize the threat and work my way through the jungle back to Flores. A couple of three-round bursts could quickly end any threat I deemed counter to our safety. Fortunately for all parties involved, on seeing my machine gun, the men kept their cool and allowed us to pass unharmed.

One of the most rewarding trips I experienced was when I accompanied the ambassador to a mountain village for the dedication of a medical clinic funded and built by the U.S. Peace Corps. The U.S. Army Black Hawk helicopter carrying Ambassador Stroock and his DSS security detail landed in a tight, makeshift helipad near the small village. Rebels were known to frequent this mountainous area in order to intimidate and frighten the inhabitants into political submission. As there were no vehicular roads into this remote region, all construction materials had to be carried in by horseback over a six-day journey.

Bullet holes from machine gun fire on the clinic's stucco walls were a reminder that the rebels were serious in their bid to win the villagers' hearts and minds for their twisted causes. Descendants of the magnificent Mayans, the tribal village inhabitants were extremely poor people who respected and appreciated the U.S. Peace Corps' efforts to help their village. Food was generally sparingly used for their own sustenance.

To honor Ambassador Stroock's visit to their community, the villagers butchered one of their few and prized cows for a village-wide celebration. It was a truly moving experience to witness some of the poorest people in this war-ravaged nation extending their boundless generosity, sharing their scarce food to honor the U.S. Ambassador. To me, this was the essence of U.S. diplomacy and foreign relations.

In the early 1990s, the U.S. Department of State and Drug Enforcement Agency (DEA) partnered to establish a counter-narcotics effort under the U.S. government's program dubbed, "Operation Snowcap." This program was specifically aimed at eradicating the increasing number of poppy fields grown in Guatemala's highlands region. It was purported that the Guatemalan poppy crop produced enough heroin to solely supply the annual need of American addicts.

To counter this threat, the U.S. Department of State's Narcotic Assistance Service (NAS) and DEA operated an aerial spraying operation aimed to kill the poppy plants before they could be harvested. This program consisted of two crop-duster spray planes piloted by civilian crop-duster pilots from West Texas. The program used commercial-grade Roundup brand herbicide to kill the poppy plants.

Because the planes were frequent targets of gunfire from the drug producers, the spray plane engines were modified to increase speed and the cockpits were armored to protect the pilots from gunfire. In addition, during the spraying missions, each plane was escorted by sky-blue-colored Huey helicopters equipped with an M60 machine gun attached at each bay door.

The escort helicopters' two-fold mission was to provide cover protection for the spray planes and prevent the growers from diluting the herbicide. Because Roundup herbicide is water soluble, the poppy growers would sometimes send men carrying water tanks strapped to their backs to quickly rinse the poppy plants of poison, hoping to save the plants before osmosis absorbed enough poison to kill the plant. Thus, the escort helicopters would hover over the sprayed plants for several minutes to allow ample time for osmosis.

I accompanied Ambassador Stroock on a Black Hawk helicopter to observe a spraying mission. In order to ensure the ambassador's safety, the Black Hawk hovered at 10,000 feet. At this altitude, it was difficult to experience the real impact of this important program. On our return to Guatemala City, I asked the DEA attaché for approval to accompany the crop duster on a future spraying mission.

Early Sunday morning, I made my way to a non-descript airplane hangar at Guatemala's international airport and met the crew I would accompany. Two planes were fueled and spray tanks were filled. The crop duster cockpit situated the pilot in the front portion of the aircraft and I sat in the second seat directly behind the pilot. We departed the airport in flying formation.

About 40 minutes into the mission, two Huey helicopters joined us. We were now in Guatemala's highland area, surrounded by large tree-topped hills with low-hanging clouds. The pilot told me of the dangers of the low clouds, as they recently lost an aircraft to poor visibility, resulting in the pilot's fatality when he crashed his plane into a hillside. As we flew over the mountains, the pilot pointed out small patches of poppy plants. His eyes were obviously adapted at spotting small plants as I could not see one red poppy. In order to avoid being hit by gunfire, the pilot would begin the spraying approach by banking hard to the right, then to the left, and banking back to the right before lining up to spray the plot at an angle on the hillside. The pilot then pulled back hard on the stick, exiting the area while pulling three g-forces, leveled out and began searching for another poppy plot.

Early in the spraying portion of the mission, the pilot lit a cigarette and filled the cockpit with smoke. I did not smoke and there was minimal ventilation inside the cockpit. I attempted to redirect a small air vent and gasped as much air as possible. Between the cigarette smoke, empty stomach, fatigue from climbing a volcano the previous day, trees and clouds quickly passing my peripheral vision, and muscles strained from resisting g-forces, I was overcome with motion sickness. With eyes watering and every ounce of energy expended, I began to wonder if my chances of survival would improve if I were on the ground, even if it meant engaging the enemy. After about an hour and forty-five minutes, my nightmare finally ended when I heard the pilot's words, "mission accomplished" and we returned to base.

On arriving back at the airport, I composed myself, thanked the two pilots, shook their hands, and told them how much fun I had and looked forward to another trip someday. Of course I lied. Although I promised myself that I would never participate in such a mission, I am grateful for the brave men and women who continually place themselves in harm's way to protect our children from illicit drugs.

The embassy's Community Liaison Office coordinated an embassy-sponsored outing for those who enjoy living on life's "ragged edge." The group would scale the active Pacaya Volcano, located 30 kilometers southwest of Guatemala City. I, along with a few other daring souls, climbed to the volcano's caldera. Sounds of popping magma made its way out of the vent hole while the group ate sack lunches as we sat on volcanic ash that was almost too hot to sit on comfortably. Hindsight being 20/20, I later learned that a group of tourists died from poisonous gases belched from the Pacaya Volcano while standing near the caldera.

Weeks prior, DSS had had the unpleasant task of debriefing a group of American tourists who had visited the Pacaya Volcano with a private tourist agency. The group consisted of over twenty tourists. Three armed men robbed the group at gunpoint near the volcano's base. After the robbers collected the loot, they took three American women and their husbands away from the main tourist group. The armed men proceeded to rape the women in front of their husbands who had been bound with ropes.

A true adventurer, Ambassador Stroock asked DSS to coordinate a trip to the base of the Pacaya Volcano. Realizing the dangers posed around the volcano, the DSS team organized a very robust protective posture for the ambassador. The long hike to the volcano was eerie as we could feel concealed eyes peering at us as we made our way through heavily wooded areas. The trip was cut short when the volcano began spitting out large rocks. There is no combating Mother Nature.

CHAPTER 12

CHARIOT OF FIRE

What seemed like a simple task
of retrieving a stolen vehicle was turning
into a dangerous fiasco.

Guatemala was an absolute haven for auto-theft cartels. During the late 1980s and early 1990s, as many as eighty percent of all vehicles in Guatemala were stolen. On one occasion, Pam and I went to one of the many used-car lots in Guatemala City. We covertly wrote down the vehicle identification numbers for eight random vehicles. Record checks through the U.S. Border Patrol revealed that all eight vehicles were reported stolen from the United States.

That year, at least a dozen people had reportedly been killed as a result of the warring auto-theft cartels. It was common to see brazen car thieves paying customs officials in broad daylight, exchanging stolen vehicles for cash. Once, while conducting embassy business at the main Guatemalan customs building, an expediter and I became lost in the vast expanse of offices and warehouses. Rounding a corner, we stumbled on a room that shone bright with an aura of new American vehicles. Chevrolet Suburbans, pickup trucks, and Jeeps filled the room. I collected the vehicle identification numbers; record checks revealed them as stolen.

I informed the National Automobile Theft Bureau (NATB) of the located stolen vehicles, but was informed that no treaty existed between the United States and Guatemala to recover stolen vehicles. I then notified the American insurance companies which held the automobile titles by virtue of paying the insurance claims—mostly in Texas, Arizona, and California—that their stolen vehicles had been located in Guatemala.

One of the vehicles was a new, cherry red Chevrolet Suburban with less than five thousand miles on the odometer. The prior owner, a California dealer, reported that two men must have stopped to make keys during an unaccompanied test drive. The men returned to the dealership that night and stole the Suburban from the lot. The dealer said that an insurance claim had been filed for the theft, so the insurance company was now the legal owner.

I informed the insurance company of the Suburban's location. The insurance company responded that it had paid $19,000 plus for the theft claim, but had no desire to hire an attorney to attempt to recover the vehicle. Perhaps tongue-in-cheek, the insurance company stated its willingness to sell the vehicle. Taking the bait, I asked what the selling price might be. The insurance company said, "Make an offer." Like a bass biting a lure, I responded $5,000. The insurance executive said, "Sold." Appraised at $35,000, I bit.

The insurance company provided one proviso. I would be required to wire the money before they would release the title. Living on thin financial margins, $5,000 was a large chunk of change. After discussing the matter with my wife, we both agreed to the risky venture. Two days after wiring the money to the insurance company, I received the original automobile title for the new Suburban.

With title in hand, I went to the Guatemalan customs building to collect my new vehicle. I approached a young customs officer and informed him that I wanted to retrieve my Suburban. The customs agent's face turned pale and he became agitated. After a moment, the customs agent calmed down and informed me that he had seized that vehicle from the suspected car thief for refusing to pay the required one-hundred percent tariff fee ($35,000). The thief told the customs agent that he would return and kill him for seizing his stolen suburban. The agent said he thought I was the assassin sent to kill him.

Wow! What seemed like a simple task of retrieving a stolen vehicle was turning into a dangerous fiasco. I was escorted in to see the colonel in charge of the entire customs operation. The colonel's dark hair— slicked straight back—looked as though this man used an entire can of Dapper Dan's hair pomade. On presenting my original automobile title, the colonel beat around the bush for a moment before getting to the crux of the matter. The colonel hinted that his office needed new computers and office equipment. Realizing that the corrupt customs official was asking for a bribe, I quickly cut him off and informed him that as a diplomat assigned to the U.S. Embassy, I was not allowed to provide the items he was requesting.

The colonel paused and said that he would allow me possession of my Suburban after I had claimed its legal entry into Guatemala. The vehicle was placed under customs custody until the paperwork could be processed at the Guatemala-Mexico border town of Ciudad Tecún Umán. My wife was now in Texas to give birth to our second son. The window of opportunity to witness my son's birth was quickly closing. As each day passed, my new vehicle acquisition dilemma was growing more complex and dangerous.

I picked up my quasi-owned vehicle from the customs building in Guatemala City. With two Guatemalan customs agents in tow, I hired heavily armed guards donning Uzi machine guns and shotguns to make the arduous trek to the Mexican border. The route to Ciudad Tecún Umán was referred to as "Bandit Alley" due to the highway bandits and guerilla attacks. While en route, we were required to go off road, driving past two bridges that the Marxist forces had destroyed with explosives.

After the four hour, one-way voyage, my customs expediter disappeared into the small customs building.

Thirty minutes later, the expediter quickly jumped into the front Suburban seat and frantically said, "Let's get out of here!"

The armed guards, expediter, and I sped away from the border in our getaway vehicle. Once at a safe distance from the border, the expediter told me that the thief who had threatened to kill the customs agent was inside the border customs office demanding the vehicle be returned to him, or else.

On the return trip to Guatemala City, we encountered a blinding tropical rain storm. Freight semi-trucks—blown onto their sides from the wind's forces—littered Bandit Alley. Somehow, we limped into Guatemala City past midnight. Passing on sleep that night, I caught an early flight to Texas for my son's birth.

Once I returned to Guatemala, I learned that the customs colonel was demanding that I pay the import tariff for the Suburban. It was then I realized the colonel had probably claimed dibs on my Suburban, perhaps to be used on his farm. With only three months remaining on my Guatemalan tour, I parked the vehicle in a warehouse and opted to drive the Suburban back to Texas.

At my going-away party—hosted by Ambassador Stroock—to highlight our incredible adventure with our new suburban, a DSS agent made a cutout poster of the red Suburban with the words, "Texas or Bust."

At the conclusion of my tour, we departed for the U.S. In order to minimize stops, I filled an ice chest with cheese and summer sausage. Passing through Ciudad Tecún Umán, a Mexican border agent told me that I was not allowed to bring the summer sausage and cheese into Mexico. I just knew the shakedown known in Mexico as the mordida (bite) would soon ensue.

Just before laying the bite boom on me, I shared that I worked at the U.S. Embassy. I did not specify which country. Assuming I was assigned to the U.S. Embassy in Mexico, the border agent's face lit and he informed that he and his spouse were planning a trip to Disney World and needed a U.S. visa. I encouraged him to call the embassy and ask for Robert. I was promptly allowed entry into Mexico. I can still envision the smiling, waving Mexican border agent in my rearview mirror. I contemplated his potential disappointment of calling the U.S. Embassy in Mexico City, only to find out that no Robert worked at that location.

Within two and a half days, I drove the entire length of Mexico. On arriving in Texas, my first stop was at the County Tax Assessor Collector's Office to legally register my new vehicle. Word quickly spread to my colleagues in the embassy in Guatemala. I was bombarded with phone calls requesting I explain how I was able to pull off the seemingly impossible feat of acquiring a vehicle for pennies on the dollar.

I strongly encouraged the eager employees to abandon any notions to follow in my footsteps, as I had lost at least five years of my life due to the stress involved with this episode.

Farewell reception. L–R: Marta Stroock, Robert W. Starnes, Pam Starnes, and Amb. Thomas Stroock.

Looking back on my assignment to the embassy in Guatemala City, I often think about my time spent with Ambassador Thomas Stroock, and gain inspiration from his leadership and friendship.

CHAPTER 13

ANDEAN HIGH

My second near-death experience in a vehicle
was on National Geographic's designated
world's most dangerous road ...

Remains of Front Gate,
Also Part of Front Wall
Damaged in Blast.

Damaged U.S. Marine residence
in La Paz, Bolivia.

The time was 11:00 p.m. on October 10, 1990. The local contract security guards had secured the two-story residence of the U.S. Marine Security Guard detachment. Two minutes later, all hell broke loose.

Members of the Néstor Paz Zamora Commission (*Comision Nestor Paz Zamora,* CNPZ), a drug trafficking organization, opened fire on two contract guards, wounding one and killing the other. Before escaping, the CNPZ attackers placed an explosive near the gate, causing significant damage to the residential structure. A few hours later, the CNPZ toppled a statute of President John F. Kennedy in a downtown plaza. Fortunately, none of the U.S. Marines were injured.[43]

During my assignment to the U.S. Embassy in Guatemala, I was temporarily reassigned to the U.S. Embassy in La Paz, Bolivia, to assist the DSS Regional Security Office in the aftermath of the U.S. Marines house bombing attack.

Boasting some of the most spectacular Andes Mountains views, Bolivia has a colorful and violent history, hosting many anti-American political and narcotic-trafficking factions. On August 8, 1988, a roadside bombing attack was carried out against the DSS security motorcade carrying Secretary of State George P. Shultz. Although Secretary Shultz was unharmed during this attack, four other motorcade vehicles were significantly damaged, including the car carrying Shultz's wife.

Perched on the side of a mountain, sitting at an elevation some 13,000 feet above sea level, La Paz boasts of having the world's

The Wild Bunch Gang, Ft. Worth, Texas, circa 1900.

highest golf course with grass greens. The thin atmosphere and lack of oxygen in the capitol city necessitates U.S. State Department employees to pass multiple medical exams in order to travel to Bolivia.

Bolivia is rich with gold deposits, evidenced by locals openly panning for gold and their daily trips to the gold market to sell their precious raw metal. This land-locked South American nation once neutralized American outlaws Butch Cassidy and the Sundance Kid.

More recently, Bolivia has become known as a safe haven for World War II exiles, protecting the likes of the infamous Nazi war criminal Nikolaus "Klaus" Barbie. Some believe that the West German intelligence recruited Klaus Barbie while U.S. intelligence assisted in his escape from Germany to South America where he was employed to assist in anti-Marxist efforts; he is believed to have abetted the CIA in the capture of Argentine revolutionary Che Guevara.

While assigned to La Paz, the terrorists kept a low profile in the wake of the U.S. Marines house bombing. Most of my adventures in Bolivia would manifest during my non-duty hours. I was encouraged by embassy staff to visit the Witches' Market in La Paz. At first I believed this to be a gag, but decided to see for myself if there really was such a market. On a weekend I hailed a taxi and I was dropped near the Cathedral. Mostly out of breath, I trekked up a large hill behind the church.

On arriving at the precipice, to my surprise, I saw several Bolivian women wearing black dresses, black vests, and black bowler hats pushing carts containing llama fetuses and other potion jars. My family members back home would never believe the sight that lay before me. I had to have proof of this most unusual scene. I raised my camera to take a photo and noticed several of the women stop what they were doing and stared at me. When I snapped a photograph, one of the witches began to pursue me.

I have received some of the world's best, state-of-the-art security training. However, never in any of my training classes was I instructed on how to deal with a 250-pound Bolivian witch. Had I stood my ground, I imagined how picture

A Guatemalan man partaking in a religious animal sacrifice.

frames would have shown the witch getting closer and closer until the final photograph would have been taken literally at ground level, a depiction of my camera and body laying spread eagle as a result of a witch's upper cut.

I would have put a smile on Sir Isaac Newton's face. Thanks to gravity, I was able to descend the hill faster than my pursuer.

While catching my breath at the base of the mountain, I had recalled another recent witch episode in Guatemala. My brave, adventurous wife and I visited the picturesque highland town of Chichicastenango, Guatemala. As with most Latin American towns, a large church is located in Chichicastenango's town center. While we walked past the market, we noticed people burning animal sacrifices at the base of the church stairs.

As I made my way through the low fog-like cloud cover, I felt like Captain Benjamin L. Willard (played by Martin Sheen), discovering Colonel Walter E. Kurtz (played by Marlon Brando) in his Cambodian jungle quasi-palace from the movie *Apocalypse Now*. Stench from burned animal flesh and xylophone music filled the air. Walking through the crowded colorful market vendors, mostly comprised of Mayan descendants, was a bit surreal. What a strange but adventurous moment. My Guatemalan assignment was my family's first overseas tour. Having been reared in America's proclaimed Bible Belt, my wife and I were astounded that people still performed animal sacrificial ceremonies.

While we were absorbing the religious ceremony before us, an elderly woman wearing indigenous Mayan clothing approached us and asked, "Do you want to go with me into the mountains? Do you want to go with me into the mountains and see the real thing?"

We politely declined the old woman's request and immediately departed the area.

A few days after my encounter with the Bolivian witch, two visiting Federal Aviation Administration (FAA) employees, two embassy security contract employees, and I decided to rent a taxi cab for the day to visit Lake Titicaca and the Tiwanaku Aztec ruins.

Intelligence placed the anti-American insurgents about seventy kilometers from these sites and the trip was perceived to be safe. Our group proceeded to Lake Titicaca where we took a boat to an island where the famous boat of reeds—that successfully crossed the Atlantic Ocean—was constructed. Afterward, we ate freshly caught trout before moving on to the Tiwanaku ruins.

The 1969 Chevrolet Impala sedan taxi we occupied turned onto a dirt road and drove for many miles. During this trip, the taxi driver constantly boasted of American-made vehicles. Traveling about 40 mph, we crashed over an inconspicuous speed bump on the gravel road. Riding without seatbelts, our bodies flung around the taxi like rag dolls. We encouraged the taxi driver to stop and check the condition of the vehicle. Out of pride maybe, the taxi driver continued to boast of the durability of his vehicle, even though his dashboard now violently shook.

A few miles later, just as we were in the process of passing a dump truck, the taxi's rear-end differential locked, causing us to skid and narrowly miss hitting the full dump truck. The taxi and passengers came to rest in an open field. No one was injured, but the embarrassed taxi driver insisted we pay him for the full day's rental before he made his way back to La Paz to get a wrecker to tow his vehicle. Now, abandoned in the countryside, we decided to continue to walk toward the ruins. After several miles, a generous European couple had pity on us and took us in their own vehicle to the ruins and back to La Paz.

My second near-death experience in a vehicle was on National Geographic's designated world's most dangerous road, the mountain road to the remote Yungas town of Coroico. The DSS RSO drove me, the FBI special agent, and his wife to the picturesque town. On arriving, we observed several large Bolivian women sitting along the roadside chewing and spitting out coca leaves, resembling cattle chewing their cuds. When the women saw us—suspecting we were agents from the Drug Enforcement Agency (DEA)—in unison, they began yelling, "Deeah! Deeah!" In Spanish, the women were yelling, "DEA! DEA!" Fortunately, we did not encounter drug traffickers.

The RSO said that the drive to Coroico had taxed his concentration so I offered to drive for the return trip. On several occasions, we drove through a road laden with waterfalls and areas where the road was so narrow, the wheels barely passed. The danger is evident from a *Top Gear* episode when presenter Jeremy Clarkson is quite anxious as his tires narrowly escape slipping off the road. Had this event come to pass, it surely would have resulted in Clarkson's death.

At one curve, we stopped to observe a vehicle that had driven off the road, leaving vehicle parts strewn all down the mountainside. The cliff was so steep, we crawled on our stomachs to the road's edge and looked over the cliff, but could not see the bottom of the ravine. While departing Coroico, we passed a micro-bus that had recently tumbled off the road. A small four-inch diameter tree was the only thing separating the bus and its passengers from descending to the river 6,000 feet below.

This road later claimed the lives of American diplomats, resulting in an off-limits directive for all U.S. diplomats and dependents.

I will always cherish the time I spent in Bolivia, my Andean paradise.

ISLAND
LIFE

CHAPTER 14

KIWIS WHO PROTECTED A TIGER

I contacted Tiger Woods' agent, Mark Steinberg,
and informed him of the threat letter and its
potassium cyanide poison, and inquired if Tiger Woods
was aware of anyone who might wish to kill Tiger.

Soon after I was seated, I observed a man make his way to the podium. Clearing his voice, the man stated, "I should be dead now!" Now that is an icebreaker for the ages, I thought. The speaker continued by introducing himself as the scientist representing the New Zealand National Police.

The police department's scientist explained that the chemical substance I had forwarded for police evaluation had tested positive for laboratory-grade potassium cyanide. The scientist continued that he normally began testing unknown substances with acid-based chemicals. For an unexplained reason, on this day, the scientist began his test with nonacid-based chemicals. The scientist explained that if he had begun his examination with acid, the potassium cyanide would have created hydrocyanic acid fumes, the same chemical brew used for capital punishment executions in gas chambers.

Unlike its neighbor Australia, New Zealand is snake-free and void of land-borne venomous animals. That is, with the exception of a specific human serpent who remained concealed somewhere on this South Pacific island nation, stating his intent to kill Tiger Woods and New Zealand citizens.

Aotearoa, meaning "land of the long white cloud," is the most recognized Maori name for New Zealand, located seventeen hours ahead of the U.S. Eastern Time Zone. I had been assigned security responsibilities for U.S. personnel and facilities in Wellington, and the U.S. Consulate in Auckland.

I also had security responsibility for the National Science Foundation (NSF) Antarctica Program based in New Zealand's south island city of Christchurch. I fondly recall stories from those who served on the southern polar cap—those who had taken the newcomers' initiation challenge to the South Pole that consisted of the newbies stripping nude and run a short distance from a building, around the pole designating the actual South Pole coordinates and back to the building. A unique T-shirt is awarded to initiates who successfully meet the challenge. Outside of hypothermia, the biggest danger I suppose is rounding the mock "South Pole" and having an appendage stick to its bare metal. I suppose for the men, the cold weather minimizes this risk.

The rarely seen nocturnal and flightless Kiwi bird is a New Zealand national symbol. Based on its stunning natural beauty, friendly people, and intriguing Maori culture, New Zealand is a popular tourist destination. And as such, its economy relies heavily on tourism.

New Zealand is also a favorite destination for the movie filming industry. Director Peter Jackson shot both *The Hobbit* and *The Lord of the Rings* there. The Helm's Deep battle scene in *The Lord of the Rings, The Two Towers*, was filmed in an abandoned rock quarry just a few minutes' drive from our residence in Lower Hutt in the Wellington Region. Sword-wielding actors could be seen battling against the feared Orcs and Uruk-hai during our trips to the grocery store. New Zealand was certainly a beehive of activity during filming.

New Zealand was to be an assignment from which to recuperate after my whirlwind, three-year Paraguayan tour where I dealt with two separate terrorist crises, a violent coup d'état, and the capture of an elusive, escape-artist fugitive.

My first challenge at the embassy was to prepare for the Year 2000 problem (Y2K); possibilities ranged from concerns about gasoline pumps failing to a worldwide societal breakdown leading to an apocalyptic-type meltdown due to computer malfunctions on the first day of the 21st century. Because the U.S. Embassy in Wellington, New Zealand, was the first U.S. diplomatic facility to bring in the new century, we were the first embassy to report to headquarters of either continued normality of our computer systems or chaos at the last strike of midnight. There were many hours of security planning conferences and countless embassy meetings. Fortunately, the Y2K concerns started with a roar but passed with a whimper.

My family and I especially enjoyed New Zealand's outdoor activities. There were hiking and berry-eating adventures in the Akatarawa Forest near Upper Hutt, trout and deep-sea fishing, hot air ballooning, whale watching near Christchurch, walking among dozens of wild blue penguins as they made their nests in Dunedin, boating through the Milford Sound, walking the warm beaches on Bay Islands, skiing at the Southern Alps mountain range, soaking in the warm, geothermal waters at Hanmer Springs during snowfalls, and taking a helicopter flight that landed on top of a mountain peak snow field. One of our favorite outings was seal-watching at Red Rocks, located along Wellington's south coast at the treacherous Cook Strait.

New Zealand did not disappoint with my recuperation and will always hold a special place in my family's memories.

People ask, "Do you remember where you were during the September 11 terrorist attacks?"

Seventeen hours ahead into the United States' future, on September 12, 2001, New Zealand time, my sleep was disturbed by a telephone call on September 11, Washington, D.C., time. Struggling to transition from my deep sleep, I recognized the voice of the DSS overseas desk officer responsible for supporting embassies throughout the Asia-Pacific region, including New Zealand.

Skipping normal salutations, with a shaky voice, the DSS desk officer stated, "Robert, we are under attack!"

My mind in a state of surreality, I struggled to awaken, but could not comprehend what he said.

I replied, "I don't understand."

The DSS desk officer simply suggested I watch the CNN news broadcast. I stumbled into the living room and sat shocked at the sight of the collapse of two World Trade Center buildings and the fire that engulfed the Pentagon. Having visited both sites, this was personal. I was well aware that while serving as a DSS RSO, I was responsible for protecting a mission terrorists considered a jewel for an attack against America, a U.S. Embassy.

The day my family and I spent on September 11, 2001, in New Zealand was completely uneventful. Now, the day after, temporarily detached from my immediate surroundings, something kept niggling at me. Finally, snapping to my senses, I realized that I was responsible for the security of U.S. diplomats and diplomatic facilities. I quickly made my way to the embassy to prepare for any potential copycat attacks against American interests.

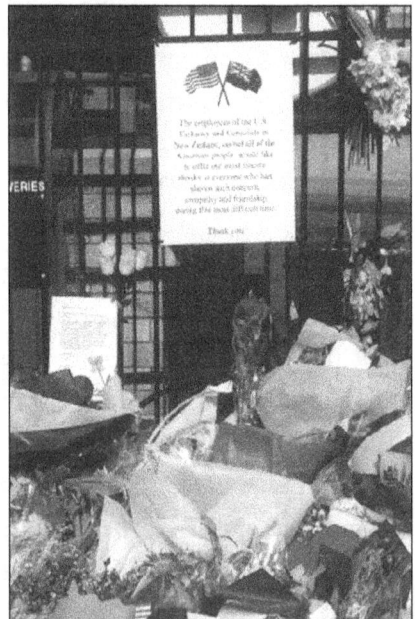

Flowers of condolences at the U.S. embassy in Wellington, New Zealand

I arrived at the U.S. Embassy around 4:00 a.m. The contract local guard who greeted me at the gate informed me that Phil Goff, New Zealand Minister of Foreign Affairs, who lived in a house adjacent to the embassy's perimeter wall, had just stopped by the embassy to offer his condolences to the American people. The people of New Zealand also laid flowers and wreaths in front of the embassy to pay respects to those who perished in the attacks.

Just as Japan had declared war against the United States in World War II and conducted a sneak attack on Pearl Harbor, al-Qaeda had declared war and conducted its own sneak attack on September 11. Although separated by years and generations, both attacks were a kick in the gut that evoked a spectrum of emotions from anger, empathy, sympathy, and sadness—but mostly anger.

Just a few weeks earlier, I had completed a fiction action adventure novel manuscript, partly based on my DSS experiences while serving in Paraguay. My Hollywood-based agent informed me that filmmaker Michael Bay had expressed interest in my manuscript, but opted to produce the movie *Pearl Harbor* instead.

I had also traveled to Honolulu, Hawaii, to attend an East Asia-Pacific RSO regional conference. During the week-long conference, the Director of DSS scheduled a wreath-laying ceremony at the *USS Arizona* Memorial to pay tribute to those who made the ultimate sacrifice at Pearl Harbor.

While crossing the harbor on a U.S. Naval shuttle boat, three WWII-vintage Japanese "Zero" fighter planes circled and passed directly overhead while making mock strafe runs along Battleship Row and Ford Island. Michael Bay was filming the movie *Pearl Harbor,* recreating the December 7, 1941 day that continues to live in infamy.

The sight of the movie's replicated black smoke rising from Ford Island and the circling Japanese Zero attack planes—as I was standing above the *USS Arizona*—proved to be a special moment. It was a reminder of the recent attacks against America on 9/11. For me, it was a convergence of snapshots in time, exhibiting the pain of loss and honor of heroism.

In 2001, Tiger Woods, PGA's top-rated professional golfer world-wide, announced he would participate in the 2002 New Zealand Open tournament at the Paraparaumu Beach Golf Club near Wellington. During this era, Tiger Woods shared a close friendship with his caddie, New Zealander Steve Williams. Steve Williams, New Zealand's top-earning sports figure by virtue of his ten-percent winning cut for toting Tiger's golf bag, had scheduled his wedding in conjunction with the New Zealand Open in order to allow Tiger Woods to participate as his best man.

On December 18, 2001, the secretary for U.S. Ambassador Charles Swindells notified me of a threat letter she had received that morning addressed to the U.S. ambassador. Serving as the first-ever RSO permanently assigned to New Zealand, I accepted all threat letters routinely passed to my office for a threat assessment. I suspected that Tiger Woods' highly publicized visit to New Zealand might give an opportunity to deranged or disgruntled voices generally expressing political, economic, or religious dissent.

This letter's ramblings included the opinion that America had not learned its lesson on September 11, accusing America's foreign policy of suppressing the weak and powerless. The letter expressed dismay of Israeli leaders who committed genocide against the Palestinian people. The letter's author claimed to be an enemy of America, the Great Satan, as well as the Israeli regime, and claimed allegiance to Islamic Jihad.

The author expressed a view of New Zealand's lax security for the planned golf tournament. The author stated a belief that Tiger Woods represents the American suppression and exploitation of the Islamic people of Southeast Asia. The letter inferred that suicide attacks would ensue against Tiger Woods and New Zealand citizens via fire bombings, train derailments, and poisoning the tournament's spectators. The writer concluded by referring to the enclosed product (a sugar packet) be handled with care, or better yet, pour the contents into "your coffee."

(L–R): RSO Robert W. Starnes, NZ Police Commissioner Rob Robinson, Ambassador Charles Swindells, NZ Police John White, Foreign Service National Investigator (FSNI) Raymond Millar, surrounded by the New Zealand Police Special Tactical Group (STG) at the U.S. Embassy in Wellington.

Threat letters received by U.S. embassies containing anti-American and anti-Israeli views are not uncommon. However, the specific mentioning of a desire to accomplish suicide attacks and acts of violence against Tiger Woods and New Zealand citizens elevated security concerns for both the New Zealand government and United States.

Field assessments of threat indicators for suspicious letters and packages are generally based on excess postage, poor handwriting, misspelled names, titles, and common words, lopsided or uneven packages, oily stains, strange odors, protruding wires or tin foil, ticking sounds, excess securing tape or string, and restrictive markings such as Confidential or Personal. This letter was assessed on the credibility of the author's intent, motive, capability, and opportunity.

The letter's envelope exhibited poor handwriting with misspelled words and no return address. Of course, the enclosed packet elevated my concerns.

Taking custody of the letter from the Ambassador's secretary, I processed the threat letter as evidence and transmitted it to the New Zealand police for testing and investigation.

Adding to security concerns after the 9/11 terrorist attacks, a new threat emerged. U.S. State Department employees had died from anthrax chemical attacks inside the State Department's headquarters mailroom in Washington, D.C.

New Zealand's land mass is the approximate size of California with a population slightly above that of Los Angeles. Operating with limited human resources, New Zealand has very capable police and military forces that helped train the security forces of their neighboring island nations to the north.

Any harm that might be unleashed against the international golfing star while in New Zealand would certainly deliver a devastating—if not mortal —financial blow to tourism.

The onus of protecting the world's top-rated golfer now rested with the New Zealand police and DSS. In an effort to retain the element of surprise by not alerting the threat letter's author, law enforcement kept a tight hold on information pertaining to the investigation.

The New Zealand police tried to identify the author and began security planning on an unprecedented scale to protect Tiger Woods and others attending the golf tournament.

After navigating through the sports representation bureaucracy, I contacted Tiger Woods' agent, Mark Steinberg, and informed him of the threat letter and its potassium cyanide poison, and inquired if Tiger Woods was aware of anyone who might wish to kill Tiger. Mark Steinberg responded that neither he nor Woods was aware of anyone wanting to harm him.

The New Zealand government asked the embassy to not go public about the threat letter. From a law enforcement perspective, I completely understood the importance of holding the information close so as not to telegraph or compromise their investigation and security plans to the letter's author.

The U.S. Embassy in Wellington, wanting to assist the New Zealand police, now faced a quandary. A sharing policy had been created as a result of information initially withheld from the public leading to the suspected Libyan sponsored bombing of Pan Am Flight 103 over Lockerbie, Scotland.

Tiger Woods escorted by New Zealand police.

Under this protocol, the U.S. Department of State's "No Double Standard" policy[44] requires information about credible or significant security threats— if shared with the U.S. community (for example, U.S. employees serving abroad)—must be made available to the wider American community if the threat pertains to both official and non-official Americans.

After several meetings and bureaucratic hand-wringing, the decision was made to enact the "No Double Standard" policy. The U.S. consular office, in unison with the U.S. public affairs office, released a statement informing the public of the threat, the mention of Tiger Woods, the New Zealand Open, and the potassium cyanide received by the U.S. Embassy in Wellington.

After the cyanide threat was made public, Tiger Woods responded to a reporter, "Things like this do happen. You have to go on living your life. It's unfortunate that people have these types of views and do these types of acts. I'm going to go down there and enjoy myself."[45]

The gravity of the situation called for unprecedented human resources. The New Zealand police and military cancelled all scheduled personnel leave in order to enhance protection for the Open. The police's comprehensive security plans included securing every road, train track, public transportation route, event venue access, and strict monitoring of all food and beverages brought into the golfing event.

Tiger Woods' arrival in New Zealand on a private jet was carried live on national television, and he was shuttled around the countryside in a motorcade befitting a head of state. More than 400 New Zealand police officers were assigned to the golf tournament. Tiger Woods' gallery included plain clothes police officers carrying firearms stashed in duffel bags.[46] Police manpower for Tiger Woods' executive protective security detail far exceeded the support normally used to protect the Queen of England on her prior visits.

Fresh off al-Qaeda's 9/11 attacks in the United States, nationwide tension in New Zealand still ran high leading to the golf open. Some people opted not to attend the tournament out of fear. The estimated financial cost for security during the New Zealand Open exceeded $500,000, a significant amount of expended capital for the small island nation.

Not playing at the top of his game, Tiger Woods almost missed the cut and finished the Open fifth overall. Regardless of the cyanide threat against Tiger Woods, the event was well attended, and the course galleries swarmed with fans under the protective umbrella of the New Zealand police and military.

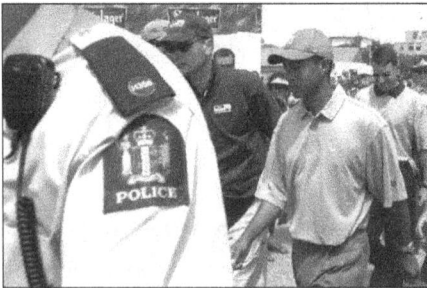

Thanks to the Kiwis who protected a Tiger.

Tiger Woods protected by plain clothes and uniformed New Zealand police.

CHAPTER 15

DR. MOREAU MEETS LORD OF THE FLIES

Like horror scenes from the movie
The Terminator, Evan Ebel exited his mangled vehicle
while continuing to engage the Texas peace officers in gunfire.

O n March 21, 2013, as the sun shone brightly on Montague County, Texas, Deputy Sheriff James Boyd made what he thought would be a routine traffic stop on a 1991 Cadillac de Ville. Little did Deputy Boyd know at the time, but he had just pulled over 28-year old Evan Spencer Ebel, a seasoned and disturbed career criminal who was on the run for recently murdering Tom Clements, the state of Colorado's prison chief, and Collin Leon, a Denver-area pizza delivery employee.

Deputy Sheriff James Boyd's gunshot wound.

As Deputy Boyd exited his patrol vehicle, the red and blue emergency lights reflected off the Cadillac's chrome trim. Shortly after both vehicles rolled to a stop, a lawman's most dreaded sound was heard. Evan Ebel shot Deputy Boyd three times, almost fatally wounding the ambushed peace officer near Bowie, Texas.

Evan Ebel's wrecked car after high speed chase from Texas peace officers.

Spotted later by a Texas state trooper, Evan Ebel led law enforcement on a wild high-speed chase, often exceeding 100 mph. Evan Ebel was a seemingly lost soul whom a dozen years earlier I had helped rescue from an abusive behavior modification camp in the South Pacific island nation of Samoa.

Mimicking something out of a mobster movie, Evan Ebel drove his car with his right hand while shooting at his pursuers with his left hand. Nearing the Wise County sheriff's headquarters building, a collision with a tractor trailer brought Ebel's vehicle to an abrupt stop.

(L–R): Tom Clements, Evan Ebel, Nathan Collin Leon.

Like horror scenes from the movie *The Terminator*, Evan Ebel exited his mangled vehicle while continuing to engage the Texas peace officers in gunfire. Moments later, a debilitating shot from a Texas highway patrolman brought Evan Ebel's crime spree to a halt. Hours later, Evan Ebel was pronounced dead. An investigation confirmed Evan Ebel had indeed murdered Tom Clements and Nathan Collin Leon.

Because the U.S. Ambassador in Wellington was also credentialed for Samoa, I had U.S. security responsibilities for both New Zealand and Samoa. In the ambassador's absence from Samoa, the ranking American diplomat holds the title of chargé d'affaires.

Consisting of two main islands located northwest of Fiji, in 2001, Samoa had a population of less than 200,000 people. Samoan Polynesians are generally a friendly, family-oriented, and peaceful people. Tribal tattoos adorn Samoan chiefs. Known for painful tattooing by hammering ink into the skin with an "au ta"—a serrated, wooden-handled bone comb and a tapping mallet. A rite-of-passage for young Samoan men is to receive dense tattoos reaching from both ankles to the waist while enduring the pain without the aid of the root-based sedative called *kava*.

A three-hour flight from New Zealand, a trip to Samoa was always filled with adventure. Inhabitants of Samoa are quick to point out the crime and deteriorating Polynesian culture on the neighboring island of American Samoa. I found Samoa full of friendly people surrounded by jungle-type foliage and crystal-clear ocean waters. On its surface, many lush island nations are viewed in a light of a utopian paradise, especially during short vacation stays. However, island communities have undercurrent cultures invisible to vacationers.

While scuba diving the warm, clear South Pacific Samoan waters for my diving certification, I witnessed pristine ocean wildlife, including giant clams, barracudas, and sharks. My diving instructor was a retired

American IBM executive who decided to uproot to Samoa to live a more quiet life.

Prior to making my final certified dive, I asked the scuba diving instructor's nineteen-year-old son if he had experienced anything unusual while living in Samoa. Adjusting my air tank, the dive master's son solemnly responded, "I recently had a 'Bernie' experience." Clearly affected by a bad experience, he was referring to actor Terry Kiser who played the character of Bernie Lomax in the comedy movie *Weekend at Bernie's*. In this movie plot, Bernie Lomax is killed during his beach party. In an effort to save their own lives from a planned "hit," characters Richard and Larry pretend to keep Bernie alive by transporting his corpse from place to place.

The dive master's son continued, "In Samoa, it is common to discover vagrants sleeping off an alcoholic binge in one's front yard. One morning, I noticed a man lying in the front yard. I walked over and nudged the man with my foot. The man did not respond. On further examination, I discovered the man was dead."

The dive master's son paused and said, "I called and informed the Samoan police. Because they lack patrol vehicles, the police instructed me to transport the corpse to the local hospital. Following their instructions, I summoned a taxi cab, loaded the body into the back seat (extra cab fare was required) and accompanied the deceased to the hospital."

While visiting Samoa, American diplomats would usually reside at the historic Aggie Grey Hotel, which in 1953 hosted actor Gary Cooper while shooting the Hollywood film *Return to Paradise*. The hotel is located on the same side of the island as the estate of Robert Louis Stevenson, author of *Treasure Island* and *The Strange Case of Dr. Jekyll and Mr. Hyde*. After contracting tuberculosis, Mr. Stevenson moved to Samoa, where he later died. His grave site is on the top of a large hill overlooking the Pacific Ocean.

Ambassador Carol Moseley-Braun was the American ambassador accredited to both New Zealand and Western Samoa. Ambassador

(F) Amb. Mosely-Braun and Adm. Dennis Blair, CINC PACOM, sign security memorandum.
(R) Robert W. Starnes and U.S. military attaché.

Moseley-Braun was a caring and no-nonsense diplomat from a law enforcement family. She had previously served as a U.S. Assistant Attorney and her father and brother both served with the Chicago Police Department.

On a typical day in July 2001, I provided an out-briefing to the U.S. chargé d'affaires in Samoa regarding my review of the security posture of the U.S. Embassy building and official residence. Looking ahead, I was excited at the opportunity to support the U.S. Secretary of State's DSS protective detail in Darwin, Australia.

Jim Derrick, serving as chargé d'affaires, was a retired Department of State annuitant brought back to active duty to fill in for the vacationing foreign service officer permanently assigned to the embassy. Jim Derrick listened intently while I checked off my security briefing items. At the conclusion of my briefing, Jim Derrick paused a moment, his slightly lazy eye making contact with my eyes, and he stated, "I would like to show you something before you depart Samoa."

Adjusting his black-frame glasses, Jim Derrick opened his safe drawer and produced a video cassette. He explained, "This was just passed to me by Bob Delancy, an American citizen who was visiting his son at the juvenile behavior camp called the Pacific Coast Academy."

According to Jim Derrick, for several years, the consular officials at the U.S. Department of State expressed concerned about juvenile behavior camps similar to the Pacific Coast Academy, but lacked a basis for U.S. government intervention. Jim Derrick shared that in 2000, Ambassador Mosley-Braun had visited the Pacific Coast Academy in Samoa out of a widespread concern about the camp.

Earlier in 2001, the senior consular officer assigned to the U.S. consulate in Auckland, New Zealand reported serious concerns about his visit to the Pacific Coast Academy. Frustrated at the camp's "stage managed aspect" of his visit, the Pacific Coast Academy failed to provide their camp's accreditation. The camp's staff did not permit the consular officer to have private conversations with the American students. The consular officer was only able to speak to a group of students in private when he excused himself from the camp staff for a bathroom break. The consular officer's quiet conversation with the students continued until camp staff members became suspicious of the consular officer's long absence and quickly sought him out to prevent his alone time with students.

U.S. Ambassador Carol Moseley-Braun presents Chicago P.D. shirt to RSO Robert W. Starnes.

On July 1, 2001, American citizen Bob Delancy called the embassy and shared that prior to visiting his son at the Pacific Coast Academy, he had received an anonymous tip of abuses against students at the camp. Mr. Delancy brought along his personal video recorder and taped students at the Pacific Coast Academy without staff's permission or knowledge. Mr. Delancy was now concerned that he and his wife were being barred

James Derrick, U.S. Chargé d'affaires, U.S. Embassy, Apia, Samoa.

from departing Samoa for having videoed students at the camp. Jim Derrick and Mr. Delancy met at the Aggie Grey Hotel to discuss Delancy's visit to the camp. Appalled at having heard of potential abuses against the students, Jim Derrick asked Bob Delancy to make a duplicate copy of his videotape. Concerned about the nature of their sensitive conversation, Jim asked Mr. Delancy to meet him at the safe confines of the embassy a few blocks away.

At the embassy, Mr. Delancy informed that Pacific Coast Academy students said they had been punished for sharing their camp experiences with consular officials. According to Jim Derrick, "... the fact that (consular) access was apparently restricted, plus the content of the (Delancy) videotape, providing indications of physical and mental abuse, medical neglect and sexual assaults, gave the basis for official action."[47]

Likely alerted by Pacific Coast Academy staff members of the video, the Samoan police became involved, intent on seizing the potentially damaging video.

After Bob Delancy had passed the video to Jim Derrick for safe-keeping, Bob and his wife traveled to the airport to board a flight back to the United States. However, while standing at the airline ticket counter, the Delancys were denied boarding privileges and temporarily detained by the Samoan police. Once the police had learned that the video was now in the custody of the American Embassy, they reluctantly allowed the Delancys to board the aircraft.

Top: Pacific Coast Academy.
Below: A Pacific Coast Academy detainee stands next to this primitive jungle living quarters.

To the Delancys' surprise, sitting on the same row in the aircraft was a Pacific Coast Academy staff member who was intently watching their every move. Bob Delancy learned that Utah Governor Mike Leavitt was on the same flight. Making his way to the rear of the aircraft, Bob shared his ordeal with the governor's security team, who appeared shocked at his distress.

Plugging the cassette into the video player, Jim Derrick asked me to view the tape. Anxious to return to New Zealand, I indulged Jim Derrick by seeming genuinely interested, while my mind really focused on the piles of work that awaited me in Wellington.

The video began with a view from the inside of a vehicle bouncing down a secluded, pothole-filled dirt road. The vehicle's dashboard and white hood jump up and down with each pothole as it passed banana trees and dense jungle.

The voice of a boy enrolled in the behavior modification camp narrates the guided tour: first noting the bridge leading into the academy, and scenes of campers moving rocks and packing dirt—labor forced on the children by the academy staff. As the vehicle approaches the camp's entrance guard shack, the boy points out the access restriction sign and a Samoan man who serves as the Pacific Coast Academy's security guard. The boy sarcastically makes reference to the small wooden sign delineating Pacific Coast Academy as a far cry from the images portrayed in the academy's marketing brochures.

The next scene focuses on a teenage girl wearing a white T-shirt and gray baggy sweats, sitting on the ground in tears as she shares

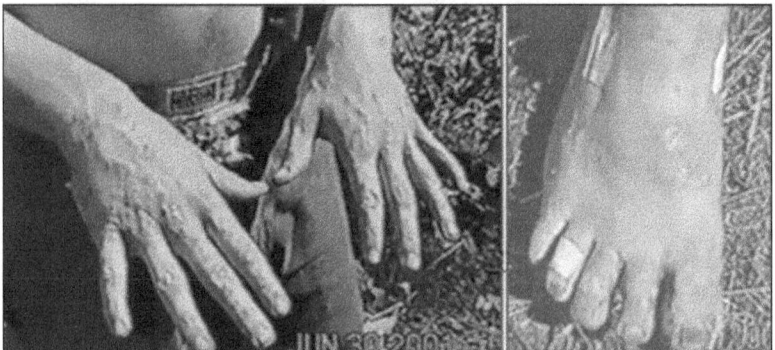

Juveniles' infected hands and feet at the Pacific Coast Academy.

that she has been in isolation for more than a week for saying "damn." In a sad, hopeless voice, this girl looks into the camera and shares instances where she has been inappropriately sexually touched by Pacific Coast Academy staff members. She pleads to the camera that she wants to leave Samoa and go home.

The camera then pans to three juvenile boys: one shirtless boy in blue jeans, the other two boys were wearing T-shirts and shorts. Each boy contributed their version of performing forced hard labor for 12 hours a day and having to bathe in a nearby river. The camera zooms in on one boy who shows dozens of infected welts caused by mosquito bites. Another boy displays oozing boils on his legs while the third boy points to infected sores on his feet.

Standing in a patch of sunlight, contrasted by the dense Samoan jungle, these juveniles explained how after escaping from the academy, they were captured, returned, "had the crap beat out of them," were made to kneel with their hands above their heads, and placed in isolation. One boy quipped that he believed isolation was illegal in the United States. The visiting parent responded, "… unfortunately, guys, you are not in the United States."

A smoky haze from their camp fire hung still in their windless confines. The camera panned around, revealing thickets of banana trees surrounding a rustic lean-to shelter constructed of branches and palm leaves draped with old, holey mosquito netting. A few blankets sprawled on top of the rocky soil served as these three boys' beds. Exposing them to unrelenting nightly mosquito bites without the aid of repellant, they revealed how they used smoke from a camp fire to attempt to keep the mosquitos at bay. Asked to hold up his hands, one boy shows grotesque and infected bumps covering both hands, claiming the academy staff does not administer antibiotics.

The video cuts from the three boys in the jungle to a young Evan Ebel. Wearing a white short-sleeve shirt, black shorts, and sporting a burr haircut, Ebel speaks into the camera, explaining how he received seven beatings from Pacific Coast Academy staff, accusing several offending members by name, and claiming that nothing is ever done to discipline the staff members for his beatings.

Driving over an earthen roadway dam to a garden area, the camera films a juvenile girl dressed in a blue sleeveless shirt and blue jeans while standing in the open-air yard. This teenage girl explains that during her sixteen-month stay at the Pacific Coast Academy, she was disciplined by being "hog tied," slammed on the rocky ground with her hands tied to her feet. This girl claimed that she was kept in this position for two days, having to urinate and defecate on herself.

The young girl maintained that the ropes binding her hands were tied so tightly that her hands swelled and turned blue. In order to induce sleep deprivation, the girl said staff members poured water on her face, first beginning with mugs of water, progressing to pitchers of water, to eventually five-gallon buckets of water, making it nearly impossible for the girl to breathe.

In a *Lord of the Flies*-type scene, the girl stated that in order to avoid child abuse charges, the camp's staff ordered other juvenile campers—who were under the age of 18-to beat her with their fists and kick her while still tied. Her voice trembling with emotion, the girl explained how she was taken across the island to a place called the "Veil," where she was sexually assaulted by the village chief—while still bound in ropes. The girl abruptly stopped her interview, apparently due to a Pacific Coast Academy staff member listening to her conversation. The girl paused for a moment and, while wiping tears from her face, said that she had told the Pacific Coast Academy director the same day (Sunday) of the sexual assault. However, the director took the chief's word over hers, accusing her of being pregnant, and left her at this site for a couple more days until realizing that it was unsafe to leave her at this remote location.

At the conclusion of the tape, Jim Derrick and I sat silently trying to absorb the juveniles' accusations of physical abuse and sexual assaults. If these accusations were true, not only had this behavioral modification camp violated law and basic decency, it may have violated human rights. Even prisoners serving debts to society are subjected to better treatment. Heck, even the rattlesnakes I had captured years earlier were treated better.

Jim Derrick said he suspected officials from the Pacific Coast Academy were pressuring the Samoan police to retrieve the damaging video of their boot-camp/prison/torture-chamber-style behavior modification academy. Having a responsibility for Amer-

An American teenager in tears as she shares her ordeal.

ican citizens' well-being, Jim Derrick promptly reported the incident to the U.S. Department of State in Washington, D.C.

Little did either of us know at that time, things in Samoa were about to become more heated. Washington instructed Jim Derrick and me to engage the Samoan government to investigate the serious allegations concerning the health, safety, and welfare of more than 25 American teenagers who were forcibly held at the Pacific Coast Academy. The concerns included consistent and credible allegations of physical, mental, and sexual abuse, as well as denial of medical treatment and medication.

While attending several high-level meetings with Samoan government officials, it was apparent that the Pacific Coast Academy had convinced senior government officials to their way of business. The main prosecutor was an Australian who was very defensive regarding the questions posed to the Samoan government Jim and I had received from headquarters. When Jim Derrick asked the prosecutor what type of justice system Samoa instituted, the prosecutor began a diatribe about the lack of professionalism of the U.S. Supreme Court.

Sensing this meeting was beginning to spin out of control, I stopped the prosecutor and told him that Jim and I were only the messengers, trying to acquire information for our headquarters in Washington, D.C. I insisted that we shared the same desire—an eagerness to protect the children's welfare. The prosecutor paused, and from that moment on he became supportive of the U.S. effort to investigate and repatriate those children who so chose.

Samoa's initial pushback quickly softened when embarrassing news articles reported the abuse allegations in Samoa and about a string of other behavior modification camps allegedly organized and operated by Utah-native Stephen Cartisano.

Stephen A. Cartisano (also known as *Stephen Michaels*) was no stranger to behavior modification camp controversies. He was a former manager of the Utah-based Challenger Foundation, one of the initial U.S. boot camp-style behavioral therapy camps. In 1990, Stephen Cartisano was charged with negligent homicide for the death of student Kristin Chase. The camp was closed 63 days after its opening and Cartisano's criminal trial ended in a mistrial and acquittal. A slew of civil lawsuits and eventually bankruptcy followed.

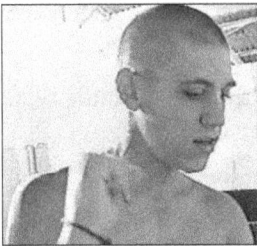

A young Evan Ebel demonstrates how Pacific Coast Academy staff beat him.

Based on additional child abuse allegations and the operation of camps without proper licenses, Stephen Cartisano was barred from participating in any future behavioral camps in Utah and later Hawaii, Puerto Rico, and the Virgin Islands.

Several U.S. Embassy staff members from New Zealand were mobilized and sent to Samoa to assist with the students' repatriation.

American teenagers covertly assemble at the Pacific Coast Academy for a group photo prior to their abrupt departure.

The Department of State's legal department instructed Jim Derrick and me to locate, identify, and inform the American juveniles that they could immediately depart the Pacific Coast Academy camp, and stay in Apia, Samoa, until they had been returned to their parents and/or guardians. In directives from the State Department attorneys, we were to ensure the juveniles' well-being without assuming their custodial control.

After the host government's agreement to rescind the camp license, I dispatched Ray Millar—the Foreign Service National Investigator (FSNI) assigned to the RSO office in New Zealand—to locate the students. Having been forewarned of the United States' inquiry, Pacific Coast Academy staff had quickly mobilized and hid the students at a remote Samoan beach. Ray Millar, a former New Zealand police officer, was a natural sleuth and quickly located the students. When provided with the repatriation option, each and every student decided

Raymond Millar, Foreign Service National Investigator.

to immediately depart the academy, creating an exodus toward the small U.S. Embassy office in Apia (about 25 kids in total).

The newly liberated, but frightened juveniles huddled on the embassy's lobby floor. The children were clearly in fear of their former overseers, including the camp's former military disciplinarian called "Wolf" or the "Wolfman." I ordered pizza for the seemingly starved students. The teens gobbled up the pizzas as if they had been on a deserted island for years.

After all traces of the pizzas disappeared, I escorted the juveniles to a nearby hotel. The "Wolfman" was sitting in his late-model Ford pickup, eyeing each former camp enrollee as they left the building. From his bushy sideburns down to his cowboy boots and pickup truck, the "Wolfman" closely resembled the character Mr. Sir (portrayed by Jon Voight) in the 2003 movie *Holes*. We made it safely to the hotel without incident from Samoan's version of Mr. Sir.

For the next two weeks, the six embassy team members from Samoa and New Zealand worked diligently to repatriate the students. Parental response was mostly positive toward the U.S. government's actions. Sadly, however, perhaps jaded by years of their child's misconduct and anti-social behavior, some parents were irate at the embassy's action in facilitating the students' departure, in spite of their child's plight.

Implementing advanced negotiating skills, Jim Derrick, Ray Millar, and I were able to calm the students and convince them of the need to behave in their unanticipated and non-chaperoned environment, pending their departure. Out of precaution, I arranged for police protection at their resident hotel.

After several days of boredom, the unsupervised teens began revealing traits that had landed them in the unpleasant confines of the behavioral modification camp in the first place. Of particular concern was a wild girl who broke the ribs of another girl during a fight in the hotel lobby. One day, we received word that the same girl was "turning tricks" behind a hardware store in order to earn enough money to buy and get high on roach spray. Sure enough, when dispatched to the hardware store, a line of men was seen wrapped around the storefront.

A U.S. Embassy Samoan staff member pointed out two of the juveniles who had recently disrupted a Catholic church service in Apia. Samoan islanders are quite religious. After the church service, the rather large Samoan altar boys met the offenders outside and gave them the age-old "spare the rod, spoil the child" Sunday school lesson. The former campers never again disrespected the church's sanctity.

To protect their interests, the Pacific Coast Academy quickly initiated legal action. The legal situation became fluid and confusing for all concerned. James Derrick and I coordinated certain aspects of the inquiry with a Samoan attorney who worked *pro bono*, representing the students' legal interests in the Samoan courts.

On October 29, 2002, The Salt Lake Tribune reported, the U.S. Department of Justice had initiated a grand jury investigation into the Pacific Coast Academy in Los Angeles, California. According to grand jury witnesses who spoke to The Salt Lake Tribune, federal investigators from the U.S. Postal Service, Internal Revenue Service, Justice Department and other agencies seemed to be focusing on white-collar crimes rather than allegations of child abuse or neglect. "The type of information that has been sought from us as witnesses is going strongly toward mail fraud, money laundering and income tax evasion," said Pamela Elliott, a California attorney who had sued Pacific Coast Academy on behalf of her son and other parents whose children were clients of the Samoan camp.

If there was an indictment, it would be the first criminal prosecution of the former Utah teen therapist since he was acquitted in 1992 of negligent homicide in the Kane County death of a 16-year-old girl in his care, reported the Salt Lake Tribune.

Started in November 1998, Pacific Coast Academy was the latest in a rocky legacy of boot-camp style outdoor "schools" involving Cartisano in Utah, Hawaii, the U.S. Virgin Islands, Puerto Rico, Costa Rica, and elsewhere in Samoa. In sales pitches made to parents, the ventures claimed to offer professional counseling, nurturing environments and no corporal punishment. All the programs collapsed, however, amid allegations of child abuse, misrepresentation and missing money. Inspired by an outdoor program he took while a student at Brigham Young University, Cartisano made millions marketing "tough love" camp outs for troubled teens in Utah in the late 1980s. Although the former Air Force "Para rescue" instructor was acquitted of negligent homicide charges in the heat-exhaustion death of 16-year-old Kristen Chase while she was enrolled in Cartisano's Challenger Foundation Program in 1990, his empire crumbled after he was placed on a Utah registry of suspected child abusers who are forbidden to work with children in the state.

But in a legal deposition Cartisano gave in the civil case May 7, he describes Pacific Coast Academy as his brainchild and calls himself a "partner" of David Weston of Logan and Lonnie Fuller of Arizona. Weston and Fuller, who did not respond to requests by The Salt Lake Tribune for comment, also are named as defendants in the civil case.

According to a transcript of Cartisano's deposition obtained by The Tribune, Cartisano said he wrote and designed a Pacific Coast Academy brochure that he mailed to prospective clients. Although the brochure showed Pacific Coast Academy offered activities such as scuba diving, cattle ranching, horseback riding and schooner sailing at the Samoan camp, Cartisano acknowledged in the deposition that the photos were of child actors on the Caribbean island of Nevis.

Cartisano set up multiple bank accounts for Pacific Coast Academy, including a company account in California in his son's name. He said he used a debit card drawn on those accounts, cashed payments to Pacific Coast Academy from parents and wired funds to the Samoa camp "all the time." Cartisano helped parents arrange bank financing for the camp's annual tuition, upward of $25,000 to $30,000, by referring them to Key Bank for a student loan. More than a dozen families took out the loans, even though Pacific Coast Academy was never an accredited school. On company letterhead, Pacific Coast Academy was billed as a "non-profit organization," an arm of the "Pacific Coast Foundation," of which Cartisano's mother-in-law in Oklahoma, Geneva Carr, was a director. But when asked if Pacific Coast Academy was truly a nonprofit organization, Cartisano replied: "That's a good question. It was supposed to be."

He acknowledged he was unaware of any income tax returns filed for Pacific Coast Academy or of the filing of IRS Form 8300, required when nonprofits receive cash payments of $10,000 or more in a trade or business transaction. On where all the money went-when the State Department raided the camp it had 23 students, an estimated tuition income of more than half a million dollars-Cartisano's attorney Amidon said his client pocketed less than $70,000 during the entire run of Pacific Coast Academy. In his deposition, Cartisano contended, "There isn't a pot of gold somewhere in this deal" and that "while I was starving, [Fuller] went to Vegas and Disneyland.[48]

A federal grand jury investigation directed by the U.S. Department of Justice was convened out of Los Angeles. However, during this investigation, America came under attack on September 11, 2001. According to Bob Delancy, as a result of shifting focus on the war on terror, the grand jury investigation took a back seat to "higher" priorities.

During this episode, Jim Derrick earned his nickname "The Cleaner," for initiating and cleaning up the Pacific Coast Academy crisis during his temporary assignment in Samoa.

I suppose it's natural to ask, "what if?" in the case of historical events in our lives. Though justified as a practice of tough love, the violence allegedly administered against its juvenile subjects by the Pacific Coast Academy staff violated the principles of morality through the infliction of pain, cruelty, and denigration of humanity.

Just as Doctor Moreau's torturous experiments to change animal nature to human nature had backfired in H. G. Wells' 1896 science fiction novel, *The Island of Doctor Moreau*, the Pacific Coast Academy's tactics to create a more socially accepted state backfired, and in some instances, may have helped propel criminal behavior of at least one impressionable kid, Evan Ebel.

To what extent the Pacific Coast Academy's tactics aided in Evan Ebel's violent Colorado and Texas crime spree may never be known. Perhaps the isolation he was subjected to on the small island of Samoa triggered his need to spread his wings in a twisted form of anti-social behavior. Or regardless of his experiences in Samoa, perhaps Evan Ebel simply chose a life of crime.

After his arrest, Evan Ebel's time in prison included solitary confinement, which his father testified to lawmakers was destroying his son's psyche. In prison, Ebel was a member of the 211 Crew, a white supremacist prison gang in Colorado.[49]

No one will ever know how much mental, physical, and spiritual damage Evan Ebel suffered at the hands of the Pacific Coast Academy staff, and the effects the damage may have contributed to his life of violence. However, one thing is certain: The Pacific Coast Academy experiment is no longer open for business on the island of Samoa.

CHAPTER 16

THE BEARDED TREE

Crime exists everywhere,
even amidst a volcano eruption.

arbados, meaning *bearded tree*, purportedly received its name by Portuguese explorers. The native tree's roots extend downward from its branches, giving the appearance of a beard.

The tiny island nation of Barbados is the only place President George Washington visited outside of the North American mainland. In 1751, at the age of nineteen, George Washington accompanied his half-brother Lawrence, who was suffering from tuberculosis, to the tiny island nation of Barbados. Due to the captain's navigational error, the sloop *Success* almost met with disaster when crew members sighted the island around four o'clock in the morning off Barbados' treacherous east coast. An aristocrat, George Washington was permitted to view the British military training

George Washington's Portrait

The residence once occupied by George Washington in Bridgetown, Barbados.

tactics, greatly assisting his future Revolutionary military career. During his time spent in Barbados, George Washington contracted small pox. His immunity to this disease prevented him from the deadly illness during the war for American independence.[50]

When I reminisce about walking across the grounds of the historic British Garrison in Bridgetown, the site where George Washington likely studied the British military training tactics that would some-day be used against the American Revolutionary Army, I am reminded of an ancestor who served in an elite military unit in Washington's army. William Bigbie, my great grandfather (x4), was a cavalry dragoon assigned to the 3rd troop of the Partisan Corps commanded by Henry ("Lighthorse Harry") Lee,[51] father of Civil War General Robert E. Lee. Colonel Lee's Legion received multiple commendations from General George Washington.

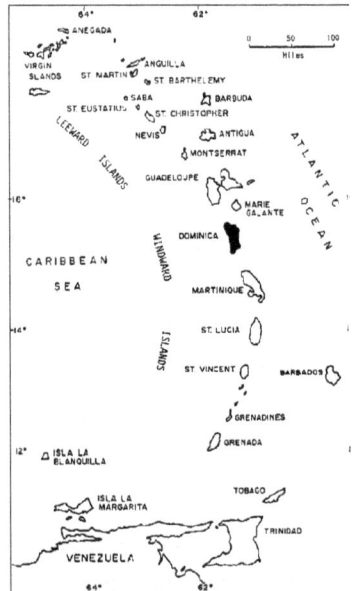

Map of the Eastern Caribbean

During my three-year assignment to the U.S. Embassy in Bridge-town, the capital of Barbados, I had security responsibilities for fourteen Caribbean islands, and the distinct honor of serving with two exceptional Ambassadors. The Ambassador serving in Barbados is credentialed in seven Eastern Caribbean island nations, including Antigua/Barbuda, Barbados, Dominica, Grenada, St. Kitts/Nevis, St. Lucia, and St. Vincent/the Grenadines.

In addition to these seven islands, I had security responsibilities for seven additional British and French territorial islands including Anguilla, British Virgin Islands, Guadalupe, Martinique, Montserrat, St. Barthélemy, and St. Martin.

Serving at the U.S. Embassy in Barbados was not a lounge on the beach sipping Mai Tais. Given its deceiving vacationing atmosphere, Barbados offered many security challenges, including hosting the 2007 Cricket World Cup and the U.S. Soccer Team World Cup. Security planning for these large events—especially given the world's counter-terrorism concerns—was daunting but rewarding.

Of course, life on a small island is full of unexpected setbacks, or as I like to call them, small adventures. Once, while refueling my vehicle's diesel tank, the attendant became distracted at Barbados native Rihanna's presence inside the gas station. As a result, the attendant mistakenly filled my diesel tank with gasoline, resulting in a long night spent with my mechanic draining the bad fuel from my tank.

On occasion, an unexpected wild case would come my way.

Drunken Sailors

One afternoon, I received a telephone call from the Barbados police department inquiring if a visiting ship carrying U.S. Merchant Marine trainees was under the protection of diplomatic immunity. I thought the request was a bit odd, but I informed the police that the ship was not granted immunity status under the Vienna Convention of Diplomatic Relations. The following day, while attending services at a local church, I was approached by a South African church member who worked as the security director for Eugene Melnyk. Mr. Melnyk was a part-time Barbados resident and owner of the Ottawa Senators hockey team.

Before the sermon began, Mr. Melnyk's security director quipped that one of my "boys" was caught trying to spy on Mr. Melnyk. At first I thought the security director was making some type of odd joke, so I dismissed his off-the-cuff accusation as his strange sense of humor. However, in the words of the late, great radio host Paul Harvey, I later learned, the *Rest of the Story*.

According to a very reliable source, three drunken Merchant Marine trainees made their way from their ship to Eugene Melnyk's residence and took a dip in his personal swimming pool. Afterward, the mariners entered Mr. Melnyk's home, walked to a back bedroom, and made off with a large stuffed animal. I was told that Mr. Melnyk was watching television at the time and was completely oblivious to the three inebriated intruders. As the drunken sailors departed the Melnyk residence via the front door, they passed Mrs. Melnyk, who had just returned home. Thinking the sailors were guests of her husband, the sailors were not confronted. When Mrs. Melnyk asked her husband about his visitors, they both realized the situation at hand.

A few high-level phone calls to the Barbados police initiated an investigation that revealed the identities of the three intoxicated Merchant Marine trainees who had breached Mr. Melnyk's residential security. The South African security director insisted the entire incident was an attempt by the United States government to commit espionage against Mr. Melnyk. I found it both comical and absurd that corporate espionage was advanced as an excuse by the security director in lieu of confessing his program's incompetence for securing a major North American sports figure. In the end, I am uncertain if the South African retained his private security position. An apology to Mr. Melnyk from the Merchant Marine trainees, and the return of the stuffed animal, put this international "espionage" caper to rest.

RESILIENCY DEFINED

I had always heard how friendly and resilient the islanders are in the Caribbean. The hearsay turned to firsthand experience when I traveled to the British protectorate island of Montserrat in order to assess security training needs.

While in Montserrat, a senior police officer informed me that I had just missed Prince Charles, who had recently visited the island and toured Plymouth, Montserrat's former capitol city. Plymouth is now a ghost town, abandoned and covered in ash from Volcano Soufriere's continual eruptions since 1995. Some two-thirds of Montserrat is uninhabitable due to threats posed by the active volcano.

As a gesture of friendship, the Montserrat police officer offered to provide a rare personal tour of Plymouth, which is located within the "Exclusion Zone"—off-limits to the public. I graciously accepted his offer.

The police officer and I made our way through the lightly-traveled roads. Several minutes later, our trek was temporarily stopped at a security gate erected by the police. After passing this security point, we continued to drive past a ravine that had previously served as the island's former golf course and country club. The once-green fairways now resembled the aftermath of a California mudslide. We continued up a hillside, passing many residences that had been vacant since the volcano's first eruption.

Reaching the hill's crest, the former capitol city spread out before us. For a moment, I was speechless at the devastation I saw. As we made our way down the hill, I saw that the entire town had been covered in ash. Now standing at rooftop level, the hands of a large clock face on top of a buried bank building still reflected the time of the town's demise.

Eerily, the smoking volcano loomed in the background from the now still clock. Just then, the Montserrat police officer informed me of the risk we had assumed. Similar to the Romans who had died in Pompeii as a result of the eruption from Mount Vesuvius, given the tremendous speed of pyroclastic flows, it would have been virtually impossible to survive an eruption at that precise moment.

Although futile, my security training kicked in. I began devising potential escape routes in the event of an eruption. I suggested a plan of action to quickly run to the nearby coastline and submerge ourselves in the cool water for a few moments until the danger would pass. My makeshift plan was dashed when the police officer told me that superheated ash and rocks carried by pyroclastic flows in the past had extended above the ocean water as far out as a mile off the coastline. We were truly at the mercy of God and nature.

I found it quite surreal as we made our way through untouched neighborhoods built along the hillside. The police officer stopped a moment in order to pick large, ripe guava fruit from trees once cultivated by its residents. Most residents had been uprooted as a result of the active volcano.

Crime exists everywhere, even amidst a volcano eruption. The Montserrat police officer shared that after the eruption, several people were arrested while attempting to steal weapons from the former police armory, as well as cash from the banks in Plymouth. At the same time, other people had died in superheated ash flows when they tried to return to their homes—within the Exclusion Zone—to collect their personal belongings.

I think the Montserratians are the most resilient people I have ever met. Given their dire circumstances, Monserratians retain friendly nature with a "can do" attitude.

A HAWK-EYED LEADER

Ambassador Mary Kramer and I shared a common Texas bond. She had visited the Texas Governor's Mansion in Austin, and I had worked at the Mansion as a state trooper. In February 1999, then president of the Iowa Senate, Mary Kramer—accompanied by several Iowan lawmakers—traveled to the Texas Governor's Mansion to encourage then-Governor George W. Bush to become a U.S. presidential candidate in 2000.

Now, assigned to the U.S. Embassy in Barbados, Ambassador Kramer possessed a unique managerial team-building style as well as a great sense of humor.

Once, while waiting for Ambassador Kramer to arrive for an embassy country team meeting, I noticed how the three photographs of the administration, President Bush, Vice President Cheney, and Secretary of State Rice, were hanging off-center to the left. When it was my turn to speak, I paused and, pointing to the executives' portraits, I asked Ambassador Kramer if it appeared to her that the administration was "leaning to the left." A good-natured Republican, Ambassador Kramer laughed at my lighthearted observation.

After a significant spike in violent crimes on the island nation of St. Lucia, Ambassador Kramer summoned me to her office to meet with St. Lucian Prime Minister Dr. Kenny Anthony. Prime Minister Anthony's graying mustache expanded with his wide Caribbean smile. The Prime Minister explained his concerns about declining tourism revenues which he attributed to rising crime on his island nation, including rapes, burglaries, and assaults. Prime Minister Anthony asked my advice about how to increase hotel security on his island. I suggested that it might best serve his nation's interests by training a member of his police force to specialize in facility security—or hire a private security consultant specializing in hotel security—to conduct security surveys and hold educational seminars for hotel staff and police officials. Prime Minister Anthony was gracious and thanked me for my advice.

Texan Ambassador

Mary Ourisman followed Ambassador Mary Kramer's assignment to Barbados. Appointed by President George W. Bush, Ambassador Ourisman is a fellow Texan from the town of Mexia, Texas, located not far from my first Texas highway patrol assignment. Anna Nicole Smith (deceased) was raised in Mexia, often

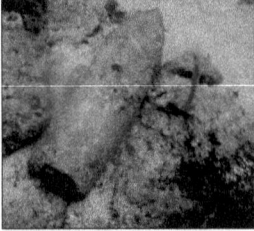
Underwater unexploded WWII shell.

mispronounced "Mex-i-a" by most non-Texans, instead of its correct pronunciation of "Me'-he-a." Ambassador Ourisman and her husband Mandy Ourisman were kind and generous philanthropists who supported their community wherever they may live.

Serving as an RSO, one never knows what will float across the desk. Neil Hinds, local embassy investigator, received a photograph taken by a tourist while scuba diving on the island of St. Vincent. The tourist had discovered an unexploded WWII ordnance near a popular beach, a potential threat to the safety of tourists and locals.

I first contacted and sent a photograph of the explosive to the DS/ATA bomb technician in Baton Rouge, Louisiana. The instructor identified the shell as either a British- or American-made WWII artillery shell. He gave two potential options: protect the coral reefs by securing a line onto the shell and dragging it to deeper waters where it could be safely destroyed, or place a quarter-size, shaped charge of plastic explosives and detonate the artillery shell in place.

(R-L): Amb. Mary Ourisman, Mandy Ourisman, and U.S. naval commander.

The DS/ATA instructor noted that the Barbados police underwater explosives demolition team possessed the skills to render the bomb safe. However, the Barbados police commissioner opted not to allow his agency to participate.

This situation was not a scene filmed to reproduce actions during WWII, as I had seen during my visit to Pearl Harbor just a few years earlier. This unexploded artillery shell lying among the colorful Caribbean coral could easily kill or maim unsuspecting swimmers or boaters. Time was of the essence. There was a solution to dispose of this sixty-year-old artillery shell—I simply had to locate the appropriate resource.

I turned to the U.S. military office at the embassy to inquire if a U.S. Navy team—specializing in underwater explosives—was scheduled to sail in the Eastern Caribbean. As fate would have it, such a team was due to arrive within a few months. In order to publicize U.S. assistance to Caribbean citizens, I had asked the Navy to allow Ambassador Ourisman to accompany the ship and ignite the charge that would destroy the artillery shell.

In true "can-do" U.S. military fashion of accomplishing missions, the visiting U.S. Navy team wired the underwater ordnance and allowed Ambassador Ourisman to detonate the explosive while standing aboard the naval vessel, rendering the channel safe for swimmers.

A CARIBBEAN SUNSET

The most memorable event I had in Barbados was during the decommissioning phase and final inspection of the old embassy, when I noticed the American flag was still flying in the fading afternoon sunlight.

Barbados sunset.

Two Navy Seabees, a DSS security engineering officer, and I climbed on top of the old downtown embassy building, surrounded by other multi-story buildings. In the orange glow of the setting sun over the Caribbean Sea, we stood at attention as a Seabee lowered the American flag. The two Seabees then folded Old Glory.

Although it was a humble flag-lowering ceremony, I believe it was a fitting closure for the historic building that sheltered many U.S. diplomats and government employees.

DOMESTIC
DENS

CHAPTER 17

LOVE BANDIT

*With less than three years remaining
on the ten-year statute of limitations for passport fraud,
time was of the essence.*

On July 28, 1992, I crawled into my bed (in a Houston suburb) after a long day at the office. While in deep sleep, I received a telephone call from DSS special agent Tom Borisch, who was assigned to the Phoenix, Arizona, office. Struggling to awaken, I managed greetings and pleasantries for my DSS brethren.

Agent Borisch informed me that while stalking graveyards and copying names from tombstones, a man and woman made numerous inquiries about deceased persons' birth certificates, raising the suspicion of the New Mexico Bureau of Vital Statistics (BVS) clerk. The BVS clerk quickly alerted the FBI. The FBI surveilled the couple,

Left: The thief: Mark Lanson aka Randy Fuchs aka Randy Fox. Right: The accomplice. Lois Elaine Fuchs.

who were now living in Phoenix. Initially, the FBI had targeted the female, Lois Elaine Fuchs, as the main player of the duo, and thought her male companion was merely an accomplice.

While attempting to locate Lois Elaine Fuchs, the FBI brought in her partner to their Phoenix office for questioning. The man made a critical error this day. As proof of his identity, he presented the FBI an Arkansas driver license in the name of Randy Lee Fuchs. A quick check of the law enforcement computer data banks revealed an entry for my DSS arrest warrant for John Doe, also known as Randy Lee Fuchs, issued by a federal magistrate in Austin, Texas.

"Tom, do you know who you have in custody?" I asked.

Tom answered, "No."

I told Agent Borisch, "Get your hands on a copy of the latest edition of *Redbook Magazine*. Everything you need to know about the alias of Randy Lee Fuchs can be learned from the article titled 'Love Bandit.'"

Almost two years earlier, in Austin's nearby town of Round Rock, Texas, a mirror reflected a middle-aged woman staring at her modest white wedding dress. Maryann Markle[52, 53] was nearing age 40, was still single, and had been lonely. Wanting to turn a new chapter in her life, she and her newly found fiancé, Mark Lanson—whom she had recently met on *The Dating Connection* personal ads—had already chosen the church, pastor, wedding gown, cake, and had ordered invitations for their wedding. Charming and easy to talk with, Mark Lanson quickly captured her heart.

Wedding vows swirl through the minds of most brides-to-be, vows that would be recited before family and friends: "To have and to hold, from this day forward, for better or for worse, for richer or for poorer, in sickness and in health, to

Maryann Markle tried to return her wedding dress, but the store wouldn't take it back. Now 42 and still alone, she fears she'll never have a reason to wear it.

love and to cherish until death do us part." It is natural for butterflies to swarm inside a stomach as the "moment" most women cherish, the lasting moment that would hopefully be consummated by word, deed, and law.

In addition to her affections for her partner, Maryann Markle was relieved that her financial future would be secure. She admired the large diamond ring, sapphire necklace, and mink stole Mark Lanson had given her. Her life partner-to-be had convinced her that he was a Harvard-educated lawyer, investor, and self-purported Baptist church deacon who owned property in New York City and a homestead on a lake near Toronto, Canada.

Maryann had introduced Mark Lanson to her family and friends, all of whom gave him their stamp of approval. As the couple bonded, Mark Larson convinced Maryann to allow him to invest her money that was safely tucked away in bank accounts. Blinded by "love," Maryann followed Lanson's advice and began to write checks for real estate property investments near El Paso, Texas. In total, Maryann invested more than $10,000 through Lanson, her quasi-broker, or so she thought.

Most of Maryann Markle's personal checks were made out to Lois Fuchs, who, Mark Lanson had convinced her was his business associate from Oklahoma City, Oklahoma. A seasoned con man, Lanson reassured Maryann that the investments she made through him were valid and issued her untraceable cashier checks in small amounts, claiming they were returns on her original property investments.

A pathological liar, Mark Lanson put Maryann's suspicions and fears to rest with answers delivered in a cool and confident manner. However, a few months after their engagement, the diamond in her engagement ring became loose and disappeared. Maryann was upset over the loss, but Lanson calmed her by reminding her that the ring had been insured for $4,000. Maryann gave her fiancé the $4,000 insurance money to reimburse the purchase of another engagement ring. However, that ring never came. At this point, Mark Lanson's money well was almost dry.

Claiming he was diagnosed with throat cancer, Mark Lanson told Maryann Markle he was planning to travel to Toronto for additional medical tests. The last message Maryann received from Mark Lanson was a telephone voice message telling her that he was preparing for surgery, and in a soft voice he said, "Good-bye, I love you."

Maryann and her father made the seven-hour drive to the site of her investment property, an hour outside of El Paso. The property turned out to be nothing. In total, Maryann had lost more than $29,500 to the man who would become known as the infamous "Love Bandit."

After Maryann Markle reported the crimes to the Williamson County, Texas, district attorney's office, other victims began to surface.

Elizabeth Rosenburg,[54] age 38, also sought love in personal ads. Twice divorced, Miss Rosenburg was quickly swept off her feet by a man who introduced himself as Randy Fuchs, a Harvard lawyer and investor. Her affection grew when Randy Fuchs showered attention and gifts on Miss Rosenburg's two children, ages 17 and 8.

Randy Fuchs convinced Elizabeth Rosenburg to quit her job, sell her belongings, and temporarily move in with her mother while he made arrangements for Miss

When she realized she'd been conned, Elizabeth Rosenburg was too humiliated to face her friends. She spent her last few dollars moving to a city where no one knew her.

Rosenburg and her children to live with him in Spain. Until their move to Europe, Randy Fuchs asked Elizabeth Rosenburg to open accounts at three jewelry stores. These accounts were mostly used to purchase gifts for himself and his aunt "Lois." So convincing was Randy Fuchs, he also conned Rosenburg's mother to invest $30,000 in Oklahoma real estate.

Several months later, Randy Fuchs told Elizabeth Rosenburg that he and his aunt Lois had contracted the same rare blood disease and needed to travel overseas to acquire medication. Fearing Elizabeth was suspicious at his strange blood-disease story, Randy Fuchs quickly added that he was traveling to Germany to meet with investors to purchase Elizabeth's mother's Texas ranch.

Randy Fuchs never contacted Elizabeth Rosenburg again. In the wake of his confidence scheme, Elizabeth Rosenburg's daughter attempted suicide, and her mother blamed Elizabeth for her financial ruin and the family's embarrassment. Miss Rosenburg was so humiliated after being scammed, she could no longer face her friends. She spent her remaining money to move to a city where no one knew her. The "Love Bandit" had struck again, leaving another victim crushed in the wake of his deceit.

Some 18 years after her divorce, Karen Sue Procter dated and fell in love with Randy Fox, from Austin, who provided much-wanted attention to Karen and her three children. Randy Fox solidified their growing relationship by presenting Karen with a $7,000 emerald ring and offered to move Karen's entire family with him to either Mexico or Belize.

As a result of falling for the wrong man, Karen Sue Procter ended up in the hospital. When she got out, everything was gone-her money, her job, her home, her children.

Randy Fox traveled with Karen Sue Procter[55] and her family through Austin, Oklahoma City, Kansas City, and Little Rock, Arkansas. His "aunt," Lois Fuchs, joined them, claiming that her fiancé had been killed in an aircraft accident. Meanwhile, Randy Fox and Auntie Lois lived on the proceeds from Karen Sue Procter's property that she had sold under Fox's promise of financial security, and her $2,000 monthly veterans disability benefits she received for the lupus she contracted during her Army service.

Karen's youngest child was mentally challenged. Randy Fox assured Karen that he would enroll the child in a private, special-needs school. Karen's oldest daughter became fed up with Fox's promises that never materialized and returned to Austin to live with her boyfriend; Karen's son moved to Missouri to live with his father.

When Fox's photograph appeared on the television show *Crime Stoppers*, Karen Sue Procter confronted Randy, but he quickly dismissed it as an angry girlfriend trying to get even with him. He even boasted that if captured, he would outsmart law enforcement officials by pleading insanity.

Then the emerald jewel fell out of Karen Sue Procter's prized ring. Just as Karen's suspicion was aroused to the point of action, she ran out of the medicine that kept her lupus in check. As soon as her next disability check arrived, Karen planned to take her remaining daughter and leave Randy Fox and Lois Fuchs. Unfortunately, Karen's lupus intervened. For fear of being captured, Randy Fox refused to transport Karen to the military hospital to renew her medication prescription. Eventually, Karen Sue Procter's condition deteriorated to the point at which she was taken to the emergency room.

Lois Fuchs convinced the medical staff at the veterans hospital that Karen's family had disowned her. As Karen Sue Procter lay unconscious, like a vulture picking at a carcass, Lois Fuchs removed Karen's valuable watch and jewelry from her limp body.

The hospital staff eventually discovered Karen Sue Procter's medical file and notified her family of her medical condition. The family retrieved Karen's youngest daughter from Randy Fox's custody. All total, Karen Sue Procter was scammed out of more than $40,000 in jewelry, cash, furniture, and clothing. Even worse, Karen Sue Procter lost all of her children. The "Love Bandit" had struck again.

The "Love Bandit" also swindled a male victim out of $15,000 in a Hawaii real estate scam. Through corrupt creativity, the "Love Bandit" spun a story to the victim's sister that he smuggled South American Indian artifacts into the United States. The "Love Bandit" also told the sister that his grandfather was a Nazi officer during World War II, and that he was now responsible for recovering German artifacts lost during the war. The sister victim lost more than $10,000 to the "Love Bandit" when she purchased two paintings that he told her had survived the Chicago Cold Storage Building Fire of 1871.

While assigned to the DSS office in Houston, Texas, I was informed of an ongoing investigation of the "Love Bandit," who had illegally acquired a U.S. passport in the name of Randy Lee Fuchs, and had used at least fifteen alias names during the commission of various crimes.

Ed Nendell has tracked the suspect through Oklahoma, Texas, New Mexico, Colorado, Missouri, and Kansas. "I'll bet he knows my name. I hope so. I'll do anything to catch him."

I was asked to contact the lead investigator, Ed Nendell, Williamson County District Attorney, Georgetown, Texas.

After listening to a synopsis of the case, I quickly came to the conclusion that Ed Nendell was a caring, tenacious investigator who possessed the spirit of a pit bull. Ed Nendell filled me in on the "Love

The Love Bandit's passport photograph.

Bandit": a man and woman team had used multiple aliases to con women into marriage in order to steal the victims' cash, jewelry, valuable art, and crystal glassware; the bandit subjugated the women further with the resulting emotional damage.

Through a routine record check, I confirmed that in July 1985, our John Doe (Randy Lee Fuchs) had applied for and received a U.S. passport under the death identity of his partner Lois Elaine Fuchs' infant nephew. Two-year-old Randy Lee Fuchs died in 1957.

With less than three years remaining on the ten-year statute of limitations for passport fraud, time was of the essence.

With the passport fraud case now front and center, I threw in my investigative hat to assist Ed Nendell with piecing together the puzzle that would lead to the capture and prosecution of the "Love Bandit" and his accomplice, as well as assist the victims by recouping some of their losses. This would hopefully bring a degree of closure for this chapter of their lives. Of course complete closure would be difficult; only time and internal healing would help the victims deal with the betrayal of one's deepest trust.

Now referred to by law enforcement agencies as "John DOE and Jane DOE," the nefarious couple, neither which had known prior criminal histories, had become adept at identity theft, stealing and operating under many different aliases. In addition to Randy Lee Fuchs, the "Love Bandit" had committed crimes under the aliases Randy Fox, Joseph L. Cook, and Mark Lanson. The woman bandit had used the name Lois Elaine Fuchs and Cathy Dawn Marks. The trail of their crime spree spread through Texas, New Mexico, Kansas, Arizona, and Canada.

Ed Nendell had informed communities of the fugitive couple's crimes by sharing their photographs via newspapers, appearances on the nationally syndicated ABC 20/20 television series, and the Joan Rivers Show. In August 1992, *Redbook Magazine* journalist Emily Benedek penned an outstanding article about the "Love Bandit" that greatly assisted in the infamous couple's capture.

Up until that point, regardless of the national exposure about the "Love Bandit" case, investigative leads fizzled and the trail became stale. Eager to bring our bandit to justice, networking and patience were the only courses of action.

As fate would have it, the FBI office in Phoenix, Arizona, had a copy of the *Redbook Magazine* edition. Once DSS Agent Tom Borisch read the article about the "Love Bandit," he responded, "Wow! The man in FBI custody is the "Love Bandit!" Learning of the enormity of their catch, the FBI quickly rounded up the "Love Bandit's" partner in crime, Lois Elaine Fuchs.

The midnight oil would be burning in Phoenix, Arizona. During the days that followed, DSS Agent Tom Borisch obtained two federal search warrants: one for the criminal's shared apartment in Tempe, Arizona, and the second for a storage unit in Mesa, Arizona. DSS agents had to move quickly before Lois Elaine Fuchs moved evidence from the Tempe apartment—via an acquaintance—on the same day the search warrant was executed. Thousands of dollars of precious gems, gold, collector art items, and a deed to a 15-acre cottage property near Toronto, Canada, were recovered.

The fraudulent U.S. passport, numerous birth certificates of deceased people, and graveyard maps in New Mexico and Arizona were also discovered. The "Love Bandit" and his sidekick had been preparing to strike again.

At the "Love Bandit's" initial court appearance in Phoenix, Special Agent Tom Borisch provided the magistrate judge a copy of Randy Fuchs' death certificate and the *Redbook Magazine* article. Asking for his true identity, the "Love Bandit" responded to the magistrate that his name was Randy Fuchs. The judge asked the "Love Bandit" a series of questions, including his date and place of birth, and the name of his parents. After each response, the judge looked down at the death certificate. The judge then asked the suspect if he knew the meaning of perjury. The "Love Bandit" replied in the affirmative. Pointing to Tom Borisch, the magistrate judge informed the "Love Bandit" that Borisch had just provided a certificate that stated that "you [Love Bandit] are dead." The judge then held up the copy of the *Redbook Magazine* and asked the suspect if the photo was his. When he did not receive a response, the magistrate thumbed to the article and, pointing to another photograph of the subject, asked the "Love Bandit" if he could see this photograph better. Now busted by the judge, the "Love Bandit's" silence was deafening.

Tom Borisch quickly led another DSS team to serve a search warrant for a storage unit in Wichita, Kansas. There DSS agents discovered stolen jewelry, artwork, furniture, valuable crystal glassware, and additional aliases.

Lois Fuchs, the "Love Bandit's" female partner in crime, was considering fighting extradition to Texas. I flew to Arizona to interview Lois Elaine Fuchs at the Maricopa County Jail. I immediately noticed a defiant sneer on Lois Fuchs' face. I found the heavy-set, big-boned woman to be arrogant and unrepentant

DSS Agents Tom Borisch (R) and Robert W. Starnes (L) display recovered jewelry from the "Love Bandit."

in the wake of victims left in her trail of deceit, including her attempt to scam her own mother and brother. Just before I departed the jail, Lois Fuchs cocked her head and told me that a fellow inmate suggested she write a book about her exploits and title the book, *My Train to Durango.* I had the distinct privilege of informing Lois Fuchs that her train to Durango was merely a brief stop. Her final destination would be Texas.

The "Love Bandit" was transported back to Williamson County to stand trial in state court. Scores of angry victims had learned of the "Love Bandit's" flight schedule to Austin. In order to protect the "Love Bandit" from harm and ensure he received justice, I implemented a protection plan at the Austin airport. On arrival in Austin, the "Love Bandit" was indeed greeted by angry victims congregated at the arrival terminal. Still reeling from their financial and emotional losses, jeers were hurled at the "Bandit."

During his initial Georgetown, Texas, hearing, the "Love Bandit's" capture strategy prediction came to pass as he claimed insanity for his legal defense. The "Love Bandit" told Texas State District Judge Burt Carnes that he did not know his true identity and signed his arrest booking card with the letter "X." Incredibly, up until this time, the "Love Bandit's" true identity was still unknown.

Several days later, Lois Elaine Fuchs was extradited to Williamson County, Texas. I chuckled when I received Lois' sheriff office booking photo. As Lois refused to cooperate, three deputy sheriffs held her and propped her head up for a priceless photograph.

Tony Ruggiero was a veteran investigator for the Louisiana Attorney General's Office. His copy of *The Progressive Farmer's Magazine* had not yet arrived. Passing time, he picked up his wife's August 1992 *Redbook* edition, and happened on the "Love Bandit" article. For more than a decade, investigator Ruggiero had been on the trail of the man now known as the "Love Bandit." As soon as Ruggiero saw the photograph in the article, he knew it was the man named Marion J. Ducote, who had been indicted in

Williamson County, Texas, deputies assist a defiant Lois Fuchs with her jail booking photograph.

Baton Rouge in 1984 for 19 counts of selling unregistered securities and two counts of felony theft. Ducote was accused of scamming more than 100 investors out of more than $400,000 by selling worthless oil and gas leases. Ruggiero gladly sent Ducote's dental records, handwriting samples, and photograph to Texas to confirm his true identity. Speaking about Marion Ducote's Louisiana victims, Tony Ruggiero stated, "I know the victims are still here," he said. "Some are very anxious to testify against him."[56]

The Williamson County district attorney sought financial restitution for only one of the several "Love Bandit" victims. On January 7, 1993, Texas State District Judge Burt Carnes sentenced Marion Ducote to 2–10 years in confinement for document fraud and theft. Ducote was ordered to pay one victim $29,550. No state charges were filed against Lois Elaine Fuchs.

Obtaining restitution for additional victims and charging Lois Elaine Fuchs now fell on the shoulders of Ron Sievert, an incredibly bright and gifted Assistant U.S. Attorney in Austin, Texas, who was assigned to prosecute the passport fraud for the "Love Bandit."

Leading up to the federal prosecution, I requested the U.S. Justice Department file a Multi-Legal Assistance Treaty (MLAT) requesting the Canadian authorities seize and auction the 15-acre cottage property in Toronto, Canada, for victim restitution. This was the first instance that DSS had requested seizure of foreign property to be returned to victims of a crime in the United States.

In order to seek maximum federal sentencing, it would be paramount to convince the judge of the victims' pain and suffering resulting from the passport fraud charge. It is sometimes assumed that the victimization of a deceased person's identity can no longer be counted as a true crime. However, I shared with AUSA Ron Sievert that when a person steals the identity of a deceased person (even an infant), for the purpose of perpetrating crime, the family of the deceased becomes the victim of the identity theft due to the soiled honor of the family name. To bolster this untested legal argument in hopes of obtaining a stiffer court sentence, I encouraged the family of the deceased infant Randy Lee Fuchs to write to the federal district judge, complaining about Ducote defiling their family member's name. This strategy worked.

Assistant U.S. Attorney Ron Sievert, (ret.)

On September 19, 1993, Marion Joseph Ducote was sentenced to eight years in Federal prison and fined $50,000 for passport fraud and conspiracy to commit passport fraud.

He also was ordered to pay restitution of $42,800 to Karen Sue Procter; $3,500 to Elizabeth Rosenburg; and $31,795 to another victim—total restitution of $78,095. At that time, Marion Ducote received the longest jail sentence for passport fraud in the history of the United States. It was also the first time that restitution was ordered to victims of theft under passport fraud charges.

Left: Lois Elaine Fuchs arrest booking photograph. Right: Marion DuCote (aka Randy Fuchs) arrest booking photograph.

A detainer was issued by the Louisiana authorities for Marion Ducote—after serving his federal sentence, Ducote was to be transferred to Louisiana to stand trial for the theft and securities charges. The Internal Revenue Service was also awaiting his return to Louisiana.

Lois Elaine Fuchs, who had purportedly abandoned her children for Marion Joseph Ducote, was sentenced to nine months in federal prison for social security and identification fraud and ordered to pay $34,000 to the U.S. Department of Housing and Urban Development for a defaulted loan and foreclosure on a house.[58]

Although this case may have brought a sense of closure for some of the "Love Bandit's" victims, it may be advisable for people to occasionally kiss while their eyes are open.

CHAPTER 18

OPERATION WURSTFEST

He set his sights on obtaining
one of the world's most highly sought documents:
a U.S. passport.

For his army of company "solicitors," George Dudov recruited Europeans who had overstayed their visas and were vulnerable to deportation. With the threat of exposing their illegal immigration status, these weak, desperate men were at Dudov's mercy. Working like indentured servants, the solicitors spent most of their days cold calling unsuspecting investors in hopes of landing victims to provide money to Dudov based on false promises of high financial yields from the rich oil fields of Texas.

George Peter Dudov

George Dudov was proud of the international Ponzi scheme he had created under the storefront name of First Eagle Oil Production Corporation, in the Heritage Plaza Building, 7800 N. MoPac Expressway, Austin, Texas, which he used to launder millions of dollars allegedly selling oil and gas leases in the United States to investors in Europe and Brazil.[59]

Dudov was living a high roller's life. Between April 21, 1993 and Feburary 1, 1994 alone, First Eagle Corp. made deposits of $2.3 million in accounts in two Austin banks. Dudov told First Eagle employees he had access to millions of dollars in illegal drug money and was washing such funds through the company.[60] His company financial books revealed his investors had been defrauded out of more than $2.5 million.

The tall, lanky German national, Dudov was a seasoned criminal who cut his teeth on European organized crime. In September 1987, Mr. Dudov was arrested in Germany for narcotics smuggling and sentenced to 42 months' detention. Shortly after his release, Dudov was convicted again on charges in Germany of false statement and larceny. He was imprisoned, but this time he escaped and fled to the United States.

As a fugitive, Dudov was stopped for a traffic violation in Florida in October. He presented the identification documents of a well-known German international criminal and had in his possession a handgun and false credit cards. Dudov was arrested and extradited to Germany to serve the remainder of his prison sentence. Dudov was released from the German prison in February 1993 and returned to the United States under the visa waiver program. The U.S. Visa Waiver Program allows citizens of select countries, including most Europeans, to travel to the United States for business or tourism for up to ninety days without being subjected to the normal visa issuance process.

Dudov, sporting long, dark, bushy eyebrows that covered both eyes and his large nose, resembled a chain-smoking Russian mafia thug. Dudov loved Central Texas: Austin, Fredericksburg, Pflugerville, Luckenbach, and New Braunfels.

Texas is rich in Germanic culture: its German festivals, including Germanfest, Wurstfest, and May Pole celebrations; Germanic architecture—distinct construction (*fachwerk*) of heavy timber frame with diagonal bracing with limestone infill—and many restaurants created by German, Prussian, and Austrian migrants; and, of course, the abundance of beer gardens made Dudov feel at home.

Speaking in his thick Düsseldorf accent, Dudov once shared with his guest that the prior year, his former First Eagle Oil business associate had been arrested by the FBI in Austin while in possession of stolen financial bonds worth more than $500,000. Fearing that his former associate would implicate him in the crime, Dudov confidently proclaimed that he could no longer trust him and was willing to pay $10,000 to have him "eliminated."

Dudov desired to eliminate his former associate by way of a murder-for-hire scheme. Using information obtained from wiretaps and an inside informant wearing a listening device,[61] the FBI began building a case against him.

Dudov had taken the bait from the now engaged law enforcement agencies, including the FBI and IRS/CID. It was time to set the hook.

With the concurrence of the Assistant U.S. Attorney, the next and crucial step toward his arrest and prosecution was to solidify his desire to effect the murder. Once Dudov committed to the solicitation for murder scheme, the long arm of the law could apprehend him.

At the last moment, Dudov became apprehensive and backed away from his desire to pay a "hit man." Because Dudov had withdrawn his hit-for-hire request, the Assistant U.S. Attorney advised that a solicitation for capital murder charge was no longer viable. Dudov's unexpected move jeopardized the heart of the federal investigation.

After a cooling-off period of several months, Dudov became emboldened and signaled his desire to travel to Peru and Switzerland to purportedly smuggle $12 million in U.S. currency from drug cartels that he would launder through his Austin-based Ponzi business. In order to facilitate his travel to South America, Dudov needed a passport in a fraudulent name so that he could travel and conduct his illegal business and conceal his immigration status.

He set his sights on obtaining one of the world's most highly sought documents: a U.S. passport. Based on case law, a passport denotes proof of citizenship and is accepted by virtually all government entities and private corporations as a valid identification document.

Dudov's quest to obtain a fraudulent U.S. passport opened the door for a new investigative strategy of possible bribery and document fraud charges, working toward ensuring a dangerous man was taken off the streets long enough for the FBI and IRS/CID to conduct their money-laundering investigation.

Based on his request for assistance with acquiring a U.S. passport, the FBI contacted me at the DSS Houston field office to determine if DSS could issue a U.S. passport for Dudov to assist with their undercover investigation. Having attended the annual German festival of Wurstfest in New Braunfels, Texas, I felt it fitting to name the DSS investigation of Dudov, "Operation Wurstfest."

Desperate to travel to Peru to inject $4 million into his cash-starved Ponzi scheme, Dudov took the bait. Dudov agreed to pay $30,000 for a U.S. passport in a bogus name, at that time, the most money ever offered for a U.S. passport. More importantly, if issued, this passport would pass law enforcement scrutiny because it would be processed internally within the U.S. State Department's passport computer systems.

The investigative parameters required Dudov to provide half of the payment up front and the remaining upon delivery of the U.S. passport. Dudov initially agreed and provided a completed passport application with his actual biographical information and his passport photographs, along with a company check in the full amount of $30,000. Dudov asked his contact to wait before cashing the check until he returned from Peru.

DSS intentionally balked at Dudov's newly established payment request. Desperate at the real possibility of losing his opportunity of acquiring the U.S. passport, Dudov endorsed the automobile title to his fiancé's new Mercedes-Benz sedan as collateral. Just like that, Dudov had swallowed the *hook, line, and sinker*.

On a cold and rainy night on January 20, 1994, in the parking lot of the U.S. Post Office in Jollyville, Texas, several FBI agents and I huddled behind bushes awaiting Dudov's arrival to pick up his fraudulent U.S. passport at a pre-arranged clandestine meeting.

Just like clockwork, his Mercedes E-Class slowly and cautiously made its way into the post office parking lot. To Dudov's surprise, dozens of armed special agents appeared from the foliage and descended upon his idling Mercedes. I pulled him out of his expensive ride and cuffed and Mirandized the confused German. As a result of the federal bribery charges, George Dudov's Ponzi business was shut down. Twenty computers valued at more than $50,000 and two German luxury automobiles—with an approximate combined value of $120,000—were forfeited to the FBI and IRS/CID.

U.S. District Judge James R. Nowlin sentenced George Dudov to 120 months for money laundering and 60 months for false statements in an application for a U.S. passport, and fined $50,000.[62]

Several weeks after Dudov's sentencing, the FBI's lead case agent called and informed that he had stopped by to visit the incarcerated German in the Bell County Jail in Belton, Texas. It was a cold central Texas day. The FBI agent noted that Dudov was squatting in the corner of his jail cell. The prisoner was delighted at the sight of his visitor, even though he had assisted in placing him behind bars. When the FBI agent removed his winter coat, he held it tightly in his arms, not wishing to lay it down in Dudov's roach-infested holding cell. It's ironic and I suppose fitting that a blood-sucking parasite was now surrounded by and living among roaches, giving credence that crime does not pay.

Based on George Dudov's arrest and prosecution, I now have a greater sense of celebration when attending New Braunfels' Wurstfest.

CHAPTER 19

CAPONE-IZED

*Ezekor collapsed in the arms of the two police officers
while exhaling a groan of a thousand sins escaping his soul.*

D ue to prolific armed conflict, extremely high rates of poverty, porous borders, and inefficient and corrupt governmental leadership, in West African nations, primarily Nigeria, organized crime syndicates have become a worldwide concern in drugs, arms and human trafficking.[63]

Because of their illegal creativity, investigations involving Nigerian organized criminals are often complex and wide-reaching.

Americans are daily deluged with email scams originating from Nigerian criminals informing of a made-up Prince who is about to inherit a large sum of money. Generally, the phony Prince claims he needs a small investment to free up his inheritance monies, thus promising to share his inheritance with his trusted investors. Surprisingly, some people, primarily motivated by greed, still fall victim to this preposterous scam.

Once, while serving as the Regional Security Officer in Western Samoa, I witnessed Nigerian criminal creativity first hand. The

Samoan police called and informed me of a Nigerian national visitor who was claiming to have millions of dollars in U.S. currency. In this scheme, the con man's pitch was a claim that the CIA had coated currency in a tar-like substance to protect monies designated for use in covert intelligence operations.

Accordingly, the U.S. government's covert currency was totally worthless as long as the tar substance coated the paper bills. The con man's hook was to sell a highly "secretive chemical" designed to dissolve and remove the tar from the money, rendering the greenbacks again useable. To succeed with this scam, the Nigerian used a small device resembling a plastic cigarette roller telemarketed in the United States during the 1970's.

With an audience of gullible police officers, this Nigerian poured a small amount of the "secret chemical" into the roller device tray. While rolling a single tar-coated bill on one side of the roller device, using a mechanical "sleight-of-hand," a clean bill exited the device on the other side, lending the appearance that the "secret chemical" had actually washed away the tar coating the currency, exposing a crisp $100 bill.

Of course, the Nigerian had brought along and donated a suitcase brimming with tar-coated currency. For a nominal fee of $90,000, the Nigerian was offering to sell his victims the highly sought "secret chemical".

The Samoan police contacted me once they began suspecting this was a scam. After I confirmed the magician-type trick was indeed a scam, the tables were turned and the angry Samoans expelled the Nigerian crook, allowing him to depart with only the shirt on his back. I suppose he who laughs last, laughs loudest.

Another common scam used by Nigerian criminals residing in the United States is homeowner's insurance fraud. During the days of residential mold scare, criminals would drag a water hose into their house, turn on the water and allow the humid Gulf coast air to grow mold, thus positioning the criminal to file fraudulent homeowner insurance claims.

In an even deadlier scheme, some Nigerians would crash their automobiles into unsuspecting drivers, claiming themselves injured in order to defraud auto insurance companies.

Because of DSS' ability to quickly acquire answers to investigative leads worldwide via the vast network of DSS special agents serving as RSOs, a lasting relationship between DSS and the Houston Police Department's Violent Gangs Task Force was forged. As a result of this successful collaboration, prominent Nigerian mafia members were investigated in an effort to protect citizens from a multitude of crimes.

In 1993, the office receptionist at the DSS field office in Houston, Texas, announced that Nigerian Peter Ezekor had arrived and was in the waiting room.

Peter Ezekor, a self-purported Nigerian Prince, had arrived in the United States in the mid-1980s on a student visa and was a suspected member of a local Nigerian organized crime syndicate. In 1989, Peter Ezekor and his Nigerian spouse had been convicted and sentenced to 10 years on felony state charges of forgery and theft. Taking advantage of a broken immigration system, Peter was allowed to remain in the United States under a claim of political asylum while his Nigerian wife was deported.

In an attempt to assist his Nigerian wife to illegally re-enter the United States, Peter Ezekor committed polygamy with an American woman. Peter conspired to

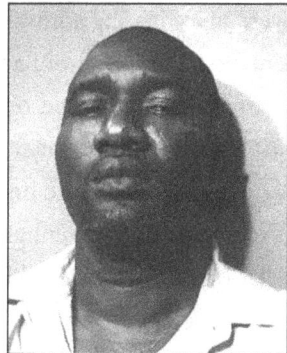
Peter O. Ezekor's arrest photograph

fraudulently apply for a U.S. passport, photo substituting his American wife's photograph while using his Nigerian wife's identity.

The U.S. Secret Service, FBI, and Health and Human Services were aware that Peter Ezekor was a major crime player in numerous fraud rings, but to date, these federal agencies were unable to make a criminal case.

Although I had proven a passport fraud case beyond a reasonable doubt, the U.S. Attorney's Office in Houston declined to prosecute Peter Ezekor, a previously convicted state felon. Indignant at the thought of allowing a criminal to escape justice by literally walking free to continue his crime spree, I convinced Peter Ezekor that his reprieve from prosecution would only be achieved by him stopping by the DSS office monthly to report any crimes he may have witnessed.

Like clockwork, in a game of cat and mouse, Peter dropped by the DSS Houston Field Office, pretended to not have information, while I pretended to be his informant handler. An exercise in futility, I thought, until fate appeared on my front doorstep.

A few days before my final meeting with Peter, I received a telephone call from an FBI agent informing me that he was investigating Peter Ezekor for fraudulent automobile insurance claims in excess of six million dollars throughout Texas and Louisiana. The FBI agent also informed me that separate to their inquiry, the Texas Rangers were investigating administrators working at a nearby state-sponsored university suspected of an improper academic grade changing scam, and admissions based on fraudulent immigration status for foreign students, including Peter Ezekor, in exchange for money.

The FBI agent said he had heard that I was working Peter Ezekor as an informant. After enlightening the FBI agent of my quasi-informant relationship with Peter, I offered a strategy whereby I would video record Peter admitting to using aliases in the FBI's ongoing insurance fraud investigation.

In a choreographed effort, the Houston Police Department's Violent Gangs Task Force secured an arrest warrant for document fraud for one of Peter Ezekor's fraudulent state driver licenses. In order to engage in a psychological operation to spread confusion within the Nigerian crime syndicates, the Houston Police officers planned a scenario to arrest Peter Ezekor in a way that would lend the impression that a mole within his circle of influence had snitched him out.

With a video camera erected in the DSS conference room, I politely asked Peter Ezekor to be seated. I put Peter at ease by congratulating him on his final DSS office visit. Peter's wide grin telegraphed his delight of this welcomed news. I told Peter that as a result of the February 1993 terrorist attack against New York's World Trade Tower, DSS headquarters was now requiring video taping for all informant debriefings. A bit uncomfortable at this new procedure, Peter sat motionless while I read him the Miranda warning and received his acknowledgment that he voluntarily agreed to the video interview.

With the requisite code of criminal procedures now satisfied, I began reciting the alias names and social security numbers I had discovered during my passport fraud investigation of Peter Ezekor. Still smiling, Peter confidently admitted to using these aliases. I then began reading off the aliases and social security numbers provided to me by the FBI. Pausing a moment, a puzzled look suddenly appeared on Peter's face as he quietly wondered how I had become aware of these aliases. Perhaps not wanting to ruin his last DSS informant interview, Peter unwittingly admitted to using eighteen different aliases, multiple fraudulent driver licenses, and social security numbers he had used in the insurance fraud scams.

At the conclusion of my video interview, Peter began to lift himself from his chair in hopes of escaping the now uncomfortable environs. I quickly informed Peter that two gentlemen waiting outside the conference room wanted to speak with him before he departed the DSS office.

At that moment, I mused at how I loved my job.

Sitting at the opposite end of the conference room, now blocking Peter's exit, I introduced the FBI agent and Texas Ranger. Peter knew his "gig" was up. He spent the next six hours admitting to and explaining his role in the insurance fraud scheme and university bribery scam. I also secured a voluntary consent from Peter to search his automobile and apartment.

Following Peter to his apartment, waiting DSS and FBI special agents descended upon his habitat. There we discovered the existence of a large document-making laboratory and seized numerous fraudulent identification documents, immigration cards, and document-making implements. We also uncovered fraudulent insurance claims related to the FBI's investigation.

After collecting the evidence, we walked with Peter to the parking lot, where the FBI agent and I bade him farewell. As we entered our vehicles, I gave a thumbs-up signal to the waiting Houston police officers concealed in a nearby white van. As we drove away, the Houston police officers enacted their psychological operations plan by surrounding Peter and informing him that he was under arrest. Resembling the "Grim Reaper," a plainclothes police officer wearing black trousers, a black shirt, and a black ski mask pretended to be a police informant, walked up to Peter, pointed his long, boney finger at Peter and said, "That's him, officer."

The theatrical ruse worked. Peter Ezekor thought he had been "ratted out" by an unknown person within his organized criminal network. Maybe because of the stress of walking a fine line with DSS and the FBI that day, or maybe the strain of guilt, Ezekor collapsed in the arms of two police officers while exhaling a groan of a thousand sins escaping his soul.

Regaining his composure for a moment, Ezekor was desperate to remain free. He quickly pointed towards my departing tail lights, insisting to the Houston police officers that the FBI and State Department had just left his apartment. Continuing the ruse, the police officer played Ezekor's claim as delusional. While in jail, Peter Ezekor was left to "breed reptiles of the mind" in his attempt to figure out who in his band had snitched.

Word quickly spread throughout the Nigerian organized criminal networks of the unsettling perception of the existence of an enemy within. We knew our plan had worked when we later learned that members of the Nigerian criminal community were now lying low, not knowing who within their sphere had turned traitor on their royal Prince.

Oblivious to our orchestrated tag team arrest, a few days later, Peter Ezekor called me from jail to tell me that an informant had identified him as a criminal. Chuckling under my breath, I told him I was clueless to his claim and broke off all communications. While awaiting trail, Peter's ankle was broken in jail after an altercation with a Houston street gang member.

On June 21, 1994, Peter Ezekor pled guilty to passport fraud, mail fraud, and conspiracy to commit mail fraud in the Southern District of Texas. Peter was sentenced to 33 months for passport fraud and 33 months for mail fraud and conspiracy, sentences to be served concurrently. Ezekor also pled guilty to a state charge of tampering with a government record and was sentenced to one year.[64] A warrant was also issued for parole violation by the Harris County District Attorney's Office.

Not content with his fate of remaining in Nigeria, Peter Ezekor illegally re-entered the United States, where he was again arrested, this time for participating in an automobile insurance accident scam. On December 17, 2007, Peter Ezekor was sentenced for his role in a fake auto accident scheme where he amassed more than $400,000 in false claims from insurance companies. Now, age 49, Peter Ezekor received a 94-month federal sentence and a deportation order from U.S. District Judge Vanessa D. Gilmore for illegally re-entering the country, and for conspiracy to launder money obtained by fraud. Peter's former U.S. naturalized spouse, Catherine Jacobs, received a sentence of 14 months for conspiracy to commit mail fraud in 2007. From February 1999 to September 2004, Peter Ezekor and his wife Catherine Jacobs utilized fake driver's licenses, identification cards and Social Security cards to purchase auto insurance policies. Ezekor and Jacobs then staged more than 50 accidents, filing claims under the insurance policies using false identities. Court documents revealed that 337 checks totaling $427,622 were issued for the false physical injuries.[65]

The DSS and Houston police task force's next order of business was to counter a major Nigerian heroin dealer. Rigby, a naturalized Nigerian, was suspected by many federal law enforcement agencies as being Houston's most notorious heroin kingpin.

Months prior, the U.S. Secret Service's excitement purportedly turned to disappointment at not having discovered fruits of crime in Rigby's residence while executing a search warrant. According to intelligence later collected, Rigby had stashed fraudulent credit cards in a hidden ceiling compartment. Like a cat with nine lives, Rigby had once again narrowly escaped the long arm of the law and had gained the perception of being untouchable by several unsuccessful investigations into his drug-dealing activities.

If DSS and the Houston police department had any chance of breaking Rigby's heroin smuggling ring, we would have to implement a completely different and fresh strategy. Fittingly, Albert Einstein's definition of insanity is doing the same thing over and over again and expecting different results. We sought different results by shifting our focus from drug dealing to document fraud.

Like a mythical dragon's chink in his armor, every criminal has weaknesses. We spent several days studying prior investigations and habits in an attempt to better understand Rigby's world. Having served in multiple overseas assignments, our DSS team knew document fraud is often an accepted way of life for criminals, especially in developing countries. We decided that document fraud and identity theft would be Rigby's blind spot.

In the same way that Elliott Nest (and the Untouchables) had taken down the infamous Chicago gangster, Al Capone, by attacking his blind spot, thus charging him with tax evasion, we would use document fraud to take down Rigby's organization.

Determined that document fraud (i.e. selling or using illegal identification cards, fraudulent credit cards and bank loans, etc.), was the Nigerian organized crime network's chink in the beast's underbelly, we focused on first taking out the lower echelon, then working

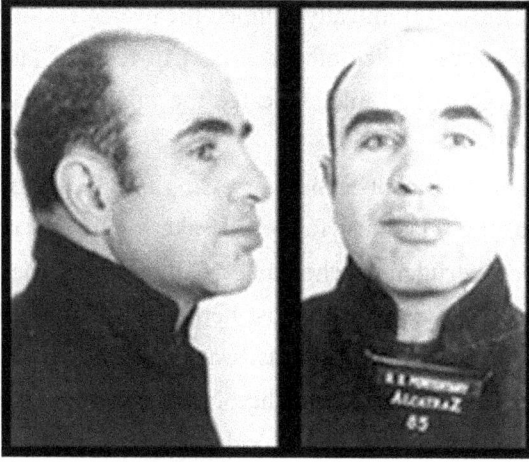

Gangster Al Capone's booking photograph

our way towards Rigby. Given Rigby's organizational insulation, this feat would prove to be difficult and time-consuming. However, we were confident that if we applied enough pressure on his henchmen, we could force Rigby to expose himself by taking risks he would not normally take. Hundreds of hours of late-night surveillance would be required.

Once, during a stakeout, a Houston police officer and I were surveilling a woman with suspected Rigby gang ties. This woman delivered fast food fried chicken meals to customers using a white cargo van with a large, plastic, yellow chicken attached to the van's rooftop. We had planned on stopping the woman during her next delivery in hopes of convincing her to turn informant.

Given the bright optics of the large yellow chicken, I quipped to the police officer how degrading it would be to our law enforcement colleagues if we lost this fowl shrouded van. Impossible!

Just then, almost like in a scripted movie, a tractor trailer pulled directly in front of our parked Jeep Cherokee. Blocking all four lanes, the truck slowly backed into a building's loading dock. Seeming like eternity, once a gap had finally appeared, I sped past the truck, only to learn that the chicken van (and our female target) had departed the restaurant. Desperate to locate our missing yellow chicken, in a face-saving move, I frantically combed the nearby residential streets. With the Houston police officer almost in tears of laughter, relief flooded my ego when I finally located the van, the chicken, and our future informant.

Our next informant-to-be, possessing knowledge of the heroin kingpin was the infamous "Record Breaker." The "Record Breaker" was a Nigerian drug mule who had earned his nickname by breaking the record of swallowing the most heroin filled condoms, each the size of a golf ball. Also referred to as "swallowers," heroin smugglers had sometimes died instantly when a heroin-filled condom erupted inside their stomachs, flooding their blood system with fatal doses of the deadly narcotic. Suspected "swallowers" entering the airport were routinely granted free night stays by U.S. Customs to allow ample time to pass their internally stashed illegal cargo.

The next criminal in the batter's box was one of Rigby's lieutenants, responsible for selling fraudulent identity cards. After witnessing the lieutenant selling false driver licenses at a local mall, we conducted a search on his apartment in Houston. There we discovered a small portable shredding machine, its plastic catch bag full of shredded financial documents and credit cards. Like assembling a jigsaw

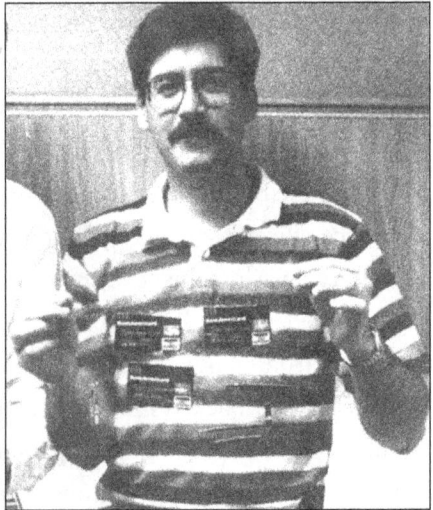

Left: Robert W. Starnes pieces together shredded cards and ID documents. Right: Robert W. Starnes displays fraudulent credit cards.

puzzle, we used a clear sheet of sticky contact paper to reassemble eight shredded fraudulent credit cards.

We then executed a second search warrant on this lieutenant's storage facility, also located in Houston. This search netted over five thousand blank Texas temporary driver license permit forms. This discovery was the largest such seizure for Texas driver licenses to date. The news of this bust quickly made its way to Rigby's ears.

With fortuitous timing, a DSS agent discovered visa fraud committed by Rigby's brother-in-law. The brother-in-law was being held by the U.S. Immigration and Naturalization Service (INS) at the Houston INS detention center and was scheduled to be released soon. The Houston Police Department obtained an arrest warrant for the brother-in-law for obtaining a fraudulent license. On the day of his release, I was the lead surveillant at the INS detention center. Sporting a big smile, I radioed to the other DSS agents and Houston police officers that Rigby was a passenger in a car driven by another of his lieutenants.

After Rigby picked up his brother-in-law and drove a short distance, a uniformed Houston Police officer stopped the vehicle in order to execute their arrest warrant. During the traffic stop, Rigby's driver could not sufficiently prove his vehicle was insured. As a result, the driver and Rigby's brother-in-law were both arrested and the vehicle was inventoried and impounded.

Rigby, now standing on the sidewalk, had unintentionally left his cellular phone inside the vehicle that was now in the Houston Police department's custody. Rigby pleaded that he be allowed the retrieve his cellular phone. In what could have been a Hollywood movie scene, a Houston police officer pulled a quarter from his pocket, flipped it to the notorious drug dealer and said, "This phone call is on me."

Rigby was a heroin kingpin who was not ashamed at destroying countless lives through his narcotics smuggling operation. Giving us his version of a rock-jawed dirty look, wearing Bermuda shorts and flip-flop sandals, Rigby turned and began walking away. Unexpectedly and unrehearsed, all law enforcement officers present simultaneously burst out humming our own adaptations to Manfred Mann's song, *Do Wah Diddy Diddy*.

As he departed, Rigby's long strides, swinging arms, and occasional stop and backwards peek, resembled a sad and dejected man.

Although my Houston assignment ended before Rigby's fate was formally sealed, I later heard that our investigative strategy against Rigby had worked, as he purportedly took risks he had not previously taken, resulting in his arrest for narcotics crimes.

Our hunch of attacking the dragon's chink had worked. Rigby had been "*Capone-ized*."

For those English language majors, dropping the "e" in the word *Capone-ized* would perhaps be improved grammar, resulting in the word "*Capon-ized*"-meaning a neutered young male chicken.

I can envision either fate fitting for a major heroin dealer.

CHAPTER 20

A WALTER MITTY COMPLEX

*Mancuso's actions eventually
cost the taxpayers at least $750,000.*

In late 1995, in the DSS Washington field office, an expression of frustration had spread across a young DSS agent's face. He had exhausted all investigative leads in a passport fraud case. Now serving in a supervisory special agent capacity, in one final effort to identify the "perp" before closing the case as "unable to locate," I encouraged the DSS agent assigned to my unit to distribute a copy of the photograph attached to the bogus passport application to the Middle Atlantic-Great Lakes Organized Crime Law Enforcement Network's (MAGLO-CLEN) monthly newsletter.

Presto! Within hours of distributing the photograph, our passport fraud offender had

Larry Joe Hollingsworth

been identified in the MAGLOCLEN publication by a special agent working for the Defense Criminal Investigative Service (DCIS). I was contacted by a supervisor assigned to the U.S. Department of

State, Office of Inspector General (OIG), and summoned to his office. On entering the State Department's OIG office, I was introduced to Donald Mancuso, the outgoing director of the DCIS, DOD's largest Office of Inspector General. Clearly dejected and concerned, Mancuso informed me that the person in the photograph we had distributed was none other than supervisory special agent Larry Joe Hollingsworth, DCIS' acting director. With 28 years of law enforcement experience, Hollingsworth was a seasoned bureaucrat.

Perhaps believing he could steer another OIG agency's investigation to protect his friend and coworker Hollingsworth, Donald Mancuso made a plea for the State Department's OIG office to act as a co-investigative agency with the DSS. I found his request odd and wondered why Mancuso wanted another inspector general's office to participate in the investigation. I promptly denied Mancuso's request as DSS was and would remain the lead investigative agency.

Hollingsworth's motive was DSS' primary focus.

As I later testified before the Texas State Senate committee chaired by Senator Steve Ogden,[66] rarely a crime unto itself, obtaining a U.S. passport fraudulently is almost always a crime intended to facilitate other crimes which generally fall into one or more of the following categories:

1. Flight from justice

2. International terrorism

3. Hostile intelligence

4. Smuggling (narcotics, weapons, illegal aliens, and so on)

5. Economic crimes (bank fraud, insurance fraud, credit card fraud, and so on)

Given these and other possible motives, time was of the essence to secure a search warrant, especially since the suspect was soon likely to be informed of the investigation and potentially become a flight risk.

The facts that we had uncovered were that Hollingsworth used his prowess to travel to South Carolina to search for a suitable identity from which to commit fraud. Searching through local vital statistics, Hollingsworth finally settled on the identity of Charles William Drew, a child who had died before his tenth birthday as a result of an automobile accident while riding his bicycle.

Nervous at knowing his actions were felonious, Hollingsworth's hand shook while he completed the DSP-11 (passport application) form, making his handwriting difficult to read. Using the dead child's information that he copied from the birth certificate, Hollingsworth affixed his own photograph to the passport application. Possibly due to anxiety, Hollingsworth subconsciously signed his own name on the application instead of the name of the deceased child, Charles William Drew.

In drafting the search warrant, I reviewed the facts that the DSS case agent had developed during his investigation. Hollingsworth had gone to great lengths to obtain a fraudulent passport. He first traveled to a South Carolina library to research the death identity he planned to use. He opened up a postal "drop box" in which to apply for and receive the illegal passport. He used a bogus social security number.

Questions raced through our minds: What was Hollingsworth's motive—especially while holding one of the highest security clearances and serving in a position of exceptional trust? Was Hollingsworth a spy? Had he absconded with millions of dollars? Was he planning to leave the country after committing a heinous crime?

In November 1983, Mr. Hollingsworth was under investigation by the IRS for perjury. That very same month—November 1983—he was hired by DCIS to be the agent in charge of the Chicago field office. The IRS concluded that Hollingsworth had "committed perjury during rebuttal testimony." On December 5, 1983, the IRS referred the matter to the U.S. Attorney in New Orleans for prosecution.[67]

Uncovering criminal activity by any member of the law enforcement community was disconcerting. However, Larry Hollingsworth was no ordinary police officer. He was the acting director of the Department of Defense's largest investigative agency.

We all knew this high-profile investigation would quickly garner intense scrutiny by our headquarters superiors. As I sat at the computer drafting an affidavit for a search warrant of Hollingsworth's Northern Virginia apartment, the DSS assistant agent-in-charge (ASAC) nervously paced up and down, periodically asking if I was near completion of my affidavit.

After the Assistant U.S. Attorney (AUSA) had reviewed my affidavit, a federal magistrate from the northern District of Virginia approved our search warrant application. The AUSA instructed me to place the search warrant in my back pocket. I would first request that Hollingsworth agree to a voluntary consent to search. If he refused to a voluntary consent to search, I would then execute a search under the warrant.

A team of DSS agents had been surveilling Hollingsworth's cherry red Corvette convertible parked at the DCIS office. After 5 p.m., Hollingsworth departed his office to his apartment, not knowing there were a dozen DSS special agents trailing him. A DSS colleague later quipped that the type of vehicle and age of the owner screamed of a "middle-age" crisis.

At Hollingsworth's apartment, the DSS search team intended to conduct a search and follow-up interview. Hollingsworth greeted us at the door and I noticed that given the seriousness of the matter at hand, Hollingsworth seemed too calm about the situation. I suspected that Hollingsworth had been tipped off to our discovery of his crime. A search of his vehicle and apartment did not yield any additional clues as to his motive.

Immediately after searching his apartment, the DSS ASAC and I interviewed Larry Hollingsworth.

During our interview, Larry Joe Hollingsworth gave three separate reasons why he had applied for a U.S. passport under fraudulent pretenses. Included among his reasons was his claim to "test" the

Department of States' passport issuance counter measures. He finally settled on suffering from a "Walter Mitty" complex—a desire to elevate his self-importance in his own mind.

When we approached DCIS headquarters, it was clear we were unwelcome guests. I asked a senior DCIS agent to allow us access to Hollingsworth's computer files. The agent quipped that he was unable to provide the files as they were privacy-protected and contained classified information. DSS special agents hold Top Secret/Sensitive Compartment Information security clearances. Unless Hollingsworth had compartmentalized information containing intelligence sources and methods deemed too sensitive for outside agents to view, DSS security clearances were sufficient to allow us to view Hollingsworth's files. I informed the DCIS agent that, if necessary, I was willing to secure a federal search warrant. The senior agent acquiesced to my request and allowed us access to Larry Hollingsworth's computer files.

Unfortunately, a search of Hollingsworth's office and computers did not develop any additional information as to his motive. We never proved to our satisfaction Hollingsworth's true intentions of his passport fraud.

Pertaining to the passport fraud crime, Larry Hollingsworth committed about twelve overt acts of fraud between 1992 and 1994. He was the Director of Internal Affairs at DCIS from April 1991 until his retirement in September 1996. While he was hammering rank-and-file agents for minor administrative offenses, Hollingsworth was deeply involved in a criminal enterprise of his own.

Larry Joe Hollingsworth was pronounced guilty by U.S. District Judge T.S. Ellis III of felony passport fraud. Applying the sentencing strategy I used in the "Love Bandit" case, I directed the DSS case agent to contact family members of the deceased child whose identity Hollingsworth had used when perpetrating passport fraud.

Two brothers of the deceased child, both highly decorated WWII veterans, wrote letters to the federal judge denouncing the defamation of their deceased brother's name, especially by a government bureaucrat.

Partly due to these letters, in one of the most unique sentencings I have witnessed, the judge sentenced Hollingsworth to 30 days in jail, to be served on consecutive weekends.[68]

Larry Hollingsworth, a seasoned law enforcement agent, was subjected to the humiliation of having to check in at the jail in Alexandria, Virginia, for fifteen consecutive weekends, but was allowed to file for law enforcement retirement due to perceived protection by his friend and supervisor, Donald Mancuso.

After the prosecution, DSS closed the investigation of Larry Joe Hollingsworth. However, Mancuso's actions were to be elevated to a congressional inquiry[69] by Senator Chuck Grassley (R–Iowa) resulting in the passage of a federal law. This congressional inquiry discovered several eye-opening and questionable actions by DCIS leadership such as allowing their colleague and friend, Hollingsworth, to retire with full law enforcement benefits, even after Hollingsworth had been indicted for felony passport fraud.

Seemingly pursuant to some routine DCIS document destruction schedule, the DCIS destroyed Larry Joe Hollingsworth's employment records. I find this practice especially odd, as the United States government requires ten-year retention of official files. Fortunately, the U.S. Probations Office obtained a copy of Hollingsworth's employment record before the DCIS destroyed them.

Senator Charles Grassley (R-IA).

In April 2000, matters pertaining to the Larry Hollingsworth investigation were catapulted past DSS headquarters, past the U.S. Congress, and all the way to the President of the United States.[70]

Senator Grassley shared with the President his Majority Staff Report, completed in November 1999, which substantiated allegations of misconduct by senior officials at the Defense Criminal Investigative Service—or DCIS— between 1993 and 1996.

He informed the President that the Hollingsworth case was the driving force behind introducing to the Committee on Governmental Affairs his bill, S. 2404, to amend chapter 75 of title 5, United States Code, to provide that any federal law enforcement officer who is convicted of a felony shall be terminated from employment.

The Hollingsworth case served as a catalyst for Senator Grassley to oppose Donald Mancuso's nomination for the DOD DCIS Inspector General position because of alleged misconduct. The alleged misconduct included Mancuso personally approving a series of administrative actions that kept Hollingsworth, a convicted felon, in an employed status at DCIS for six months. Instead, Mancuso chose to protect Hollingsworth until he reached his 50th birthday, at which time he could retire, shielding Hollingsworth from the law for at least six months. Mancuso's actions eventually cost the taxpayers at least $750,000.00 through the year 2008. According to Senator Grassley, this was money that Hollingsworth should never have collected had Mancuso exercised sound judgment under the law.

Donald Mancuso, former DCIS Director.

In a letter to the judge, Mancuso asked the judge to consider extenuating circumstances for Hollingsworth. He told the judge that Hollingsworth had taken a half day's leave to file the fraudulent passport application. Mr. Mancuso praised the convicted felon for this unselfish act. Can you believe that?

Mancuso said to Judge Ellis, "Mr. Hollingsworth could have come and gone as he pleased, [but he] took leave to commit a felony."

In Mancuso's mind, the use of personal leave to commit a felony was a sign of moral excellence.

According to Senator Grassley, documents in Hollingsworth's case file indicated that Mancuso was communicating with defense attorneys during the criminal court proceedings against Hollingsworth. For example, it contained a fax transmittal memo addressed personally to Mancuso from the defense attorney. Attached was a motion to dismiss charges against Hollingsworth. But there was no court date stamp or attorney signature on the document. And there were handwritten notes on it. This was a rough draft. This really bothered me.

Mancuso—the director of a federal law enforcement agency—was furnished with a rough draft of a motion to dismiss felony charges that the U.S. Attorney was attempting to prosecute. This was unethical conduct. The file contained other damaging documents. They suggested that the current Director of DCIS, John Keenan, had returned 11 confiscated handguns to the convicted felon—Hollingsworth—in direct contravention of a federal court judgment and statutory law. DCIS allegedly returned the guns to Hollingsworth on September 23, 1997, while he was still on supervised probation. This reckless act could have put a probation officer in harm's way.

I never discovered why—beyond his friendship with and loyalty to Hollingsworth—Donald Mancuso went to extraordinary lengths to protect a convicted felon.

Mancuso was eventually nominated for the position of the DCIS Inspector General. Senator Grassley led the opposition to Mancuso's nomination.

Larry Joe Hollingsworth currently resides in Fleming Island, Florida, where he serves as President for Lamar Enterprises, Inc., a consulting company he started in 2010.[71]

CHAPTER 21

THE KING'S WINETASTERS

My favorite foreign dignitary was
Great Britain's former Prime Minister Margaret Thatcher.

I have had the honor of protecting many well-known foreign dignitaries including Nelson Mandela (South Africa), Queen Noor (Jordan), Princess Chulabhorn Walailak (Thailand), Mikhail Gorbachev (Russia), Crown Prince Akihito (Japan), First Lady Sheikha Mozah (Qatar), and many others.

While providing executive protection, agents serve in a "tip of the spear" capacity, often working behind unfriendly boundaries and the hostile intelligence services' prying eyes. The strain of being constantly watched and followed can quickly demoralize agents.

Occupational folklore and "war stories" sometimes serve as a prescription that helps one cope with the time lost, missing their child's first spoken word or a Little League home run, listening to taped music recitals, and celebrating wedding anniversaries alone. The grinding mundaneness of standing in long airport lines, sleeping in unfamiliar beds, lost holidays, and living out of suitcases is exhausting and draining on one's morale.

The Iron Lady

I greatly enjoyed protecting British diplomats and working with Scotland Yard protection officers. During my law enforcement career, I had protected Prince Charles on three separate occasions: one with the Texas state police in Austin, and twice while working for the DSS (New York City and Houston).

Without question, my favorite foreign dignitary was Great Britain's former Prime Minister Margaret Thatcher. I was assigned to protect Prime Minister Thatcher during her visit to the College of William and Mary in Williamsburg, Virginia. In April 1996, while serving as the university's chancellor, Margaret Thatcher spoke at an international conference titled, "Quests for Western Security Amid Global Uncertainty," which was co-sponsored by NATO and the College of William and Mary.

This conference hosted by the College of William and Mary was attended by Lawrence S. Eagleburger, former U.S. Secretary of State and a true friend of the DSS and its mission, whom I had formerly protected during the signing of the North American Free Trade Agreement (NAFTA) in San Antonio, Texas.

Senator John Warner (R–VA) and David Gergen, editor-at-large for *U.S. News & World Report* and former advisor to Presidents Reagan and Clinton, were also in attendance. During his presentation, David Gergen blamed the rising tide of "isms"—isolationism, protectionism, and nativism—on a foreign policy that has strayed since the end of the Cold War.

(L–R): Margaret Thatcher, Senator John Warner (R–VA), David Gergen, and David Finifter.

When Mr. Gergen completed his presentation, Prime Minister Thatcher slowly made her way to the podium, leaned to one side with her head slightly cocked, wagged her finger at him, and said, "Mr. Gergen. Mr. Gergen. You are a pessimist. Then again, most journalists are pessimists." Prime Minister Thatcher went on to share her belief that a strong defense is a formula for peace. "Ideas never stopped a dictator. Only stronger weaponry will deter him...It's not strength that causes war, it's weakness that attracts an aggressor." said Thatcher.[72] Prime Minister Thatcher still possessed the starch that earned her the nickname, "The Iron Lady."

She went on to provide a most intriguing and uplifting pro-American speech praising the United States for its role in countering communism and protecting the cause of freedom.

After completing her speech, Prime Minister Thatcher informed the DSS detail that she wished to return to her room on campus and rest. While making her way from the conference to a holding room, a class of some twenty handheld tape recorder-wielding elementary students approached her, and each student asked a question, such as what about America did she enjoy most, where was she from, and what was her favorite color.

With a broad smile, Prime Minister Thatcher agreed to answer these questions, and not one child was turned away; Thatcher answered each of the students' questions.

Margaret Thatcher speaking at Western security conference, co-sponsored by NATO and the College of William and Mary.

As Prime Minister Thatcher prepared to board the helicopter that was scheduled to fly her to Monticello, Virginia, she paused a moment as if she had forgotten something. She then quickly approached the line of agents and police officers who solidified her protection detail. Eyes are often referred to as the window to one's soul. Walking down the line, and looking into their eyes, Margaret Thatcher thanked each man and woman, briskly shaking his or her hand. I found it refreshing for a dignitary to exhibit sincerity to the law enforcement officers and agents who had worked alongside her. Politics aside, I believe Prime Minister Thatcher was a person who inspired those around her.

LOVE FROM RUSSIA

The DSS agent sat patiently on an Aeroflot plane, waiting for repairs to be finished. He was part of the advance team that would protect the Secretary of State on her visit to Moscow, Russia. It had been about three hours since he boarded and the cabin air had become stuffy. He asked the flight attendant to crack the door open. The attendant walked away and returned with the captain.

In a thick Russian accent, the tall, brawny pilot asked the agent, "What can I do for you, comrade?" The agent again made his fresh air request. Nodding his head in an understanding motion, the captain responded, "I know exactly what you need." The captain reached into his jacket pocket, removed a half-empty bottle of vodka, and offered the DSS agent a drink. Shaking his head in disbelief, the agent turned to the other DSS team members and proclaimed, "We're all going to die!"

A DUTCH ADVENTURE

Exchanging our weapons, earpieces, and suits for more comfortable summer clothing, three DSS special agents and I boarded a train from the Holiday Inn motel in Lieden, Holland, to the wild city of Amsterdam. Tired from working a midnight shift while protecting U.S. Secretary of State Warren Christopher, we hoped to squeeze in as much sightseeing as possible.

Lieden, known for its historic university, is an exceptionally pristine and picturesque city with significant ties to the United States. Fleeing religious persecution, 135 immigrants—mostly English religious separatists (Pilgrims) residing in Lieden—boarded the *Mayflower* ship for the voyage that would bring them to the New World, landing at Cape Cod.

On exiting the train station in Amsterdam, we observed a wide street lined with restaurants with sidewalk tables and chairs. This ancient city, whose name was derived from a dam on the Amstel River, was home to many notable people, including the diarist Anne Frank and painters Rembrandt and Vincent van Gogh.

Excited at the opportunity to take a walk down history's paths, we walked along the first block. We observed a restaurant employee throwing an unwelcome beggar onto the street, causing the man to stumble into the tables and chairs that lined the sidewalk. Based on this startling event, we elevated our threat level from condition white (relaxed) to condition yellow (relaxed but more aware).

As we walked the second block, a young man walked up to our group, focused on the one of us wearing a sleeveless muscle shirt, and said, "Hey, nice tits." Our threat level went from condition yellow to condition orange.

Now on a higher state of alert, we walked onward to the third block. There, a man fluttered toward us and asked if we wanted to purchase cocaine. After emphatically saying "no," we transitioned from condition orange to condition red (identifying a threat).

Now, beginning to rethink our trip to Amsterdam, we decided to continue onward. At block four, we stopped at a small shop to purchase a city tourist map. An agent unfolded the map on the cashier counter and asked the store employee if he could point out places of interest. The store employee responded, "I am not sure about interesting tourist places, but I can show you the location of my apartment." Comically shaking his head, the agent folded the map and we departed the shop. Condition black (death), the only remaining color code, was one we certainly wanted to avoid.

Fortunately, we were not deterred again and took in the city's spectacular and historic *grachtengordel* (literally, belt of canals).

CHAPTER 22

TEXAS TREASURE BURNING

The orange glow illuminated the
Texas Governor's Mansion and its stately columns.

The blinking red light alerted me to pick up the telephone; the receptionist had just announced my incoming call. The year was 2004, and I was serving as the DSS Special Agent-in-Charge in Houston, Texas. The person on the phone introduced himself as Lt. David Armistead, with the Texas Department of Public Safety (DPS), Texas Governor's Protective Detail.

Lt. Armistead asked me to assist him with restructuring the Governor's Protective Detail by enhancing its capabilities, a goal that had been sought for years by countless DPS detail agents who had served on this same protective detail, including myself.

For years, Texas State Troopers assigned to the Governor's Protective Detail had encouraged DPS hierarchy to transition its command structure from the Texas highway patrol division to the state police director's immediate chain of command. I had been recruited by the Diplomatic Security Service while I served with DPS' Executive Protection Detail during Prince Charles' 1986 visit to Austin, Texas.

Now I relished the opportunity to give back to one of the most highly respected law enforcement agencies in the United States.

I explained to Lt. Armistead that, generally, two separate executive protection models exist within the U.S. government. One approach is the manpower-intensive practice used by the U.S. Secret Service of posting every street, searching drainage systems, and perching security atop buildings. Provided with the immense human and financial resources, the U.S. Secret Service is able to incorporate multiple robust and effective protective perimeters.

The DSS—operating many more executive protective details than the U.S. Secret Service—lacks the human and financial resources to act as its sister agency. As a result, DSS' executive protective details operate in a leaner fashion. The smaller and more nimble DSS protective packages (agents and motorcades) must maintain protective advantages of streamlined intelligence, communications, and fallback responses. Operating in hostile overseas environments, DSS cannot always rely on host government support to prevent or respond to attacks.

Having been exposed to both protective models, Lt. David Armistead considered that the DSS executive protective model was best suited for the Texas DPS Governor's Protective Detail and chose to incorporate much of DSS' procedures into his protective detail. I agreed.

Based on my experiences, the Governor's Protective Detail was often headed by supervisors hand-selected by incoming governors-elect, resulting in a lack of operational and leadership continuity. For decades, the Governor's Protective Detail operated under limited support from the DPS executive command structure and lacked comprehensive regulations specific to executive protection discipline.

During my tenure on the detail from 1985–1987, the highway patrol executives treated the Governor's Protective Detail like a square peg in a round hole. Because of the lack of command support, the protective detail was consistently susceptible to stagnation. Many troopers assigned to this detail became belligerent—leading to disciplinary problems and low morale. Unfortunately, the protective detail was eventually viewed as a "pariah assignment" by other troopers throughout the state, at least until Lt. David Armistead assumed operational supervision.

The Texas highway patrol executive command invited me to a working lunch at the famous Dirty Martin's Place near the University of Texas main campus. Sitting across the table, the assistant chief of Traffic Law Enforcement shared his and the regional commander's predicament—neither of them fully understood executive protection related to their mission of investigating accidents, processing citations, enforcing Department of Transportation regulations, issuing driver licenses, and other law enforcement duties pertaining to public safety on the state highways and byways.

I emphatically stated, "I am familiar with the problems faced by the protective detail, and I am confident professionalism and operational techniques can be injected into the protective detail. Frankly, the state's CEO and First Family deserve better."

The relief registered on the two DPS executives' faces telegraphed their desperation to improve the Governor's Protective Detail. On finishing our juicy hamburgers, I was formally commissioned to work directly with the protective detail's leadership to bring about changes.

My first order of business for a baseline assessment was to begin peeling the layers from the onion by verifying the entire top-to-bottom command structure for the Governor's Protective Detail. On the surface, this might have seemed easy. However, out of the gate I discovered confusion within the detail's chain of command.

A highway patrol captain assigned to the DPS inspection and planning division—an officer who had previously temporarily served on the Governor's Protective Detail—was representing himself to me as the operational commander. Further exacerbating the dysfunction of the Governor's detail command structure was the DPS regional commander for the Capitol Complex (state-owned buildings in downtown Austin) and the chief of Traffic Enforcement—both of whom were oblivious of the operational supervisory conflict within the detail. Frankly, I was perplexed at this obvious disconnection, especially given the importance of protecting the state's Chief Executive Officer, the Governor.

A bit frustrated, prior to providing any further DSS advisory support to the DPS detail, I asked Lt. Armistead to point me to the person ultimately responsibility for the detail's operational security. Aware of the regional commander's and the assistant chief's stated desire of undertaking a thorough DSS assessment to improve the Governor's detail, Lt. Armistead directly contacted the Chief of Traffic Enforcement and emphatically inquired who had operational responsibility for the Governor's Protective Detail: Lt. Armistead, or the invading captain?

The chief informed Lt. Armistead that he (Armistead) had operational security responsibility. We had now established a working foundation from which to begin the restructuring process.

Lt. Armistead and I rolled up our sleeves to begin the revamping process by first developing a macro-level strategy document focusing on six main protective security elements: 1. physical security; 2. technical security; 3. procedural security; 4. executive protection; 5. emergency response; and 6. training.

Using this strategic document, we fleshed out each element in the six-point strategy. On many nights of working into the early morning hours, David Armistead and I developed comprehensive protection manuals, training curriculums, and memorandums of agreement for the Texas Governor, and eventually for Texas' Lt. Governor, Attorney General, and Speaker-of-the-House.

In order to create a train-the-trainer program, I arranged for two agents from the Governor's Protective Detail (Lt. David Armistead and Sgt. Chris Brannen) to attend the full executive protection training course offered to DSS special agent trainees conducted primarily at the DSS training facility in Virginia.

Chris Brannen (far L), David Armistead (far R) protect Gov. George W. Bush (C) and Austin mayor Kirk Watson (CR) during a charity run in Austin.

The DSS training course incorporates executive protection theory and practice, antiterrorism driver training, and advanced firearms training with a live final examination occurring in Washington, D.C., and West Virginia.

The theoretical portion of DSS training provides a comprehensive breakdown of suspected motives for assassinations and attacks, and ranges from disgruntled individuals, to political, religious, criminal, and other ideological positions. In addition, trainees learn about terrorist tactics, logistics, and methods used to carry out random or planned attacks, including kidnapping and/or assassinating their targets.

The executive protection practical exercises include exhaustive agent formations to provide body cover for the protectee, methods to neutralize attacks, detecting suspicious activities, evacuating the protectee from an attack, and advanced firearms training with an array of weapons.

The arduous antiterrorism driving course pushes trainees to the brink of their offensive driving capabilities. Using a commercial competitive race track in West Virginia, agents travel at speeds exceeding 100 mph, while highly trained driving instructors bump and attempt to pass the trainees' vehicles.

Students are introduced to bone jarring vehicle ramming techniques to evade potential kill zone paths by ramming one's vehicle into other static vehicles blocking escape routes. Hollywood-type stunts of 180-turns while driving forward and then backward (known as J-turns and bootleg turns) deliver a sudden adrenaline spike, sometimes causing nausea due to extreme motion and the smell of burning tire rubber. I had previously completed the antiterrorist driving course three separate times and enjoyed every minute.

I could not help but laugh when I heard about Lt. Armistead and Sgt. Brannen's adventures while visiting the Washington, D.C., area during the DSS executive protection course. Because the rental car company was running short on inventory for their compact cars, Lt. Armistead was given a Jaguar sedan instead. A few days later, Sgt. Brannen discovered a small amount of marijuana residue in the Jaguar's console that had purportedly been left by high school prom-goers days prior. A quick vacuum remedied the situation.

Near the end of a training session, the lead DSS training officer pulled alongside, and eyeing their Jaguar, the training officer rolled down his window and quipped that the State of Texas' financial situation must be doing well. Sgt. Brannen responded, "Oil money, baby!"

I occasionally called the DSS training center to inquire as to the status of my two Texas Department of Public Safety brethren. From my time in the state police academy, to highway patrol, to executive protection, I am proud of and have fond memories of serving with the Texas State Police. Now, I was intent on ensuring Texas Department of Public Safety detail agents received state-of-the-art executive protection training, partly to give back to the agency that helped launch my DSS career, but mostly because of the importance of protecting the Texas governor.

I could not contain my laughter when a DSS training officer shared how David Armistead's dedication was extremely focused on learning all facets of the DSS curriculum, not wanting to miss a single minute of the training course. During one day of the three-week training course, the DSS Training Center received a phone call from President George W. Bush's secretary. Lt. Armistead had previously protected then-Governor Bush. The President's secretary informed Lt. Armistead that President Bush had learned of David's presence in the Washington, D.C., area and asked him to drop by the White House for a personal visit. Honored at the President's invitation, David Armistead explained to the secretary that he was tied up in a training course and would have to regretfully decline the invitation.

The President's secretary made it clear that David could not turn down an invitation from the President of the United States. When he shared his dilemma with the training staff, David was strongly encouraged to show up at the White House, posthaste. David Armistead told me later that he had a wonderful visit with President Bush.

"Wow! Lt. Armistead has unparalleled dedication to education and to his profession," I told the DSS training officer.

Back in Texas, Lt. Armistead delivered the executive protection training curriculum we had developed for his detail agents and all Texas Rangers throughout the state.

An all-important security fact: Lt. Armistead and I completed the first-ever comprehensive physical security assessment for the historic Texas Governor's Mansion—adapting many of the DSS physical and technical security standards from our recommendations, including improving access control points, the need to construct guard booths, enhancing the perimeter fence, installing anti-ram barriers, modern cameras, and alarm sensors.

Lt. Armistead and I met with the DPS chief of law enforcement at the DPS headquarters building to share our security recommendations for the Mansion security. The chief remained behind his desk when we entered his office, and was mystified as to why we came to discuss the Mansion security. Only a few months prior, his assistant chief had met with me to seek executive protection assistance. I was undeterred by the chief's unprofessional, cold welcome and unsupportive attitude toward Lt. Armistead.

Months later, while still serving as the DSS special agent-in-charge based in Houston, I arranged for and hosted a meeting between CIA analysts specializing in Mexican drug cartels and five of the highest-ranking DPS executives to discuss the rising cartel-related violence along the Texas/Mexican border. During a coffee break, the DPS chief of law enforcement pulled me aside and sheepishly admitted that the Governor's protective detail was an "odd fit" to the traditional highway patrol functions, and he was unsure how to manage the executive protection operations under his command.

A few years later, in October 2007, I learned the Governor's Mansion was scheduled for a major renovation project, so Governor Rick Perry and the First Family relocated to a private residence in Austin. Lt. Armistead called me to say that DPS highway patrol's Region 7 (Capitol Complex) would assume protective responsibilities for the empty Governor's Mansion during its renovation.

Unfortunately for the people of the State of Texas, the Department of Public Safety's executives were still disengaged from their field officers' chain of command that was assigned to protect the Governor's Mansion. This ill-fated disconnect would soon dearly cost the people of the State of Texas, and the nearly total destruction of a piece of Texas' treasured history.

Prior to relocating the Governor and the First Family to their private residence, Lt. Armistead sought my advice about how the Region 7 commanders should approach protection for the Mansion during the renovation. I advised Lt. Armistead that if not done correctly, the transfer of facility protection responsibility for the Governor's Mansion could easily "bite him in the ass" if the responsibilities were not clearly delineated. If something "broke bad" at the Governor's Mansion, it is likely that a scapegoat would be sought by those in command of DPS: high-level bureaucrats wanting to protect their paychecks or politicians needing to protect their constituency standing would be scrutinized by the public's desire to hold either or both accountable for incompetence.

Also, for good, bad, or indifference, Lt. Armistead would eventually resume security responsibility for the Mansion. I encouraged Lt. Armistead to draft a memorandum outlining the formal shift of responsibilities, list his concerns, and offer recommendations on how to secure the Governor's Mansion during the Governor's absence.

A "bureaucratic reality" while working with the Federal government is explained by Dean Acheson, former U.S. Secretary of State, "... a memorandum is more to protect the writer than to inform the reader..." Indeed, paper is a bureaucrat's kryptonite.

Eventually, protection responsibility for the Governor's Mansion shifted from Lt. Armistead to the DPS Region 7 commander.

Sadly, during the early morning on June 8, 2008, an intruder scaled a chain link perimeter construction fence and quickly lit a Molotov cocktail before launching it at the front door of the Governor's Mansion, igniting a huge blaze. The Mansion was originally built around 1854 in downtown Austin.

The orange glow illuminated the Mansion and its stately columns, as flames licked the residence once occupied by Sam Houston, former President of the Republic of Texas, former U.S. Congressman, and former Texas Governor.

According to news accounts, some 100 firefighters spent more than six hours battling the blaze that caused significant damage to the historic Mansion. Some speculate that the only thing that saved the Mansion was an Austin Fire Department engine returning from an unrelated emergency call, happened to be within 2 minutes' drive to the Mansion. Had this fire engine not been in a position to quickly respond to the fire, many believe the fire would have totally destroyed

Texas Governor's Mansion arson damage.

the Mansion. Citizen donations exceeding 22 million dollars would be needed to restore this historic treasure to its former glory.

Kudos to the Austin Fire Department!

Presumably protected around the clock by the Texas DPS, how could the very existence of such a treasured landmark have been jeopardized? Why were the security recommendations Lt. Armistead made not been accepted by the executives?

A DPS internal post-incident investigative report concluded that a sole attacker scaled a temporary construction fence and launched a Molotov cocktail on the Mansion's front porch. The report noted that only one trooper had been assigned to protect the Mansion during the renovation. The motive for the arson attack and identity of the attacker remain unknown.

Faulty intrusion-detection sensors and closed-circuit cameras at the vacant Mansion—which David Armistead had previously requested be repaired—were noted in the report.[73]

It seemed painfully obvious to some that Lt. Armistead and his immediate supervisor were being positioned as scapegoats in order to protect DPS executives—from the chief of Traffic Law Enforcement to the director.

I found the DPS post-incident memorandum perplexing;

- Why did the DPS investigator fail to mention in his post-incident report the multiple security recommendations to protect the Governor's Mansion made by Lt. Armistead to the DPS chief?

- Why did the memorandum not reveal the chief's decision to not implement—or even consider—Lt. Armistead's security enhancement recommendations as prescribed in his *Physical Security and Surveillance Detection* assessments prior to the arson attack?

- Why did DPS not hold the DPS Region 7 commander responsible for failure to protect the Mansion, but instead focused on Lt. Armistead, who was no longer responsible for protecting the vacated Governor's Mansion?

- Why did the DPS director appoint a former operational commander of the protective detail to conduct the investigation, when this investigator may have possibly contributed to some of the security deficiencies?

- Might this investigative assignment be viewed as a conflict? I wondered.

Months after the Mansion fire, I asked a high-level state police executive why the DPS executives did not support enhanced security for the Governor's Mansion during its renovation. The executive responded that the DPS implemented the same level of security for the Mansion as any other vacant state-owned building. In my opinion, that executive revealed the crux of the problem. The DPS leadership refused to grasp the importance and difference of protecting the treasured Governor's Mansion versus a common state-owned warehouse.

Lt. Armistead was ultimately vindicated by the Chairman of the Texas Public Safety Commissioners, who praised him for the proactive security insights contained in his memorandum.

Texas Governor's Mansion post renovation.

Perhaps as a result of political pressure that came to bear due to the Governor's Mansion fire, several top state police executives retired, including the DPS director.[74]

Later, while serving in a private security consulting capacity, I was asked to assist the state police with implementing the security recommendations previously made by Lt. Armistead for the protection of the Governor and the Mansion. Now, using the state-of-the-art security systems and physical security enhancements, not a single fence-jumper has appeared to date.

Fortunately, the historic Texas Governor's Mansion was completely renovated and stands today as a true testament to Texan resilience and devotion to maintaining a Texas treasure.

I was proud of Lt. Armistead and his ability to greatly improve security for the Governor's Protective Detail. I also learned that David Armistead and I shared a common bond with the American flag.

TO THE
SHORES

CHAPTER 23

LIBYA OR BUST

Gaddafi was in love—in love with himself,
in love with attention,
and in love with his dictatorial powers.

In February 2004, serving as DSS Special Agent-in-Charge assigned to the Houston Field Office located in the downtown Mickey Leland Federal Building, I paused from my work for a moment to rest my eyes. From my office perch, I watched traffic streaming along the heavily traveled I-45, linking Galveston and Dallas. I had a partial glimpse of the Enron buildings, now mostly empty after the government seized Enron's assets, including the attractive mirror-glass buildings.

I turned my attention back to my computer and noticed I had a new email. The message announced an urgent, temporary position for a Regional Security Officer in Tripoli, Libya.

I thought, *wow*, what an opportunity of a lifetime.

Although I was in the midst of assisting Lt. Armistead with revamping the Governor's Protective Detail, I simply could not pass on this golden opportunity to travel to the country where, since the

1979 U.S. Iranian hostage crisis.

United States became a nation, the American flag had first flown over occupied territory beyond the Atlantic: it was in 1805 in Derna, Libya.

Considering the potential dangers of serving in a nation with an unpredictable dictator, I drew two separate columns on a notepad, listing PROS and CONS for accepting or rejecting this opportunity to serve as the first DSS RSO in Libya.

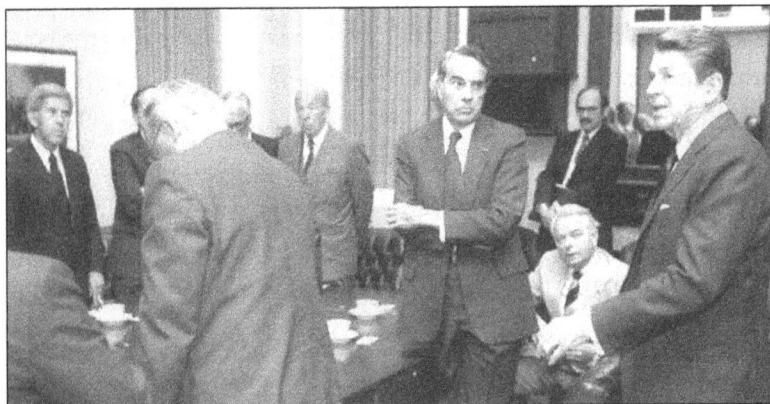

President Reagan and members of Congress discuss bombing Libya in 1986.

Typically, U.S. diplomats assigned to represent America in hostile environments understand the risks involved in serving "behind enemy lines." Like prison guards who accept risks in their jobs—such as breaking up fights or dealing with a prison riot, diplomats hope for but understand that help from the U.S. military may not deploy in a timely manner.

My mind drifted back to the year 1979. While attending Blinn College in Brenham, Texas (same *alma mater* as quarterback Cam Newton), I vividly remember listening to perspectives from some of the Iranian students about the Iran hostage crisis at the U.S. Embassy in Tehran. As the standoff between Iran and the United States dragged closer toward 444 days, the students shared how they were initially surprised at America's lack of response. In fact, one student stated that, in the early stages of the embassy takeover, Iranians were fearful that the U.S. Marines would soon be unleashed. Unfortunately, the Iranian hostage-takers' courage was emboldened as each day passed.

Under the CONS column, I listed the historically toxic American–Libyan relations dating back to the two Barbary Wars. More recently, the hurried evacuation from the U.S. Embassy in Tripoli during the 1979 Islamic Revolution, the TWA Flight 840 bombing (1986), the 1986 Berlin discotheque bombing which targeted U.S. servicemen, the bombing of Pan Am Flight 103 over Lockerbie, Scotland (1988), the many naval skirmishes during military exercises in the Gulf of Sidra, two of which (1981 and 1989) resulted in U.S. Navy fighter jets downing two Libyan jets. And there was President Ronald Reagan's bold decision to launch air strikes on Libya that resulted in the purported death of Muammar Gaddafi's four-year-old step-daughter, and the alleged Libyan hit squad plot to assassinate President Reagan.

The CONS column was overflowing.

The most important "CON" in my mind was whether the U.S. President had the fortitude to quickly dispatch U.S. military forces in the event Colonel Muammar Gaddafi detained U.S. diplomats as hostage bargaining tools.

I believed that President George Bush, a fellow Texan who had previously occupied the Texas Governor's Mansion, had exhibited a willingness to confront terrorists who were determined to kill Americans. If another embassy takeover such as the one in Tehran, Iran, was to occur, I felt confident that President Bush would not depend on diplomacy only, but would use the military if necessary.

My column titled PROS (reasons to go to Libya) contained only one entry, "opportunity for historic adventure." And in my mind's eye, this one PRO entry easily trumped the CONS.

Given my love of American history and my insatiable appetite for adventure, I received approval from my family and quickly informed DSS headquarters of my interest in this opportunity. The following day I received a telephone call from DSS headquarters, pleased with my decision to establish a security program in Libya.

Muammar Gaddafi at the African Union Summit, in Addis Ababa, Ethiopia.

I would soon be developing a security program from scratch in a nation deemed hostile toward the United States. My adventure junkie genes were delighted at having been chosen for this historic opportunity.

Later that night, I had an unexpected Hollywood prelude to my Libyan assignment. While relaxing in front of the television, watching the movie *Back to the Future*, Professor Emmett ("Doc," portrayed by Christopher Lloyd) claims the Libyans are after him and his stolen uranium, after which a high-speed shootout ensues.

A few days later, I popped a DVD into the player to watch the movie *The Dream Team*. In it, escaped mental patient Billy Caufield (portrayed by Michael Keaton) tells a storekeeper that he and his odd buddies, Henry Sikorsky (portrayed by Christopher Lloyd) and Jack McDermott (portrayed by Peter Boyle), are tracking Libyan terrorists in New York City.

It seemed like a bombardment of Hollywood versions of Libya's terrorist connections. DSS agents are capable of and have accomplished extraordinary feats: capturing terrorists, countering international crime, defending against espionage, and more. Yet the lone-man, Jason Bourne-prototype exploits occur only in movie fiction.

American diplomats' assignments can mirror those of prison guards. It is generally understood that some assignments may result in attacks against American interests, being taken hostage, and even killed. The 1979 takeover of the U.S. Embassy in Tehran, Iran, and the subsequent gut-wrenching 444-day hostage negotiations serve as a stark reminder of the risks. In Libya's case, it was the 1979 mob attack and their attempt to set fire to the American Embassy in Tripoli in December 1979, resulting in the withdrawal of America's diplomatic corps, leading the United States to formally designating Libya as a state sponsor of terrorism.

I traveled to DSS' headquarters in Rosslyn, Virginia, for out-briefings, which were concluded with a clear understanding of my objectives.

I checked into the Hilton Hotel in Washington, D.C.—often referred to as the Hinckley Hilton because it is the site of the assassination attempt against President Ronald Reagan. John Warnock Hinckley Jr. was a desperate, deranged, delusional man who was obsessed with actress Jodie Foster and was intent on drawing her attention to himself. Surrounded by U.S. Secret Service and Washington, D.C., police, Hinckley was still able to shoot six times at President Reagan—seriously wounding him—and three others.

John Hinckley FBI booking photo.

Colonel Muammar Gaddafi was also a desperate, deranged leader who was delusional in his claim to be the leader of the United States of Africa. Gaddafi was in love—in love with himself, in love with attention, and in love with his dictatorial powers. I had an uneasy feeling staying at this hotel in Washington, but thought it providential given my upcoming trip to Libya and the historic connections between President Reagan and American-Libyan relations. Partially via the impact of the 1986 bombing of Libya, President Reagan was able to contain a tyrant.

My responsibilities at the U.S. Mission in Libya would include developing a start-up security program and establishing foreign relations with security forces to protect the U.S. Mission and American diplomats. Additionally, I was tasked with decommissioning the former Chancery building and locating a stand-alone facility to be used for the temporary U.S. Mission. I would also survey multiple sites for the proposed long-term residential compound and the new U.S. Embassy.

Years of liaising with international law enforcement and security forces taught me the importance of goodwill gifts and trinkets— referred to as *chum*—as a way to communicate gratitude to those who would directly assist me with fulfilling my objectives.

During my final day in Washington, D.C., I stopped at a street vendor in Dupont Circle and purchased several white T-shirts with large red, white, and blue letters spelling "USA." I would later learn that these shirts would become a hit among the Libyan security forces.

Fittingly, my final departure point from the United States was from the Ronald Reagan Washington National Airport, which is close to Mt. Vernon, Virginia. Truth be known, I missed President Reagan's stance of confronting out-of-control dictators bent on taking away freedom.

Irrespective of the good, bad, and ugly historic relationships between our two countries, it was now Tripoli or bust!

Col. Gaddafi and Ugandan president Idi Amin Dada.

forged close links with the Soviet Union and other east European countries. Support for international terrorism was a major issue in Libya's relations with the United States and western Europe.

During the 1970s and 1980s, Libya was suspected of funding political subversion around the world. As protest raged against Washington's policies in Iran, the United States Embassy in Tripoli was stormed and burned in December 1979. American diplomats departed Tripoli and Libyan diplomats were expelled from the United States.

I remember from my college history studies the conflict between the U.S. and Libya that occurred in August 1981, when U.S. jets launched from the aircraft carrier USS *Nimitz* shot down two Libyan fighter jets during naval maneuvers about sixty miles off Libya's coast in the disputed Gulf of Sidra.[76]

During the same time that I was protecting the Texas Governor, 1984, Gaddafi told a Libyan audience that, "We are capable of exporting terrorism to the heart of America.... We have the right to fight America, and we have the right to export terrorism to them." Gaddafi followed through by planning to assassinate the U.S. Ambassador assigned to Egypt, ordering a foiled plot to bomb the American Embassy club in Khartoum, and was disrupted in 1985 in an attempt to bomb the U.S. Embassy in Cairo.[77]

Exactly one year prior to my joining the DSS, on April 5, 1986, Gaddafi exported terror to West Berlin when Libyans bombed the *La Belle* discotheque, which was frequented by U.S. servicemen. The attack killed two American soldiers and injured 230 people, 79 of whom were U.S. soldiers.

In retaliation, on April 15, 1986, President Reagan ordered the U.S. military to bomb Tripoli and Benghazi. There were forty Libyan casualties reported, purportedly including Gaddafi's adopted daughter, Hanna. Angered at the attack, Gaddafi said of President Reagan, "He is mad, he is foolish, he is an Israeli dog."

On December 21, 1988, I vividly remember the tragic downing of Pan Am Flight 103 over Scotland. Sixteen crew members, 243 passengers, and 11 pedestrians on the ground all lost their lives as

Wreckage from Pan Am Flight 103.

a result of a terrorist attack planned and authorized by Colonel Gaddafi. Especially disheartening was the loss of three DSS special agents: Daniel Emmett O'Connor, Ronald Lariviere, and Matthew Gannon.

Somewhere in Tripoli, Colonel Muammar Gaddafi and his intelligence service were celebrating another blow against the West.

As a result of Gaddafi's tyrannical worldwide tailspin, Libya became isolated, financially challenged, and the target of American retaliation.

Russian President Vladimir Putin (L) Muammar Gaddafi (R).

While I was serving a third assignment in Houston, on December 19, 2003, Gaddafi told a stunned world he was renouncing Libya's nuclear program and stated his compliance with international inspectors to disarm his nuclear program.[78]

Gaddafi and his brain trust reevaluated Libya and determined the path they had initially chosen for their nation had not met their expectations. In order to reshape their international image and strengthen their nation's finances, Libyan leadership finally relented and accepted responsibility for the Pan Am Flight 103 bombing.

CHAPTER 25

ANCIENT LANDS

.... using their cell phone cameras to snap photographs
of American diplomats—photos they would relay
to the Libyan Intelligence Services.

The low bumping of the plane's wheels hastened down the runway as we lifted off from the Ronald Reagan International Airport in D.C. I was on my way to Cairo, Egypt, where I would await the open-ended issuance of a Libyan visa to be stamped inside my diplomatic passport before proceeding to Tripoli.

I enjoyed Egypt and the Egyptian people. Years earlier, I had traveled to Cairo while protecting Secretary of State George Shultz. I spent pleasant times at the pyramids, the perfume vendors, and on the coffee breaks overlooking the Nile.

Robert W. Starnes on top of a camel at Egypt's Great Pyramid and Sphinx.

Flexing their newly-acquired diplomatic clout, the Libyans were taking their time issuing visas to American diplomats. I was told that I could wait in Egypt for several weeks—if not several months—before I received the Libyan visa. I did not really mind since each day in Egypt was a delight and provided me time to study up on Libyan and Tripolitan history.

My visits to the Regional Security Office at the U.S. Embassy in Cairo provided camaraderie and allowed me to communicate directly with the U.S. Mission in Tripoli. My first unofficial order of the day from a high-ranking diplomat at the U.S. Mission in Tripoli was to transport two bottles of the finest American wine from the embassy commissary in Cairo.

Perhaps the strain from negotiating with an unpredictable leader, who deep down despised Americans, or simply missing the freedoms from home, this diplomat simply asked I bring a familiar taste from America's fruited plains. I gladly complied.

A few days later, I received the good news that my Libyan visa had been approved and issued. I packed my luggage and made my way through the busily traveled Cairo streets. On arriving at the airport, I checked my luggage and went to the airport security screening area. I placed my carry-on bags, including two bottles of wine, on the X-ray conveyer.

I had been so focused on my upcoming security responsibilities awaiting me in Libya that I was oblivious to the fact that alcoholic beverages were prohibited in most Islamic countries, including Egypt. The tall, young, plain clothes security agent manning the X-ray machine retrieved the bag containing the two wine bottles, called me over for a personal consult, placed his arm on my shoulder, and walked with me toward the terminal. In broken English, the airport security agent nodded and said he understood. He handed me the wine bottles and wished me a safe trip to Libya. I humbly thanked the young man, boarded the aircraft, and appreciated the small reprieve I had just received.

During my three-hour flight to Tripoli, I crossed over a portion of the Sahara Desert. I have always been intrigued about the dangers and beauty offered in the Sahara Desert—forbidding sand dunes, welcoming oases, and ancient nomadic cultures living in heat exceeding temperatures greater than those of Texas' summers.

I have always been fascinated with the Barbary Coast cultures. During the Greek Empire, the Greeks named the North African area of Algiers, Tunisia, Libya, and Egypt after the ancient cities of Sabratha (western Libya), Leptis Magna (eastern Libya), and Oea (now Tripoli city).

Amazigh (modern day Berbs) were inhabitants of North Africa dating as far back as 2,000 B.C. These indigenous people had been encountered by the Greeks, Carthaginians, and Romans. It was the Arabs who unified these tribes and named them by converting the word for barbarian (speakers of languages other than Greek and Latin) into *Barbar*, the name of a race descended from Noah. Unlike the Arabs, who saw themselves as a single nation, Berbers do not conceive of a united kingdom and have no name for themselves as a people.

As a fan of the *Star Wars* movies, I recall the scene of Luke Skywalker's home on the desert planet of Tatooine. This scene was shot at the Hotel Sidi Driss, a traditional Berber "troglodyte" underground

Hotel Sidi Driss, in the village of Matmata, Tunisia.

building in the village of Matmata, Tunisia.[79] Modern-day Libyans take pride in their Berber ancestry. Learning this, I wondered if the "Force" would be with me in Libya.

The EgyptAir pilot announced our imminent arrival at Tripoli's airport, formerly the World War II U.S. Wheelus Air Base. I was

Top left and right: Hotel Corinthia in Tripoli, Libya. Above: View of mosque in Tripoli's old town Medina.

greeted by members of the U.S. Mission and whisked through the airport and into the waiting motorcade.

The local time was well after midnight when I traveled from the airport to my hotel. The highways were well lit. I was surprised to see well-manicured streets and buildings. I was told that the Libyan government maintained the highway and buildings along the main highway into downtown Tripoli as an aesthetic façade for tourists, giving the artificial impression that the entire city of Tripoli was in similar condition.

Without an embassy and without a formally accredited ambassador, the United States began its diplomatic relationship as an Interests Section before elevating its status to a U.S. Liaison Office (USLO). The U.S. Liaison Office was established in the five-star Hotel Corinthia Tripoli and operated from an entire wing with employees' rooms and miscellaneous administrative offices scattered throughout the hotel.

The Hotel Corinthia is an attractive light yellow and white building constructed with an architectural mix between a modern and Arabic design. Hotel rooms located in two high wings provide panoramic

Tripoli coppersmith.

Libyan potato vendor.

views of the Mediterranean Sea and Tripoli's old city. Adding to the experience, interior Arabesque doorways resemble Morocco's famous "gin joint"—Rick's Café Américain—operated by Rick Blaine (portrayed by Humphrey Bogart) in the 1942 movie classic *Casablanca*.

Directly across the street from the hotel, I saw a street of businesses and a street-side market where mainly poor sub-Saharan African immigrants sold clothing and trinkets such as underwear, small scissors, and various household items.

Located across another city street and directly east of the hotel is Tripoli's old city. Spanning many blocks, the old city is comprised of several acres of businesses, residences, mosques, and the Red Castle Museum, Libya's national museum. The marketplace (*souk*), which hosts coppersmiths and silver and gold dealers as well as spice markets, draws many tourists. The old city is surrounded by a large limestone wall with several entrance gates, and could have passed for Disney's fictional city of Agrabah in the movie *Aladdin*.

An open-air coffee shop occupies the Hotel Corinthia's luxurious lobby. It became obvious that many of its patrons were using their cell phone cameras to snap photographs of American diplomats—photos they would relay to the Libyan Intelligence Services. I learned from the diplomats who had arrived before me that every evening there were prostitutes wearing brightly-colored clothing, and they would saturate the hotel lobby searching for clientele. Of course, part of my responsibilities was to protect our diplomats from improper contacts that might give foreign intelligence services blackmail advantages over U.S. government employees.

As with any overseas assignment, it is imperative for DSS regional security officers to become familiar with the environment. I would devote my first few days in-country to learning as much practical knowledge about Libya, its citizens, culture, and intelligence services as possible.

Risk is the spice of life. It is here, at the tip of the spear, where the heart of adventures truly begins. I was in the city that had been forbidden to Americans for almost a quarter of a century. This was an adventurer's "Spice Market."

CHAPTER 26

A DIPLOMATIC
TIME CAPSULE

Amid the numerous ash piles—
remnants of burning classified documents—
all of the staff members escaped unharmed.

Driving along Tripoli's narrow streets, Jim Derrick and I made our way to the U.S. Embassy building that had been abandoned for some 24 years. In our small world, Jim was the administrative officer with whom I had previously served in Western Samoa during the juvenile rescue from the Pacific Coast Academy. Black char stains were still prominent on the worn walls above the embassy's large wooden double doors. It took some effort to turn the door lock after inserting the aged key inside it. The rusty hinges seemed to cry as I entered the now-quiet and lifeless embassy building in downtown Tripoli.

My plan for the vacant embassy building was to begin the decommissioning phase. Decommissioning diplomatic facilities is an arduous process; first I had to ensure that the facility was void of classified information, and then I would notify the Libyan government of our

Old U.S. Embassy in Tripoli, Libya.

Ransacked U.S. Embassy in Tripoli.

intent to sell the property. Because of deterioration and biohazards (especially the deadly *hantavirus*), all employees entering this dusty, dirty, damp building were required to wear hardhats, facemasks, and rubber gloves.

Stepping into the empty building, I could almost feel the panic and fear during that December 2, 1979, day when the diplomats were attacked. On that morning, the staff members assigned to the U.S. Embassy in Tripoli became keenly aware of the dangers that surrounded them. They did not want to become hostages like their fellow diplomats assigned to the embassy in Tehran, Iran, the month prior.

Receiving information of a planned anti-American demonstration headed toward the Chancery building, the staff hurriedly burned all classified documents, destroyed sensitive equipment, and locked down the two vault doors housing the communications centers.

I admired the cunning of the Marine security guards who tacked a cloth mail bag on the steel mesh day gate leading to the two classified vaults. The Marines attached copper wires to the mail bags and ran the wires under the large metal vault doors, giving the

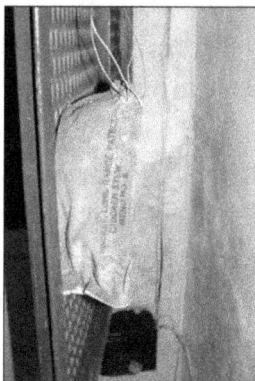

Mail bag and wires posing as explosives inside the old U.S. Embassy.

appearance of booby traps. As a result of this ruse, rumor spread, leading locals to believe that one-third of Tripoli would be destroyed by a bomb if the vaults were breeched. Since the abrupt departure from the U.S. Embassy in December 1979, for decades the Marine's shrewd ploy protected the contents of the two vaults—neither was ever opened.

Now standing in the room that served as the embassy's lobby, I could envision the frenzied crowd's fury as they marched downtown, only to stop in front of the U.S. Embassy building. Among the angry chants, American diplomatic staff knew their evacuation through a rear door was imminent. Amid the numerous ash piles—remnants

M-25 grenade on top of a desk in the old U.S. Embassy, Tripoli.

of burning classified documents—all of the staff members escaped unharmed. A sole M-25 hand grenade was placed in the center of a desk, in hopes that it would slow down any unwelcome intruder.

Now a veil of darkness was drawn over American-Libyan relations. It would remain that way for several decades. Twenty-four years later, I was looking at furniture caked in layers of dust, file cabinets overturned, books and files laying strewn on floors throughout the offices, and mummified animal carcasses littering the building. An American revolution bicentennial flag hung over cases of unopened food ra-

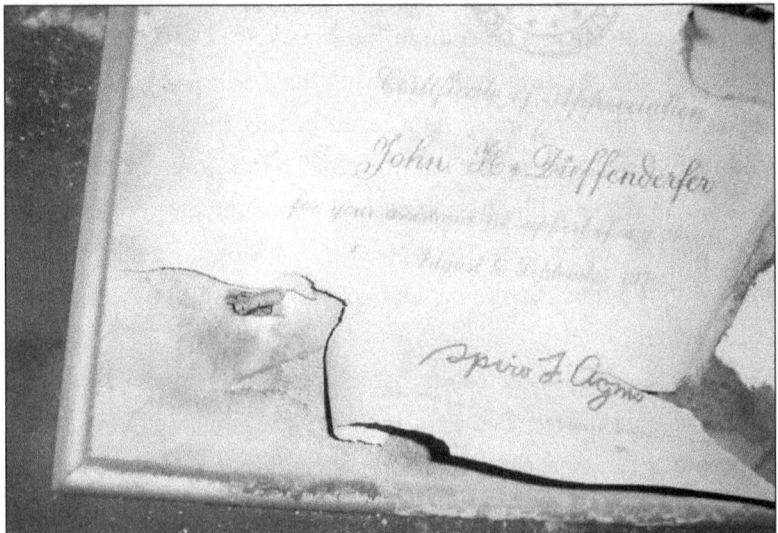

Certificate of Appreciation signed by Spiro T. Agnew.

tions that expired in 1962. A foreign service officer's half-charred certificate of appreciation, signed by Spiro Agnew, prominently hung on the wall, along with color photographs of Presidents Nixon and Carter.

As I made my way to the embassy library, I was amused by a book laying on a pile on the floor titled *Stranger Than Fiction* by Lewis Browne. Other titles among the pile were *Who's Who in the Arab World 1971–1972,* and *Diplomacy for the '70s.*

A small tattered and soiled three-inch by five-inch American flag lay on the floor among the rubble. Two aluminum casket covers sat neatly stacked against a third-story wall, still poised to be used to repatriate bodies of unfortunate Americans.

Robert W. Starnes discovers an American flag among the rubble inside the old embassy in Tripoli.

My adventure junkie genes, now in a heightened state, were temporarily choked by images of panicked American diplomats hurriedly destroying classified information and equipment amid chants of "Death to America." Protesters marched on the U.S. Embassy purportedly based on Iran's leader Ayatollah Khomeini's claim that the United States was responsible for attacking the Grand Mosque in Mecca, Saudi Arabia. Whiffs of smoke from burning the American flag—likely in effigy—permeated the offices, raising the diplomats' already heightened anxiety.

I walked down the hallway to the former ambassador's office and saw the empty flag stand next to the desk.

A month prior to my arrival in Tripoli, during my out-briefing in Washington, D.C., the administrative and communications officers who had just returned from Tripoli shared how they retrieved the American flag from the ambassador's office at the embassy. This flag had proudly stood its post since America's 1979 evacuation and was destined to be displayed in the new embassy building in Tripoli.

On a typical sunny Tripoli day, Jim Derrick retrieved the American flag tucked away in a file cabinet at the hotel for safekeeping. We pro-

Above: Robert W. Starnes (L), Jim Derrick (LC), DSS Engineer (RC), and U.S. Navy Sea-bee (R) display American flags inside ambassador's office, Tripoli. Top left: Flag discovered inside Ambassador's office in the old U.S. Embassy in Tripoli. Top right: Photograph of President Nixon inside the old U.S. Embassy in Tripoli.

ceeded to the abandoned U.S. Embassy in Tripoli. As with all trips to the embassy, the experience was surreal. The ambassador's leather furniture that once welcomed high-level officials was now cracking and covered in dust. A calendar ominously hung on the wall, still displaying the month of December 1979.

On the wall behind the former ambassador's desk, three embassy staff members and I hung the original flag retrieved from the embassy, a flag destined for the DSS museum, and a flag donated to the *USS Constitution* museum. It was a proud moment seeing the stars and stripes once again adorn the now dusty room that was occupied by the U.S. president's personal representative.

As part of the facility decommissioning process, all documents, furniture, and equipment would be destroyed. I recommended that a U.S. military explosive unit be used to safely clear the building from possible unexploded ordnance.

U.S. Mission members were allowed to collect souvenirs from the embassy building. As days passed, the photograph of President Nixon was claimed. I retrieved several U.S. federal law books, a dusty old encyclopedia set, a glass magnifying paperweight, and a small American flag I had dug out from the rubble.

Having analyzed and developed a facility decommissioning plan, my attention now turned to searching for property suitable for a new embassy. Working with a local real estate agent, my objective was to locate a 10-15 acre plot of land on which to build an embassy and residential compound. Following instructions from Colonel Gaddafi,

Gaddafi's Mediterranean vacation bungalow.

the real estate agent showed many potential building sites, mostly Libyan-owned military bases and compounds—even Gaddafi's son's Mediterranean beach retreat.

"This piece of property would be a great location for your new embassy compound," replied the Libyan real estate agent as he pointed toward the high exterior walls.

Through our local government liaison officer, we were informed that Colonel Gaddafi offered one of his many fortified compounds as a location for our new embassy compound. An unconfirmed report indicated that the compound offered was the same location where Gaddafi's adopted daughter, Hanna, was allegedly killed during the 1986 U.S. bombing raid ordered by President Reagan. If true, I was unsure how Gaddafi might have intended this offer. Was he trying to "poke America's eye" by locating our new embassy on the site where his daughter was said to have been killed by an American bomb? Or was he sincere in his offer to provide a secure facility to protect U.S. diplomats and their welcome return?

Caskets inside the old U.S. Embassy in Tripoli.

Libyan surface-to-air missiles near Tripoli.

"Let's drive on," I responded to the driver as I imagined the political fallout that would ensue at accepting an offer from Colonel Gaddafi for America to convert one of his palaces into an American Chancery building.

Our next stop was at a small Libyan military base along the Mediterranean coast. This piece of real estate was attractive because it offered an excellent escape route across the Mediterranean by aircraft, ship, or submarine.

I snapped a few photographs as we passed rusted, dilapidated trucks mounted with Russian-made surface-to-air missiles hidden beneath willow trees. A few hundred yards later, we drove by a large Scud missile laying on the ground, concealed by the high grass. Chinese- and Russian-made Scud missiles provided the Libyans long-range strike capability and a nuclear payload delivery system. Sensing that the

President Carter's photograph inside the old U.S. Embassy.

truckload of Libyan security service intelligence agents following us at a distance did not want me to photograph the Scud, I opted not to raise my camera.

Later that night, still fighting jet lag, I had difficulty sleeping. Around two o'clock in the morning, I peered out of my hotel room at the busily-traveled road that separated our hotel from the Mediterranean. Just then, I observed a Scud missile strapped to a semitruck tractor heading in the opposite direction from the military base we had visited the prior day. Perhaps Colonel Gaddafi wanted to remove any sign—including missiles—that might hinder America's return and long-term stay. He wanted to give the appearance that he and his nation were turning over a new leaf. So it was best for Gaddafi to conceal any symbol of nuclear proliferation, or as I thought—Scud proliferation.

I eventually compiled recommendations for several properties to be considered for the site of a future U.S. Embassy in Tripoli.

Interestingly, the photograph of President Jimmy Carter was never claimed as a souvenir. Maybe because he was the sitting President during the 1979 Islamic Revolution that jeopardized so many State Department employees, President Carter's photograph remained. This photograph as well as obsolete documents and files were removed from the diplomatic time capsule and destroyed in the Sahara Desert by a DSS team that followed my assignment.

CHAPTER 27

STAYIN' ALIVE

....I could visualize Al-Saadi Gaddafi's assistant
whispering in his ear that his request for a U.S. visa
had been denied. I envisioned the enraged Minister
barking, "Throw the Christians to the lions!"

Attention from bystanders was laser-focused on the two sleek black Mercedes sedans that quickly pulled up to the Hotel Corinthia's portico. Dressed in a white *thawb* (robe) and *keffiyeh* (head scarf), a young man exited the vehicle. It was clear this man was a power broker as he parted the masses that milled around the hotel lobby.

"Who is that man?" I asked my Libyan interpreter.

Smiling, the interpreter replied, "Al-Saadi —Gaddafi's son."

Al-Saadi Gaddafi, generally referred to as Libya's Minister of Sports, headed the Libyan Football Federation and was the commander of Libya's Special Forces. Al-Saadi was

Al-Saadi Gaddafi, Libya's Minister of Sports.

indeed a powerful man by virtue of his government positions and family lineage. Young, energetic, and all powerful, Al-Saadi also had a much-deserved reputation as a playboy and hard partier.

One morning, a U.S. political officer assigned to the Mission asked if I would be interested in attending the football (soccer, to Americans) match in Tripoli between the top two rival clubs of Tripoli and Benghazi. I gratefully accepted the offer. Of course, Tripoli's national football club happened to be managed by the Libyan Minister of Sports. I was told that in an effort to heighten Libya's national team's talent, many of the local football clubs were disbanded and an attempt was made to hire football-leading athletes and coaches—including Pelé, Brazil's football superstar. The political officer and I both believed the match would be an orchestrated, one-sided slaughter in Team Libya's favor.

The political officer wanted to attend the match in a low-key profile in order to simply observe and report back to Washington about a typical football game played in Libya. Unfortunately, given the Libyan intelligence service's oppressive collection and reporting mechanism, keeping information close-held proved difficult.

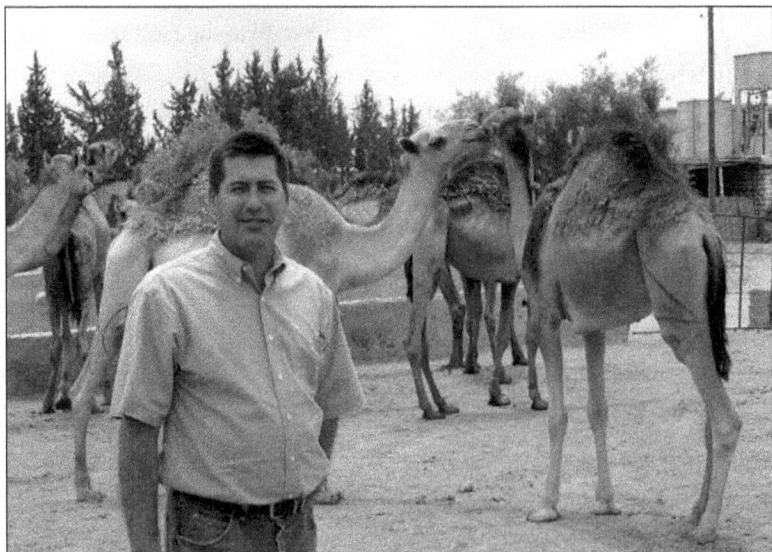

Robert W. Starnes inspects camels in Tripoli.

Days prior to the match, word had made its way to Al-Saadi Gaddafi that two American diplomats were planning to attend the much-anticipated event. Through his emissary, the Minister extended an invitation for the political officer and me to be his personal guests and watch the game from his private stadium box.

Calculating the high-level invitation, the American political officer and I informed the U.S. Chief of Mission, who responded that it was still too early in our bilateral relationship to begin interacting socially at such high governmental levels.

Following our supervisor's instruction, the political officer and I graciously declined the Minister of Sports' offer, and we did not attend the football match.

Soon after declining Al-Saadi's invitation to the match, I learned that Al-Saadi Gaddafi had applied for a U.S. visa, to be the first member of the Gaddafi ruling family to visit the United States since reestablishing our diplomatic relationship.

Coincidentally, an assistant secretary with the Department of State had denied Al-Saadi Gaddafi's visa issuance request.

I thought about the timing and possibility if we had accepted the invitation to sit in the Minister of Sports' private stadium box. I could visualize Al-Saadi Gaddafi's assistant whispering in his ear that his request for a U.S. visa had been denied. I envisioned the enraged Minister barking, "Throw the Christians to the lions!" in his coliseum with his American guests featured as the main attraction.

Overlooking the Mediterranean Sea, the city of modern-day Tripoli offered many of the conveniences of other major metropolises throughout the world. Camel lots scattered throughout Tripoli stabled the humped animals awaiting treks across the Sahara Desert. Although most foreign diplomatic facilities were located in Tripoli, Gaddafi's home town of Sirte, Libya, was the official Libyan capital.

When Jim Derrick and I made an exploratory trek into the old city marketplace, we were immediately struck with the smells of local spices. Tables covered with melons, oranges, and dates provided a colorful contrast to the dull concrete and rock buildings. The bustling market square was full of locals of all ages, milling about the open-air vendor booths and tables. Soon after entering the old city gates, a pickpocket had attempted to steal Jim's wallet from the front pocket of his shirt.

I chuckled at a vendor's tube of knockoff toothpaste called Crust, and wondered if four out of five Libyan dentists recommended this toothpaste for a brighter smile. I thought that the goal of brushing was to remove crust, not brush with it.

At that moment, I felt like Ali Baba surrounded by "the Forty Thieves." If cornered in a narrow alleyway, would the words "open sesame" provide a means of escape for Jim and me?

Our American appearance garnered much attention, as it was a well-known fact that American diplomats had returned to

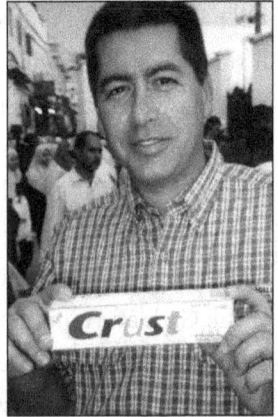

Libyan toothpaste Crust.

Libya. I visited the old city many times during my tour. In the beginning, I recall several of the vendors stopping me as I passed their shops, asking if I were American. I still held negative feelings about Libyan threats to Americans during the '70s and '80s. Not knowing if the vendors were pro- or anti-American, I lied and said I was Canadian or Texan. That answer seemed to appease the curious hosts.

In time, I came to understand that generally speaking, local Libyan businessmen were more interested in the potential commerce opportunities and less concerned with political or religious ideological differences between our two countries. Once I understood this fact, when asked if I was American, I confidently responded, "Yes."

I found the Libyan culture intriguing. Every weekend, located just outside of the old city wall and near the coastline, vendors sold their animals at the dog market and bird market. A large, open-air fish and vegetable market lined the harbor-front. Fishermen proudly

Tripoli Market.

displayed their fresh catches from the Mediterranean Sea. The brilliant colors of diverse fruits and vegetables provided a rich backdrop for buyers, sellers, and little children playing in the bright sun and cool sea breeze.

A brief walk along the shore led me to a beached, wooden-hulled boat being repaired by a Libyan man using antique tools. I held my camera up to signal my request for his permission to snap a photograph. He smiled and nodded his head with approval, allowing me to capture an iconic photographic souvenir.

The U.S. Mission staff and I frequented two restaurants near the hotel. One restaurant had a small seating area with a fire brick oven. It was relaxing to watch the baker place the flat pieces of uncooked Egyptian bread on his shovel board. As soon as it hit the oven, the bread would inflate like a balloon. Many extra pounds were added to my waistline from dipping the newly baked bread into a bowl of fresh olive oil. Not far from this restaurant was the Philadelphia Restaurant, named in honor of Libya's Barbary pirates who, in 1803—during the First Barbary War—captured an American naval sailing frigate

Libyan boat builder.

named the *USS Philadelphia* (launched in 1799). The Philadelphia Restaurant sold fried chicken and French fries, and became a favorite for U.S. Mission employees craving a little taste of home. The restaurant owner was very personable. After learning that I was an American diplomat, he presented me with a hat and polo shirt with the company's name (written in Arabic) and logo depicting a masted ship.

Eerily, Libyans proudly proclaim the original *USS Philadelphia*'s ship's mast is fixed to the top of Tripoli's old fort, now used as their national museum. To me, the mast symbolizes the U.S. naval sailors who were captured, bound, and enslaved for several years.

Tripoli's old fort and museum.

Ship mast fixed to top of Tripoli's museum.

While working for the DSS, I have met with many dangerous situations. Driving on the world's most dangerous road in Bolivia, climbing and sitting on an active volcano's caldera in Guatemala, and scuba diving in the dangerous currents of New Zealand's Cook Strait are just a few examples of the risky business I was drawn to.

However, being given the opportunity for a Libyan terrorist to kidnap an American during my visit to a back-road Turkish bathhouse in Tripoli ranks as one of the most daring actions I have ever undertaken.

In a daring mood, I rode to the far side of Tripoli to a non-descript bathhouse. My interpreter told the proprietor that I was American and to give me the "full treatment." My interpreter promptly departed, leaving me alone. Awkward, I felt as if I were in a fish bowl as the eyes of the other bathers followed my every move. The bathhouse had three separate steam rooms, each room progressing in heat levels.

After about 45 minutes, I sat in a room with showers to cool down. This room had several large marble slabs. I was oblivious to what was to come. A bathhouse employee motioned for me to lie on the hard slab. He then grabbed a brush with sharp, flexible teeth and put on a glove with plastic nodules that closely resembled a glove one would use to descale fish. I then received a 45-minute massage while listening to soft Italian music. Although living in a desert environment may seem dirty, many Libyans keep their bodies squeaky clean.

A few of the U.S. Mission staff and I were invited to the home of a staff member for a Libyan-style dinner. The hospitality was impressive as the lamb, rice, chicken, and

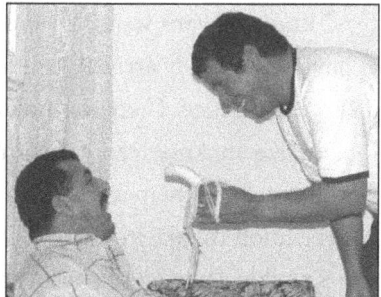

"Knuckle-Dragger" partakes in Libyan food game.

hummus were delicious and abundant. Our Libyan host proposed we play a game in which one person peeled a banana and jammed it down the throat of the other. The game was as foreign to me as the continent I was visiting, but evoked laughter from all of the dinner guests.

After six weeks in Tripoli, I was in serious need of a good old-fashioned haircut from a reputable barber. I put out the word among our local employees that I wanted to find a barber shop. Within minutes, through our staff interpreter, I learned that a driver for the U.S. Mission recommended his own barber. The driver had a stocky build and a dark, bushy mustache, to go along with his air of pretension. I guessed this driver was a Knuckle-Dragger, used for exerting his will upon others in hidden north African torture chambers.

Early afternoon in Tripoli brought dark blue skies with warm winds blowing off of the Mediterranean Sea. Our interpreter, Knuckle-Dragger, and I loaded into the U.S. Mission's rented vehicle. We drove past several blocks of familiar streets that I and other American diplomats had visited to sample the local cuisine. Twenty minutes and many unfamiliar city blocks later, we snaked our way through neighborhoods that resembled project housing. Dusty, gray concrete apartment buildings surrounded small strip centers lined along the pothole-filled streets.

Being an adventurer at heart, my excitement piqued as I knew I would soon be rubbing elbows with the locals who were not accustomed to catering to American tourists or diplomats.

I knew Libyans were still abuzz with excitement (or displeasure) at having the newly arrived American diplomats in their country after a 24-year absence. There was no disguising it. I was an American who looked like an American. Oftentimes, entire dining rooms of people, vendors selling their wares, and businessmen would stop in mid-conversation to take in a rare sight of a real-life American diplomat.

Knuckle-Dragger's favorite barber shop resembled the countless, old-style barber shops I was used to at home and in Latin America.

Real barber shops attract customers as much for the "barber experience" as for a standard haircut.

Faded pictures hung crooked on the off-color blue and white tarnished walls. Outdated, dog-eared Arabic magazines littered the stained coffee tables, and large mirrors decked the wall directly in front of the two occupied barber shop chairs. Clippers, scissors, and combs swirled in half-filled jars of disinfectant solution. Implements of the barber trade crowded the shelves just below the large mirrors.

I relished this once-in-a-lifetime opportunity of getting a haircut along the real Barbary Coast.

As we walked into the shop, in unison, the two barbers, in their white smocks, and the room full of clients, stopped talking and turned their attention toward me. The middle-class customers were dressed modestly and openly socialized with one another. The novelty of seeing an American signified their middle-class status—they would not be rubbing elbows with members of the diplomatic corps. I cautiously took the only empty chair in the waiting area.

In his concern for the American diplomat's well-being, Knuckle-Dragger walked up to a barber chair, began poking the customer on his shoulder, and in Arabic, instructed the man to get out of the chair to make room for the American.

I stopped my well-intentioned escort and reminded him that we Americans wanted to portray a good image to Libyan citizens, so I would not mind waiting my turn. I motioned to the surprised barber to continue his trade with his now confused client.

I studied the Tunisian barber sporting a contagious smile and joking manner. Just as in barber shops around the world, this is a universal refuge where men go to share their ideas, opinions, gossip, and to bond with "everyman."

When it was my turn, the barber spun his chair around and motioned for me to have a seat. My interpreter stood close by.

I relaxed at the sound of the scissors' snips and clippers' buzz. When the barber finished my haircut, he motioned for me to lean

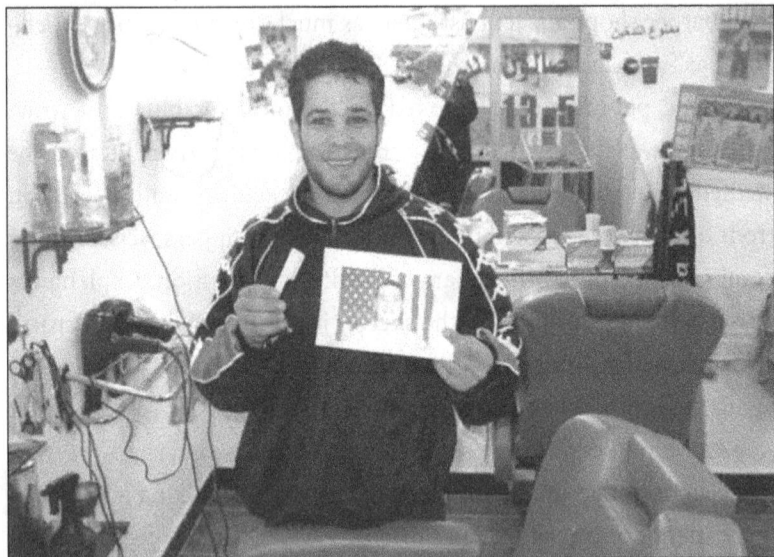

Tunisian barber in Tripoli holding his straight razor and photo of Robert W. Starnes.

my head forward into a sink to wash my hair. Used to laying my head backward when receiving a salon shampoo in America, this position of head washing was a bit awkward. I felt like King Louis XVI descending my throne to face the guillotine.

On completing the shampoo, the barber patted my head with a towel and leaned me back into the chair. My interpreter explained to me that the barber was going to shave the hair on the back of my neck. I agreed, but instructed the interpreter to ask the barber to put in a new blade—I did not want to risk disease or infection from a pre-used razor. The barber smiled and nodded his head in agreement.

Sitting upright in the blue upholstered chair, I noticed in the mirror's reflection a small black-and-white television mounted on a wall bracket. On the battlefield of the Iraq war, the Iranian-backed Shiite Muslim cleric Muqtadā al-Sadr was giving a television interview to *Al Jazeera*. The cleric, dressed in a black tunic and black turban, seemed serious as he spoke into the microphone.

I asked my interpreter what al-Sadr was saying. Choosing his words carefully, my Libyan interpreter composed himself and said the cleric had just issued a holy *fatwa* (ruling) for all Muslims to kill Americans.

I was sensitive to the recently revealed atrocities against the Iraqi prisoners of war at the Abu Ghraib prison in Iraq, perpetrated by a U.S. military unit, and how these despicable acts deflated, for a time, any diplomatic high ground and governmental integrity we had hoped to achieve in Libya. America was known for ethical treatment of prisoners of war. Now, a handful of rogue military police and officers had eroded the professionalism America stood for.

Then my barber lowered his straight razor to the back of my neck. No longer relaxed, beads of sweat formed on my forehead. I thought of the gruesome acts of the monster *Sweeney Todd, the Demon Barber of Fleet Street,* as I grew more wary of the razor scraping the nape of my neck.

After minutes that felt like a lifetime, the barber removed the lap drape and eagerly awaited payment.

Physically and mentally exhausted, the 20 minutes I spent in the barber's chair had taken its toll. I smiled, paid, and thanked the barber. I sat quietly during the ride back to the hotel and thought how my barber and I must have been the two happiest people in Tripoli that day—he was delighted with my generous tip and I was grateful to have survived al-Sadr's *fatwa.*

A year later, the barber was a good sport and agreed to have his picture taken. He was photographed with a mischievous smile holding my diplomat's I.D. card in one hand and *that* straight razor in the other.

The U.S. Mission had installed a computer with small speakers in my hotel room to allow me to conduct unclassified work after-hours. Unable to understand the lyrics, the constant drone of Arabic music gave me a hankering for American music. I asked our Libyan interpreter to accompany me to a local market where I could purchase music CDs. Albums from American musical artists were uncommon in Libya.

However, singer Celine Dion was quite popular among the locals and racks of pirated Celine Dion CDs were plentiful. Had I known earlier, I could have worked her CDs into my ruse of being Canadian.

I almost gave up my music shopping when I spotted and purchased the *Best of Bee Gees* album. By the end of my tour, I had almost worn it out.

The Bee Gee classic—"Stayin' Alive"—reminded me of a scene from the movie *Airport!:* in San Francisco's Barbary Coast district, a seedy portside bar is transformed into a disco floor. In a hilarious parody of *Saturday Night Fever*, Elaine (portrayed by Julie Hagerty) and Ted (portrayed by Robert Hays) dance, juggle, jiggle, and gyrate to the disco beat.

And now, here I was, near the shores of the real Barbary Coast, listening to the same beat. Only the disco ball was missing.

CHAPTER 28

INTO THE CUCKOO'S NEST

I can only imagine the actionable intelligence and
valuable insight about the Gaddafi regime and its
reign of terror that could have been divulged if given the
opportunity to train the Revolutionary Nuns protective detail.

L ike two unacquainted dogs who sniff each other to determine if the other is friend or foe, anxieties between Libya and the United States remained high during the early months of the U.S. diplomatic corps' return to Libya since its abrupt departure in December 1979.

On my arrival at Tripoli, my first order of business was to meet with one of Libya's most powerful officials, Minister of Foreign Affairs Moussa Koussa. The success of my tour as the regional security officer in Libya depended on gaining their government's support to evaluate the internal and external terrorist threat against Americans.

Moussa Koussa, Libyan Foreign Minister

This assessment included Libya's capability (and willingness) to protect American diplomats. How secure were Libya's borders in keeping out anti-American insurgents? What assets was Libya prepared to dedicate to our protection? Would Gaddafi's regime honor the diplomatic reciprocation with their embassy in Washington, D.C.?

Answers to these questions would provide critical information leading to reestablishing a full contingency of staff for a future U.S. Embassy in Tripoli and consulate in Benghazi.

For my meeting with Koussa, I was escorted through an inconspicuous concrete government building. The maze of hallways and offices muffled voices within Libya's intelligence nerve center. A stern-faced Libyan intelligence agent extended his arm and waved his fingers, signaling for me to have a seat in a dark reception area. I felt like I had been sent to the principal's office.

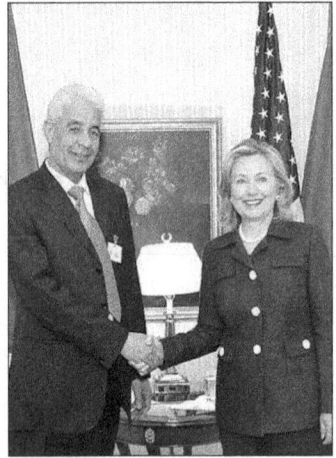

Libyan Foreign Minister Moussa Koussa (L) and U.S. Secretary of State Hillary Clinton (R).

A few minutes passed before I was motioned to enter a large office. Seated on a frayed sofa, I noticed Jim McGrath's compilation book, *Heartbeat: George Bush in His Own Words*, was open and laying on the desk. On my return to Houston, the official who was responsible for providing daily intelligence briefs included my observations in my meeting with Moussa Koussa—and the open book—to former President George H. W. Bush.

A Michigan State University alumnus, Moussa Koussa was a tall, distinguished gentleman with white hair who spoke fluent English.

Meeting Moussa Koussa, I was reminded of the unsolved murder of London's Metropolitan Police officer Yvonne Joyce Fletcher. Although no DSS investigative nexus existed, I wished justice for the family of officer Fletcher. In 1984, officer Fletcher was shot and killed while

Left: Former Libyan Embassy in London. Right: Yvonne Fletcher, London Metropolitan Police Officer.

policing a protest at the Libyan Embassy in London. In 1980, while assigned to the Libyan Embassy in London, Moussa Koussa had been expelled from England for alleged remarks appearing to support the state-sponsored assassination of Libyan dissidents within the United Kingdom. Moussa Koussa later served as Col. Gaddafi's chief intelligence officer and eventually Libya's Foreign Minister, where he was purported to have participated in planning the event that led to officer Fletcher's murder and the downing of Pan Am flight 103.[80]

Of course I would keep my thoughts to myself during our meeting. I could not stray from my mission at hand, that of protecting American diplomats in Libya. Anti-American leader Moussa Koussa did not command a mere band of thieves—he commanded an entire army of thugs and terrorists.

From our meeting, I successfully received concessions that allowed me to develop assessments and analyses to establish the foundation for U.S. diplomatic relations in Libya. The initial stage of the American-Libyan renewed and evolving relationship under the Gaddafi regime was set—with caution.

The Libyan security service agents assigned to American diplomats operated with dual functions:

1. Monitor and collect intelligence

2. Protect American diplomats

While working at the U.S. Mission from the Hotel Corinthia, I met with the Libyan security service supervisor periodically to review its security agent postings, physical security protections at the hotel, diplomatic travel protocols, and executive protection for all U.S. diplomatic staff. The supervisor, dressed in a dark brown European-style double-breasted suit, did not speak English, and I do not speak Arabic.

Frustrated by the shortcoming of communication, I smiled and asked, "Habla espanol?"

The supervisor grinned and responded, "Si."

We spoke together in Spanish—unlike the Spanglish of adding an "el" in front and an "o" at the end of words as prescribed by my DPS field training officer. My tours in Guatemala and Paraguay paid linguistic dividends. After all, the Spanish language was impacted by the Moors (Berber and Arab peoples from North Africa) during their conquest of the Iberian Peninsula during the Middle Ages. The modern-day Spanish word *ojalá* (I hope) was derived from the Arabic phrase *insha-Allah*, roughly translated (if God [Allah] wills it). My hope for the ability to communicate with my Libyan counterpart was granted.

Now the Libyan agent freely shared his agency's desire to ensure our diplomats' safety and asked that all in-country trips first be pre-coordinated with him.

At this point, it was well-known that the local intelligence security services followed the American diplomats everywhere. It became sort of a game to watch the men seated inside the vast hotel lobby as we went to our rented vehicles. As soon as our followers recognized that we were destined for the hotel parking lot, they lost their "professional coolness" and jumped out of their chairs as if jolted by an electric shock.

I briefed the American diplomats to not attempt to intentionally "lose" the security service followers—this wasn't a James Bond movie.

I remembered a foreign service officer's story of intentionally losing his KGB followers at a street-train crossing in Russia. In retaliation, the following morning, the KGB orchestrated a truckload of dirt dumped onto the uncooperative diplomat's vehicle. Message received!

Counterintelligence is a crucial role provided by DSS. Like the Spy vs Spy cartoon in *Mad Magazine,* it is not a matter of *if* hostile intelligence will attempt to probe and co-opt American diplomats, it is a matter of *when* and *how.*

DSS lore shared by other agents about hostile intelligence services can be comical. For instance, a DSS agent on a trip to Russia wanted to trade for a fur-lined Russian military hat. Due to a busy schedule, the DSS agent was unable to visit the local flea market. On the last day of his assignment, the agent shared how he walked into his hotel room, speaking to the walls plainly and loudly, stating that he wanted to trade for a hat. Within minutes, a burly man knocked on his hotel room door offering a military-style hat.

Another DSS agent shared a story about his visit to an Asian country suspected of spying on America. After taking a shower, the agent stepped in front of the bathroom mirror and began dancing. A few seconds later, a young Asian man knocked on his hotel room door and told the agent that he was only doing his job. A clear indication of a two-way mirror and perhaps a critique of the agent's dancing skills.

I instructed American diplomats that any future travel by car would need coordination. I told them they needed to wait a couple of minutes prior to departing in order to allow time for Libyan intelligence agents to get into position for their "following exercise."

Similar to many U.S. cities and states, Libyan laws prohibit driving while talking on a cell phone. Once, while en route to the Tripoli airport to meet a U.S. government support flight, our Libyan driver pulled off the road in order to receive a phone call. As our driver pulled onto the shoulder, the local intelligence security service vehicle unwittingly passed our sedan. Returning to the highway, the embassy vehicle was now positioned behind the intelligence security service vehicle, thus, the hunter became the hunted. For a few kilometers, our driver followed the security vehicle before passing it. As we pulled alongside their vehicle, the Libyan agents began laughing and waving at us as we assumed the lead position. They apparently found this maneuver amusing.

However, some of the younger intelligence agents were not so relaxed in their job. On a Sunday, I traveled to the abandoned U.S. Embassy building. I was unable to hail a taxi cab for my return trip to the hotel. While standing on the street corner, I recognized four local intelligence agents who had made their "keystone cop" hotel exit and sat in their vehicle a block away.

Hoping to solicit a ride back to the hotel, I walked up to their vehicle and knocked on the driver-side window. Feigning surprise yet seeming fearful of having been compromised, the driver rolled down his window. When I asked him for a ride, he responded, "no speak English," and took off around the corner. It was some time before I was able to catch a taxi cab to take me back to the hotel.

Like a fish to lures, law enforcement officers throughout the world are charmed by souvenirs. The "chum" (white T-shirts with a large "USA" emblem and U.S.-Libyan friendship lapel pins) I had purchased at Dupont Circle in D.C. were paying huge dividends. Word quickly spread throughout the Libyan intelligence service of the "chum" giveaway. Libyan agents increased patrols in the hallway outside of my room, hoping for a free T-shirt and lapel pin.

My goodwill gesture drew significantly increased security presence. However, my gifts had attracted so much attention from the Libyan security agents that their intelligence supervisor feared his staff would become co-opted by the Americans and he ordered his men to greatly minimize patrols on my hotel floor.

The window of opportunity to access Libyan information was briefly wide open. I was allowed to interview a range of Libyan officials from various agencies, gathering information to determine the indigenous and trans-national terrorist threat which provided valuable data to the DSS Office of Threat Analysis for its development of a threat matrix.

Libyan uranium centrifuges.

My time in Tripoli would prove to be quite productive. The Libyans permitted me to begin the decommissioning phase of the old U.S. Embassy building and to shop for property for a future Chancery compound. I evaluated crime levels and made assessments on the human and technical intelligence threats. I developed an emergency draw-down plan, completed an annual crime report, an Overseas Security Advisory Council (OSAC) report, established a foreign service national employee certification process, surveyed current diplomatic pouch delivery processes, established a lock-and-leave plan for the new office building, and developed a newly-formed local guard program. I briefed many American oil company executives seeking lucrative contracts in the oil-rich fields throughout Libya.

I was in-country when the U.S. team collected, inventoried, and transported to the United States the highly enriched uranium known as yellowcake—the real material used by *Back to the Future* character Professor Emmett Brown to power his DeLorean time machine.

Libya had purchased a turnkey facility in which foreign suppliers would provide the parts for the gas centrifuges, as well as assemble and test them. Libya was acquiring a large uranium enrichment facility capable of producing enough highly-enriched uranium for several bombs a year.

On January 27, 2004, the United States airlifted out of Libya components of the nuclear weapons program that country agreed to surrender. The White House hailed Libya for its cooperation and said its good faith in dismantling weapons would be reciprocated. The announcement was made several hours after the U.S. transport plane landed in Tennessee carrying some 25 metric tons of Libyan weapons program components, including centrifuge parts, uranium, and sensitive documentation. The airlift was the most dramatic move since Muammar Gaddafi concluded an agreement with the United States and Britain on December 19, 2003, to destroy all of Libya's weapons of mass destruction in a bid to end two decades of international isolation and U.S. sanctions.[81]

On a bright, sunny Libyan afternoon, while preparing a security report, I learned from the U.S. chief of mission that Colonel Gaddafi and Gaddafi's son were aware that a DSS special agent was in-country, and requested that I assess, analyze, and train his and his son's executive protective security details. Gaddafi's protective detail was locally referred to as the Amazonian Guards—officially known as the Revolutionary Nuns—a cadre of bodyguards made up exclusively of females.

Many believe Colonel Gaddafi surrounded himself with female security agents because he thought it would be difficult for an assassin to shoot women. Still others believed his "armed harem" quenched his eccentric appetite for young women. Hand-picked by Colonel Gaddafi himself, the women were required to take an oath of chastity and undergo extensive martial arts and firearms training.

In 1996, during a doomed assassination attempt of Colonel Gaddafi, one of his female bodyguards was killed and seven others wounded. British MI6[82] was alleged to be responsible for the attack.

Gaddafi's female guards known as the Revolutionary Nuns.

During the Libyan civil war, five of the women assigned to the eccentric unit claimed they were systematically raped by Colonel Gaddafi, and then passed on to his sons and Libyan military commanders.[83] Some of the unit's women even claimed to have been given the ultimatum to either execute captured rebels or face execution themselves.[84]

Libyan guard protects Colonel Gaddafi.

However, the reality of our strained relationship was again revealed when the U.S. chief of mission stated that he declined Colonel Gaddafi's request to provide security training to his detail because the renewed relationship between America and Libya was too new and fragile.

By virtue of proximity and trust, security agents are privy daily to sensitive meetings, back seat conversations, and highly protected communiqués. I can only imagine the actionable intelligence and valuable insight about the Gaddafi regime and its reign of terror that could have been divulged if given the opportunity to train the Revolutionary Nuns protective detail.

Golfer weathers a sandstorm at Benghazi course.

two Libyan intelligence agents tried to tell our tour guide what their responsibilities were—to report all activities with the Americans. The baffled tour guide drove away from the agents, telling them to leave him and us alone.

We were nervous knowing that there would be a "day of reckoning" for our untrained tour guide friend.

In the midst of a sandstorm, we made our way to our downtown Benghazi hotel. The storm was not blinding, but it did significantly reduce visibility and caused respiratory problems for some.

On the way from the airport, we passed a golf course. Being a golf hacker myself, I asked our driver to stop. The golf course was completely void of grass. The greens consisted of oil-soaked packed sand. Each green had rakes and rollers that were used to smooth the ground after each putt. I was convinced that only hard-core golfers with a mastery of sand pits played this course.

Although blessed with immense oil fields, Colonel Gaddafi's regime had left his country economically barren—just like this lonely golf course.

Leaving the course, I noticed a local golfer standing next to his bag of clubs, apparently waiting for his partner. Given the handicap, he deserves a lifetime PGA card for his love for and dedication to the game.

Our guide then drove us to the hotel and offered to take us to a restaurant that served local Benghazi cuisine. As we got out of the vehicle, the two Libyan intelligence agents jumped in and ordered the guide to drive away. To this day, I can recall the dazed look on the guide's face as they drove away.

We knew the guide had committed a national sin. He had unwittingly rebuffed the Libyan intelligence officers at the Benghazi airport. Stunned ourselves, Shawn, Cindy, and I looked at each other and wondered if we would ever see the guide again. Fortunately, he returned to the hotel as scheduled. He would not elaborate on the meeting with the intelligence agents, but we knew his life likely hung on a razor-thin string.

WWII headstone at War Cemetery.

After making several stops, including at the Benghazi War Cemetery, we retired for the night.

The following morning, we set out for Apollonia, Cyrenaica (or Susa), and Derna. We wound our way through the Jebel Akhdar (Green Mountain)—the mountainous region where Libya's famous freedom fighter Omar Mukhtar engaged the Italian forces. In 1911 Mukhtar pledged his life to driving out the invading Italian forces. He was eventually captured and executed by Italian forces in 1931. Shawn was responsible for coordinating recently approved U.S. military flights over Libyan air space. As we neared the town of Tocra, the embassy notified Shawn that the Libyan government returned the wrong flyover permission code for a U.S. military aircraft that was due to arrive in Libyan airspace within the hour.

Memorial honoring Omar Mukhtar.

Cellular phone service was sporadic and Shawn wasn't able to contact his Libyan counterpart to secure permission for the aircraft to fly over Libya. Shawn was extremely stressed over the possibility of the aircraft being downed as a result of not closing the loop. After a frantic search, we located a hill from where Shawn was able to pass the corrected code to Ramstein Air Base in Germany. Libyan permission was granted and the crisis averted.

I hoped that would be the final crisis we would face on this trip. That hope would soon be dashed.

CHAPTER 30

FROM THE SHORES OF TRIPOLI

"My head or yours."

My anticipation grew as we neared the port city of Derna—one of the wealthiest provinces in the Barbary States and the site of the Battle of Derna in 1805. This Mediterranean Sea city is steeped in American military history.

Beginning in 1799, the U.S. government had acquiesced to piracy extortion and agreed to pay the Barbary Coast countries $18,000 a year for the right to sail in "their" sea. This agreement broke down in 1801 when Pasha (Turkish title of high rank) Yusuf Karamanli, of

Left: Painting of USS Philadelphia grounded by Tripoli pirates. Right: Depiction of Stephen Decatur's skirmish aboard the USS Philadelphia.

Tripoli, sought to extort more money, a demand the U.S. government refused.

Under the leadership of President Thomas Jefferson, in October 1803, the frigate *USS Philadelphia* ran aground and was captured while chasing Barbary pirates.

Her captain, William Bainbridge was unsuccessful in scuttling the ship and subsequently surrendered. The U.S. crew ended up prisoners and slaves in a Libyan dungeon. Working and dying under harsh conditions, the U.S. sailors may have felt they had been abandoned. This was a stark reminder to me that freedom for Americans has never been free.

To prevent the pirates from from repairing the *USS Philadelphia* and using her against the United States' forces, on February 16, 1804, Lieutenant Stephen Decatur led a daring nighttime assault in Tripoli's harbor to reclaim or destroy the captured frigate. Using the captured corsair *Mastico*, renamed the *USS Intrepid*, Stephen Decatur and his brave crew burned the *USS Philadelphia*. The ship reportedly took three days to burn to the waterline.

On March 8, 1805, with a military commission, Continental Army General William Eaton, Marine Corps First Lieutenant Presley

Painting by Charles Waterhouse depicting the Battle of Derna, Libya.

O'Bannon and their small troop of soldiers traveled from Alexandria across the desert to Derna. With 100 camels and some mules slogging through the red-hot sand, it took them seven weeks to complete the harrowing 600-mile journey.

On April 25, 1805, they arrived at Derna. After their ordeal, was the prospect of battle more welcome than dying a miserable death in the desert? Now General Eaton sent the governor of Derna a letter asking for safe passage through the city.

In defiance, the governor replied, "My head or yours."

On April 27, Eaton and the Marines began the attack on the harbor fortress. The American force was bolstered by the flagship *USS Constitution* and offshore bombardment support from the *USS Argus*, *USS Hornet*, and *USS Nautilus* in the harbor.

On April 27, 1805, Marine First Lieutenant Presley O'Bannon, a 29-year-old Irish-American from Virginia, pulled the American flag from inside his soiled uniform jacket and attached the flag to a static pole jutting from the newly acquired fort in Derna, Libya. O'Bannon became the first man to raise a United States flag over foreign soil in time of war. Seeing the stars and stripes flying over the Berber fort in Derna, the defenders in the governor's castle took flight and by the end of the day, the entire city of Derna had fallen.

The victory is memorialized in the first line of the Marine Corps hymn, "... From the Halls of Montezuma to the shores of Tripoli ...." In recognition of his bravery, Lieutenant O'Bannon was presented the Mameluke sword, adopted in 1825 for Marine Corps officers, which is still part of the dress uniform today. It is a scimitar-like sword featuring an eagle head hilt.

Top: Consul Gen. William Eaton. Below: USMC First Lt. Presley O'Bannon.

CHAPTER 31

LEFT BUT NOT FORGOTTEN

American blood had been spilled
along these shores almost two hundred years earlier.

The cattle grazing outside the Greek ruins at the Temple of Zeus brought on a momentary homesickness for Texas. While I walked through the temple in Apollonia, overlooking the Mediterranean Sea, two Libyan intelligence agents approached and introduced themselves and ensured our safety during our trip.

We concluded our tour of Apollonia and embarked for Derna, where I planned to raise an American flag to commemorate the Marines and sailors who died or were taken prisoner during the Barbary Wars. I have many worldwide locations on my "bucket list" of places I hope to someday visit: the Great Wall of China, Antarctica, and a backpacking trip through Ireland and Wales. Given its connection to American history and the U.S. Marine Corps, Derna, Libya, ranked high on my must-see list.

In order to add a special military historic relevance, I wanted to schedule this portion of the trip for June 6, 2004, the sixtieth anniversary of D-Day. Because of a scheduling conflict, I traveled to Derna on

Cattle graze near Zeus' temple in Apollonia, Libya.

Saturday, June 5, 2004. This day proved to have a greater American-Libyan historical significance. President Ronald Wilson Reagan, the 40th president of the United States, died. He had had more than his share of conflicts with the Libyan leadership.

Our search for the location of the original fortress in Derna was futile. In lieu of flying the American flag near the location of the old fort, I opted to raise it at the Derna seaport.

I knew that not all Libyans would be thrilled to see the American flag on their shores—especially during the height of the Iraq war—so I asked the political officer to set up the camera for a quick snapshot as soon as I unfolded the flag.

On a dazzling, sunshiny day, with the sea water lapping near my feet, I unfurled the same American flag that was presented to me by the Marine Security Guard detachment at the U.S. Embassy in Cairo, Egypt, prior to my arrival in Libya. The flag's brilliant red, white, and blue colors were resplendent, almost glowing like a gorgeous comet.

American blood had been spilled along these shores almost two hundred years earlier. I encouraged the political officer to quickly

Robert W. Starnes holding the American flag raised at Derna, Libya.

take the photograph. Sensing my anxiety, the political officer began giggling, delaying the photograph for what seemed like an eternity, before finally snapping the camera.

At the precise moment the photograph was taken, the sound of screeching tires caught our attention. A determined driver was backing his vehicle against heavy traffic on the major highway that ran parallel to our port-side position. The small sedan sped into the parking lot and came to a halt near us. The driver was clearly upset. This man slammed his car door and stomped toward our group. Glaring at us and the American flag, the Libyan asked me if I was planning to occupy his country the same way Americans were occupying Iraq. Without answering, we quickly loaded back into our vehicle to return to Benghazi.

In Benghazi, we had several hours to burn before our flight to Tripoli. Compelled by a desire to document history, I wanted to locate and photograph the former American consulate in Benghazi. I found an old building of Italian architecture near the city center that matched the description I received from a retired diplomat. The day was late and darkness was descending on the city. I raised my camera, focused, and snapped a photograph.

Within seconds, a dozen men stormed from the building. Two of them confronted our guide and demanded the identity of the photographer, and more importantly, the reason for taking the picture. To our dismay, this building was the Benghazi Revolutionary Command Council (RCC) headquarters. The RCC is comprised of some of the most anti-American radicals in all of the Middle East.

To escalate the problem, our tour guide unwittingly poured proverbial gasoline on the fire when he told the revolutionists, "Everything is okay. They are Americans." Before weapons were drawn, two Libyan intelligence agents appeared from the shadows and confronted the angry RCC faction. For a moment, I thought there would be a brawl. This entire ruckus was caused by my untimely photograph. Fortunately, the intelligence agents were able to calm the RCC members down long enough for us to speed away from the scene.

The following day, I met with the assistant to the minister of interior to apologize for the misunderstanding in Benghazi and

Members of the Revolutionary Command Council (upper left) peer from the their headquarters in Benghazi, Libya.

offered to delete the digital photograph from my camera. The minister's assistant told me not to worry—if we wanted a photograph of the RCC building, American satellites are able to take such a photograph.

Whew! An international diplomatic incident averted, at least for now.

On the day of my departure from Libya, the U.S. Mission vehicle drove past Tripoli's harbor and the original fort that American sailors and Marines bombarded during the Barbary Wars.

A few miles down the road, we passed the Christian cemetery that supposedly contains the remains of some of the sailors and Marines who perished during the Barbary Wars. The cemetery walls, chipped and unpainted, surrounded weed-covered, broken and fallen headstones.

A basic tenet of the Army Soldier's Creed is, "I will never leave a fallen comrade." In those instances where comrades are left behind, they will never be forgotten. Every effort is made to return them to their families. I thought about the abandoned American flag in the ambassador's office at the U.S. Embassy. To me, this flag symbolized the long and lonely days endured by Americans held captive in foreign lands.

American cemetery in Tripoli.

As I passed the Christian cemetery in Tripoli, I thought about the captive American sailors and Marines who must have felt hope slipping away during their imprisonment. I imagined their elation at learning of General Eaton's and Lieutenant O'Bannon's victory at Derna, which ultimately led to their rescue. They were free to reunite with their families across the Atlantic.

I may be leaving Libya this day, but I will never forget the American lives sacrificed in its fractured land with a complex history.

In October 2010, after a 23-year career, I retired from the DSS. I may have left the adventures and excitement DSS provided, but I will always remember the special men and women in law enforcement and military serving as peacemakers around the globe.

Similar to the song lyrics of fellow Texas State University alumni George Strait, time had come for this DSS cowboy to ride into the sunset.

...every time I hear America's national anthem,
I think of Derna, Lt. Presley O'Bannon, Francis Scott Key,
Major George Armistead, and my friend, David Armistead.

A t last, after twelve years, now in retirement, my American flag has found a home, I thought to myself as I hung up from a call with a member of the *USS Constitution* Museum in Charlestown, Massachusetts.

Nicknamed *Old Ironsides,* the *USS Constitution* was launched in 1797 and is the oldest commissioned warship afloat in the world. She was named personally by President George Washington. Still under active command of the U.S. Navy, the *USS Constitution* was one of six initial frigates commissioned for the U.S. Navy, and was briefly commissioned as the flagship during the First Barbary War.

USS Constitution, 1845, painting by Jacob Peterson.

Especially meaningful to my family is the patriotic connection to our nation's first commanding general. From April 1778 to June 1778, my great-grandfather (*x*5), Sergeant John Bird (Byrd) served with

Left: Francis Scott Key. Right: Star Spangled Banner Flag flown at Fort McHenry, War of 1812.

General George Washington's Army at the Valley Forge encampment while assigned to the 2nd Virginia State Regiment.[85] I think of the endless drills Sergeant Bird must have marched while training under Prussian Baron Friedrich Wilhelm von Steuben—after all, the baron literally wrote the standard United States drill manual of the day.

In a "six degrees of separation" moment of recognition, I learned that David Armistead, whom I assisted in overhauling the Governor's Protective Detail, has direct ancestral lineage to Major George Armistead, the commander at Fort McHenry, Baltimore, during the battle against the British, when on September 14, 1814, Francis Scott Key penned America's national anthem, *The Star-Spangled Banner*.

During the Battle of Baltimore in the War of 1812, it was Major George Armistead who commissioned flagmaker Mary Pickersgill to

Libyan postage stamp artwork depicting battle for the captured frigate *USS Philadelphia*.

create a flag so large the British would be able to easily spot it from a distance. The largest American flag flown in battle, this historic Star Spangled Banner Flag now hangs in the Smithsonian National Museum of American History.

Not a postage stamp collector, I was fascinated with the art and graphic images on Libyan postage stamps commissioned by Colonel Gaddafi. I purchased an interesting Libyan postage stamp depicting a painting of "fearful" American naval sailors in hand-to-hand combat with "strong and brave" Berbers on board the captured *USS Philadelphia* frigate, engulfed in flames, during the U.S. military operations to scuttle the vessel in Tripoli's harbor.

Robert W. Starnes (R) presents Texas Governor Rick Perry (L) with flag flown in Libya.

On returning to Texas, I was honored to present a U.S. federal law book I had retrieved from inside the ransacked library at the U.S. Embassy in Tripoli to Michael McCaul, Assistant U.S. Attorney in the Counterterrorism Unit in Austin, Texas (now U.S. Congressman) as a souvenir for the prosecutorial assistance he provided the Diplomatic Security Service.

I was equally honored to present a flag flown in Derna, Libya, to Texas Governor Rick Perry for his unwavering service to the people of the State of Texas. An American flag I flew inside the U.S. Embassy in Tripoli, Libya, is currently on display at the Diplomatic Security Service museum in the bureau's training center in Dunn Loring, Virginia.

I am humbled and delighted that the *USS Constitution* Museum, dedicated to preserving "Old Ironsides" history, will display a second American flag I flew in Derna, Libya, alongside the rare Libyan stamp

David Armistead (L), Governor Rick Perry (C), and Robert W. Starnes (R)

depicting the scuttling of the frigate *USS Philadelphia*.

Since traveling to Libya, every time I hear America's national anthem, I think of Derna, Lt. Presley O'Bannon, Francis Scott Key, Major George Armistead, and my friend, David Armistead.

My hope for our life's next set of adventures now revolve around my wife Pam and my vision to establish a non-profit organization to support missionaries by building schools, clinics, and churches in developing countries abroad and to provide Christian ministers a refuge in Texas to rest and recuperate before returning to their ministerial assignments.

Whatever my perch in life has been or will be that allows me to see far, I will always credit the shoulders of giants on which I stand.[86]

ACKNOWLEDGMENTS

I SINCERELY ACKNOWLEDGE the love, patience, and support of my family, my wife Pam, and children Jacob, Zachariah, Rachel, and Caleb.

The completion of this memoir would not have been possible without the assistance of many people, whose names may not all be enumerated. Their contributions to this work is greatly appreciated and sincerely acknowledged.

Editorial

Merry Bilgere, Judith Briles, Catharine Fitzsimmons, Jessica McCurdy Crooks, Norah Sarsour

Graphic Design

Rebecca Finkel, Judith Briles

Contributors

David Armistead, Emily Benedek, Chris Brannen, Dale Bohren, Tom Borisch, Dana Conner, Bill Crider, Bob DeLancy, Tom Derrick, Cindy Edwards, Alvaro Freyre, Rebecca Freyre, Maura Harty, Jim Hill, Neil Hinds, Michael Hudspeth, Sue Irish Cindy Kierscht, Michelle Lambing, Joyce Lee, Katie Lentzl, Sandy Leottal, Pedro Martinez, Lisa McGahen, Paul McGahen, Raymond Millar, Mary Molineux, Margaret Potyrala, Jennifer Reibenspies, Charles Rowcliffe, Darren Sartin, Tina Sciocchetti, Jackie Sherrill, Ron Sievert, Harrie Slootbeek, Betty Stroock, Les Stroud, Kristen Tribe

Back cover David Scarbrough_HP. *Prince Charles Visits Houston.* "N.d." Photograph. ©Houston Chronicle. Used with permission.

1   Starnes, Robert W. *Gaddafi poster.* ©2004.

2   Starnes, Robert W. *U.S. Embassy ransacked.* ©2004.

3   Starnes, Robert W. *Texas State Trooper.* ©1982.

4   *Joseph P. and Polina Crider*, circa 1860. Photograph. House of Crider archives ©1976, all rights reserved. Used with permission.

5   Texas DPS. *Texas DPS headquarters.* Circa 1960. *https://www.dps.texas.gov/ PublicInformation/varietyPhotos.htm.* Web. 01-Nov-2017.

6   *New York Yankees*, circa 1924. Photograph. Cushing Memorial Library and Archives, Texas A&M University. Used with permission.

7   *Coach Jackie Sherrill*, "N.d.". Photograph. Courtesy Cushing Memorial Library and Archives, Texas A&M University. Used with permission.

8   Starnes, Robert W. *Coach Jackie Sherrill, Pam Starnes and Robert W. Starnes.* ©2017.

9   Starnes, Robert W. *University of Texas Seal.* © 2017

10   *Coach "Bully" Gilstrap*, "N.d.". Photograph. Courtesy Schreiner University. Used with permission.

11   Kilgore, John. *What do highway patrolmen do off-duty.* ©1983. Rosebud News. Used with permission.

12   Kilgore, John. *What do highway patrolmen do off-duty.* ©1983. Rosebud News. Used with permission.

13   Kilgore, John. *What do highway patrolmen do off-duty.* ©1983. Rosebud News. Used with permission.

14   Kilgore, John. *What do highway patrolmen do off-duty.* ©1983. Rosebud News. Used with permission.

15 Starnes, Robert W. *Snake Farm Zoo* © 2017.

16 Starnes, Robert W. *Snake Farm Terrariums*. © 2017.

17 Marathekedar93. Indian Cobra. 2016. Wiki Media. *https://commons.wikimedia. org/wiki/File:Indian_Spectacled_Cobra_02.jpg*. Web. 11-April-2017.

18 Hickman, Jimmy C. USMC GySgt. *U.S. Embassy Beirut*. 1983. Marines in Lebanon 1982-1984; Chapter 5: Beirut IV-- Circumstances Change, 'Presence' Remains' 15 February-29 May 1983.

19 Hickman, Jimmy C. USMC GySgt. *U.S. Sgt. Luis G. Lopez*. 1983. Marines in Lebanon 1982-1984; Chapter 5: Beirut IV-- Circumstances Change, 'Presence' Remains' 15 February-29 May 1983.

20 Central Intelligence Agency. *Admiral Bobby R. Inman*. 1983. Wiki Media. *https://commons.wikimedia.org/wiki/File:Admiral_Bobby_Ray_Inman,_official_ CIA_photo,_1983.JPEG* Web. 01-Nov-2017

21 *Prince Charles and Gov. White*. 1986. Photograph. Texas State Library and Archives Commission. Current Events Photographic Documentation Program collection1986/138-16. Used with permission.

22 *Prince Charles at Governor's Mansion*. 1986. Photograph. Texas State Library and Archives Commission. William Gregory Vimont collection, 1998/142-PP1190-F3-25. Used with permission.

23 Starnes, Robert W. *Gen. Gray, Pam and Robert Starnes*. © 1987.

24 Varidion. *Large map of South America*. 2006. Wiki Media. *https://commons. wikimedia.org/wiki/File:LocationParaguay.svg* Web. 01-Nov-2017

25 Starnes, Robert W. *Paraguay Gun Shop*. ©1996.

26 P., Patti. *Mennonite Children in Paraguay*. 2008. Wiki Media. *https://commons. wikimedia.org/wiki/File:San_Ignacio.jpg* Web. Viewed 01-Nov-2017.

27 Adomo, Jorge, *Paraguay Police Riot Squad outside U.S. embassy*. 2008. Rueters. Used with permission.

28 *Tri Border Area Map*. 2003. U.S. Federal Research Division. Terrorist and Organized Crime Groups in Tri-border Area (TBA) of South America, (revised December 2010).

29 *Josef Mengele*. 1956. Wiki Media. *https://commons.wikimedia.org/wiki/File:WP_ Josef_Mengele_1956.jpg-Web*. 01-Nov-2017.

30 *Children Survivors at Auschwitz*. "N.d". Wiki Media. U.S. Holocaust Memorial Museum, courtesy of Belarussian State Archive of Documentary Film and Photography. *https://en.wikipedia.org/wiki/Josef_Mengele* Web. Viewed 01-Nov-2017.

31 Ekem. *Paraguay and Brazil Border*. 2007. *https://commons.wikimedia.org/wiki/ File:Brazil.Paraguay.border.jpg* Web. 01-Nov-2017.

32 CMasi. *Ciudad del Este*. 2012. Wiki Media. *https://commons.wikimedia.org/wiki/ File:Ciudad_del_Este_20120427_411.jpg* Web. 01-Nov-2017.

33 *Khalid Sheikh Mohammad.* U.S. Federal Government. 2003. Wiki Media. *https://commons.wikimedia.org/wiki/File:Khalid_Shaikh_Mohammed_after_capture.jpg* Web. 01-Nov-2017.

34 Mir, Hamid. *Osama Bin Laden.* Circa 1997. Wiki Media. *https://commons.wikimedia.org/wiki/File:Hamid_Mir_interviewing_Osama_bin_Laden.jpg* Web. 01-Nov-2017.

35 *Ibrahim Malmood Awethe's Arrest.* 1996. ABC Color newspaper, Asuncion, Paraguay. Used with permission.

36 Massimiliano, W. *Omar ibn al-Chattab Mosque.* 2011. Wiki Media. *https://commons.wikimedia.org/wiki/File:Mesquita_omar_ibn_al-khattab5.JPG* Web. 01-Nov-2017.

37 *U.S. Embassy Asuncion, Paraguay.* "N.d." U.S. Department of State webpage *https://py.usembassy.gov/es/embassy-es/jobs-es/* Web. 01-Nov-2017.

38 Ekem,*Ciudad del Este Market.* 2007. Wiki Media. *https://commons.wikimedia.org/wiki/File:Ciudad-del-este.jpg* Web. 01-Nov-2017.

39 *Ibrahim Malmood Awethe's Arrest.* 1996. ABC Color newspaper, Asuncion, Paraguay. Used with permission.

40 *Ibrahim Malmood Awethe's Extradition.* 1996. ABC Color newspaper, Asuncion, Paraguay. Used with permission.

41 *Ibrahim Malmood Awethe escorted to plane.* 1996. ABC Color newspaper, Asuncion, Paraguay. Used with permission.

2 Courtesy Pedro Martinez,©2017. Used with permission.

43 *William Fourie arrested.* 1998. ABC Color newspaper, Asuncion, Paraguay. Used with permission.

44 CMasi, *Hotel Cecilia, Asuncion, Paraguay.* 2017. Wiki Media. *https://commons.wikimedia.org/wiki/File:Hotel_Cecilia.jpg* Web. 01-Nov-2017.

45 *Klause Barbie.* 1940. Wiki Media.*https://commons.wikimedia.org/wiki/File:Klaus-Barbie.jpg* Web. 01-Nov-2017.

46 *Stroessner Viewing Parade.* "N.d." Paraguayan Military. Used with permission.

47 Ekem. *Tacumbu Prison, Asuncion.* 2013. *https://commons.wikimedia.org/wiki/File:Tacumbu.prison.jpg* Web. 01-Nov-2017.

48 Stringer. *Paraguay Police arrest three escapees from the Emboscada Prisons.* 1998. Reuters. Used with permission.

49 Ekem. Bus Terminal, Asuncion. 2007. Wiki Media.*https://commons.wikimedia.org/wiki/File:Bus.Terminal.Asuncion.jpg* Web. 01-Nov-2017.

50 *William Fourie extradition.* 1998. ABC Color newspaper, Asuncion, Paraguay. Used with permission.

51 *William Fourie escorted to plane.* 1998. ABC Color newspaper, Asuncion, Paraguay. Used with permission.

52 *William Fourie loaded onto plane.* 1998. ABC Color newspaper, Asuncion, Paraguay. Used with permission.

53 IIngolfson. *Technical University in Darmstadt.* 2010. Wiki Media. *https://commons. wikimedia.org/wiki/File:Construction,_Technische_Uni_Darmstadt_I.jpg* Web. 01-Nov-2017.

54 Rufus46. *U.S. Consulate, Munich.* 2012. Wiki Media. *https://commons.wikimedia. org/wiki/File:Amerikanisches_Generalkonsulat_Muenchen-1.jpg* Web. 01-Nov-2017.

55 "N.d." *Mohammad Gharib Makki* arrest. 1998.

56 Starnes, Robert. *Mohammad Gharib Makki* arrest. 1998.

57 FFMM. *Silvio Pettirossi International Airport, Asuncion.* 2010. Wiki Media. *https://commons.wikimedia.org/wiki/File:International_Airport_Silvio_Pettirossi_by_Felipe_M%C3%A9ndez.jpg* Web. 01-Nov-2017.

58 Mariordo. *Sao Paulo, Brazil.* 2005. Wiki Media. *https://commons.wikimedia.org/wiki/S%C3%A3o_Paulo_(city)#/media/File:Sao_Paulo_Congonhas_2.jpg* Web. 01-Nov-2017.

59 *Herberts Cukurs.* circa 1934. Wiki Media. *https://lv.wikipedia.org/wiki/Att%C4%93ls:Kapteinis_Herberts_Cukurs.png* Web. 01-Nov-2017.

60 Shimgray. *Map of Lebanon.* 2010. CIA World Factbook. Wiki Media. *https://commons.wikimedia.org/wiki/File:Map_of_Lebanon.png* Web. 01-Nov-2017.

61 Khamenei, Farsi. *Hassan Naserallah.* 2005. Wiki Media. *https://commons.wikimedia.org/wiki/File:Seyyed_Hassan_Nasrallah_by_khamenei.ir_01(2005)_02_(cropped).jpg* Web. 01-Nov-2017.

62 *Mohammad Gharib Makki arrest.* 1998. U.S. Government.

63 Msanlm. *Luis Argana.* 1996. Wiki Media. *https://commons.wikimedia.org/wiki/File:Genaro_Sanchez_y_Luis_Maria_Arga%C3%B1a6.jpg* Web. 01-Nov-2017.

64 *Anastasion Samoza.* circa 1936. Wiki Media. *https://commons.wikimedia.org/wiki/File:A_Somoza-Garsia_1936.png* Web. 01-Nov-2017.

65 ABC Color Newspaper, ©17-Sept-2014. *http://www.abc.com.py/nacionales/hace-34-anos-mataron-a-somoza-en-asuncion-1286879.html* Used with permission.

66 *President Francisco Solano Lopez.* circa 1870. Wiki Media. *https://commons.wikimedia.org/wiki/File:Lopez1870.jpg* Web. 01-Nov-2017.

67 *President Andres Rodriguez* 2008. Wiki Media. *https://commons.wikimedia.org/wiki/File:Andr%C3%A9s_Rodr%C3%ADguez_Pedotti.jpg* Web. 01-Nov-2017.

68 *President Alfredo Stoessner.* "N.d." Paraguayan Stamp. Wiki Media. *https://commons.wikimedia.org/wiki/File:Alfredo_Stroessner.jpg* Web. 01-Nov-2017.

69 Cruz, Jose. *General Lino Oviedo.,* 2008. Brazil News Agency. Wiki Media. *https://commons.wikimedia.org/wiki/File:Lino_Oviedo.jpg* Web. 01-Nov-2017.

70 Rueters. *Nissan SUV.* 1999. Used with permission.

71 Adomo, Jorge, *FOPE bomb unit removes explosive devicee.* 1997. Rueters, Used with permission.

72   *President Raul Cubas.* 2011. Wiki Media. *https://commons.wikimedia.org/wiki/ File:Ra%C3%BAl_Alberto_Cubas_Grau.jpg* Web. 01-Nov-2017.

73   Padwe, Jonathan. President Carlos Wasmosy. 1990. Wiki Media. *http://www. meatradio.com/ https://commons.wikimedia.org/wiki/File:Wasmosy_1990_ (cropped).jpg* Web. 01-Nov-2017.

74   Rueters. *Military armored vehicle at Paraguay Presidential Palace.* 1999. Used with permission.

75   Rueters. *Police confront protestor after Argana's assassination..* 1999. Used with permission.

76   Rueters. *Paraguay Police and Protests.* 1999. Used with permission.

77   Rueters, *Paraguay Protesters.* 1999. Used with permission.

78   Casal, Marcello Jr. *President Gonzalez Macchi.* 2003. Brazil News Agency. Wiki Media. *https://commons.wikimedia.org/wiki/File:Gonzalez_Macchi_2003.jpg* Web. 01-Nov-2017.

79   *U.S. Ambassador Gordon Mein.* "N.d." U.S. Department of State News Letter No. 89, September 1968. Wiki Media. *https://en.wikipedia.org/wiki/File:John-Gordon-Mein.jpg* Web. 01-Nov-2017.

80   ZackClark, *Antigua, Guatemala.* 2005. Wiki Media. *https://commons.wikimedia. org/wiki/File:GT056-Antigua_HillView.jpeg* Web. 01-Nov-2017.

81   Starnes, Robert W. *Grenade damage,* Guatemala. ©1989.

82   *President Bush and Stroocks.* 1990. Courtesy Freyre Family archives. Used with permission.

83   Chixoy. *La Aurora Airport.* 2006. Wiki Media. *https://commons.wikimedia.org/ wiki/File:Aeropuertodeguate.JPG* Web. 01-Nov-2017.

84   Justiciaya. *President Jorge Serrano Elias.* 2016. Wiki Media. *https://commons. wikimedia.org/wiki/File:Jorge_Serrano_Elias.jpg* Web. 01-Nov-2017.

85   *Richard Thornburgh.* U.S. Department of Justice. Circa 1988. Wiki Media. *https:// commons.wikimedia.org/wiki/File:Dick_Thornburgh.jpg* Web. 01-Nov-2017.

86   Starnes, Robert W. *Guatemala Military Outpost.* ©1990.

87   Starnes, Robert W. *Guatemala Farewell Reception.* ©1991

88   *Bolivia Bombing.* 1990. U.S. Dept. of State, Bureau of Diplomatic Security, publication no. 9869 *"Significant Incidents of Political Violence Against Americans",* 1990 edition, released July 1991. https://www.state.gov/documents/ organization/20307.pdf Web. 01-Nov-2017.

89   *Wild Bunch.* circa 1900. Wiki Media. *https://commons.wikimedia.org/wiki/ File:Wildbunchlarge.jpg* Web. 01-Nov-2017.

90   Starnes, Robert W. *Guatemala Animal Sacrifices.* ©1989.

91   Starnes, Robert W. *NZ Condolences.* ©2001.

92   *NZ Police at U.S. Embassy*. 2002. U.S. Department of State.

93   *Tiger Woods in New Zealand*. 2002. Fairfax Media. Used with Permission.

94   *Tiger Woods golfing in New Zealand. 2002*. Fairfax Media. Used with Permission.

95   Ennis, Ron T. *Deputy James Boyd*. 2013. Fort Worth Star-Telegram, via the Associated Press. Used with permission.

96   Alford, Jimmy, Evan Ebel's wrecked car. 2013. Wise County Messenger newspaper. Used with permission.

97   *Tom Clements*. "N.d." Colorado Dept. of Corrections. Used with permission.

98   *Evan Ebel*. "N.d." Colorado Dept. of Corrections. Used with permission.

99   *Nathan Collin Leon*. "N.d." Credit Facebook

100   Courtesy U.S. embassy, Wellington, New Zealand

101   Starnes, Robert W. *U.S. Ambassador Carol Mosley-Braun*. ©2001

102   *James Derrick*. "N.d." Used with permission.

103   DeLancy, Bob. *Pacific Coast Academy*. 2001. Video. Used with permission.

104   DeLancy, Bob. *Pacific Coast Academy*. 2001. Video. Used with permission.

105   DeLancy, Bob. *Pacific Coast Academy*. 2001. Video. Used with permission.

106   DeLancy, Bob. *Pacific Coast Academy*. 2001. Video. Used with permission.

107   DeLancy, Bob. *Pacific Coast Academy*. 2001. Video. Used with permission.

108   DeLancy, Bob. *Pacific Coast Academy*. 2001. Video. Used with permission.

109   *Raymond Millar*. 2017. Used with permission.

110   *George Washington Portrait*. Circa 1772. Charles Wilson Peale, Washington and Lee University. Wiki Media. Virginia *http://www.americanmilitary historymsw.com/blog/536357-washingtons-mission/ https://commons. wikimedia.org/wiki/File:Washington_1772.jpg* Web. 01-Nov-2017.

111   Jerrye and Klotz, Roy. *George Washington House*. 2012. Wiki Media. *https:// commons.wikimedia.org/wiki/File:GEORGE_WASHINGTON_HOUSE_-_ BARBADOS.jpg* Web. 01-Nov-2017.

112   *Map of the Eastern Caribbean*. 1991. Country Environmental Profile, Dominica. CCA/IRF/USAID. National Forestry Action Programme - Dominica: Executive Summary Produced by: Forestry Department *http://www.fao.org/ docrep/x5651e/x5651e01.htm* Web. 01-Nov-2017.

113   Anonymous. Underwater Unexploded Shell. 2007.

114   Buslovich, Michael. Ambassador Mary Ourisman. 2008. Wiki Media. *https:// commons.wikimedia.org/wiki/File:US_Navy_080704-N-8943B017_Cmdr._Edwin_ Kaiser,_commanding_officer_of_the_guidedmissile_frigate_USS_Simpson_ (FFG_56)_gives_U.S._Ambassador_to_the_Eastern_Caribbean_Mary_Ourisman,_ a_tour.jpg* Web. 01-Nov-2017.

115 Starnes, Robert. *Barbados Sunset.* ©2006.

116 Benedek, Emily Benedek, *Love Bandit, aka. Lanson.* 1992. *Redbook Magazine,* 98-101 and 118-120. Used with permission.

117 Benedek, Emily Benedek, *Lois Fuchs.* 1992. *Redbook Magazine,* 98-101 and 118-120. Used with permission.

118 Benedek, Emily Benedek, *Maryann Markle.* 1992. *Redbook Magazine,* 98-101 and 118-120. Used with permission.

119 Benedek, Emily Benedek, *Elizabeth Rodenroth.* 1992. *Redbook Magazine,* 98-101 and 118-120. Used with permission.

120 Benedek, Emily Benedek, *Karen Sue Prince.* 1992. *Redbook Magazine,* 98-101 and 118-120. Used with permission.

121 Benedek, Emily Benedek, *Ed Nendell.* 1992. *Redbook Magazine,* 98-101 and 118-120. Used with permission.

122 Benedek, Emily Benedek, *Love Bandit passport photo.* 1992. *Redbook Magazine,* 98-101 and 118-120. Used with permission.

123 Starnes, Robert W. *Borisch and Starnes display jewelry.* ©1992.

124 *Lois Fuchs,* 1992. Williamson County Sheriff's Office.

125 *Sievert, Ron J.* 2017. Used with permission.

126 *Lois Fuchs.* 1992. Williamson County Sheriff's Office.

127 *Marion DuCote.* 1992. Williamson County Sheriff's Office.

128 George Dudov. 1995. U.S. Department of State, reprinted by Austin American Statesman newspaper.

129 *Peter O. Ezekor.* 2004. Harris County Sheriff's Office, 2004.

130 United States Department of Justice, circa 1931. Wiki Media *https://commons.wikimedia.org/wiki/File:Al-Capone-Alcatraz-mug-shot-front.jpg* Web. 01-Nov-2017.

131 Starnes, Robert W. *Piecing together credit cards.* ©1992.

132 Starnes, Robert W. *Displaying fraudulent credit cards.* ©1992.

133 Starnes, Robert archives, *Larry J. Hollingsworth.* ©2017.

134 U.S.Congress. *Sen. Chuck Grassley.* 2002. Wiki Media. *https://commons.wikimedia.org/wiki/File:Sen_Chuck_Grassley_official.jpg* Web. 01-Nov-2017.

135 U.S. Government, *Donald Mancuso.* 1995. Wiki Media. *https://commons.wikimedia.org/wiki/File:Donald_Mancuso.jpg* Web. 01-Nov-2017.

136 *Margaret Thatcher.* William and Mary News, volume XXV, no. 16, 24-April-1996. Used with permission.

137 *Margaret Thatcher.* William and Mary News, volume XXV, no. 16, 24-April-1996. Used with permission.

138   *President George W. Bush jogging.* 1998. Chris Brannen archives.
      Used with permission.

139   *Texas Governor's Mansion arson attack.* 2008. Courtesy Texas State Preservation
      Board. Used with permission.

140   *Texas Governor's Mansion renovated.* "N.d.". Courtesy Friends of the Governor's
      Mansion. Used with permission.

141   Unknown. *U.S. Iranian hostage crisis.* 1979. Wiki Media. *https://commons.
      wikimedia.org/wiki/File:Iran_hostage_crisis_-_November_1979.jpg* Web. 01-
      Nov-2017.

142   U.S. Government. *President Reagan discuss bombing Libya.* 1986. Wiki Media.
      *https://commons.wikimedia.org/wiki/File:Libya_Bombing_Reagan_Meeting_14_
      March_1986.jpg* Web. 01-Nov-2017.

143   Awalt, Jesse B. *Muammar Gaddafi.* 2009. Wiki Media. *https://commons.
      wikimedia.org/wiki/File:Muammar_al-Gaddafi_at_the_AU_summit-LR.jpg*
      Web. 01-Nov-2017.

144   U.S. Department of Justice, *John Hinckley.* 1981. Wiki Media. *https://commons.
      wikimedia.org/wiki/File:John_Hinckley,_Jr._Mugshot.png* Web. 01-Nov-2017.

145   Libyan Information Ministry, *Libyan King Idris.* 1964. Wiki Media. *https://
      commons.wikimedia.org/wiki/File:King_Idris_I_of_Libya_August_15,_1965.jpg*
      Web. 01-Nov-2017.

146   Unknown, *Col. Gaddafi.* 1972. Wiki Media. *https://commons.wikimedia.org/wiki/
      File:Gaddafi_1972.jpg* Web. 01-Nov-2017.

147   *Col. Gaddafi and President Idi Amin Dada.* "N.d." World History Archive,
      Alamy Stock Photograph. Used with permission.

148   *Pan Am flight 103.* Air Accident Investigation Branch, 1988. Wiki Media. *https://
      commons.wikimedia.org/wiki/File:Pan_Am_Flight_103._Crashed_Lockerbie,_
      Scotland,_21_December_1988.jpg* Web. 01-Nov-2017.

149   *President Putin and Col. Gaddafi.* "N.d." Shutter Stock. Used with permission.

150   Starnes, Robert W. *Egypt camel ride at the Pyramids.* ©1994.

151   Carvin, Andy. *Hotel Sidi Driss.* 2005. Wiki Media. *https://commons.wikimedia.org/
      wiki/File:Hotel-sididriss.jpg* Web. 01-Nov-2017.

152   Elhusuni, Abdul-Jawad. *Hotel Cornithia, Tripioli.* 2012. Wiki Media. *https://
      commons.wikimedia.org/wiki/File:Corinthia_Hotel_Tripoli_Libya.JPG* Web.
      01-Nov-2017.

153   Starnes, Robert W. *Hotel Corinthia.* ©2004.

154   Starnes, Robert W. *Tripoli Old Town.* ©2004.

155   Starnes, Robert W. *Libyan Coppersmith.* ©2004.

156   Starnes, Robert W. *Libyan potato vendor.* ©2004.

157   Starnes, Robert W. *U.S. embassy, Tripoli.* ©2004.

158   Starnes, Robert W. *U.S. embassy, Tripoli ransacked.* ©2004.

159   Starnes, Robert W. *U.S. embassy, Tripoli, fake explosives.* ©2004.

160   Starnes, Robert W. *M-25 grenade at U.S. embassy, Tripoli.* ©2004.

161   Starnes, Robert W. *Certificate signed by Spiro J. Agnew.* ©2004.

162   Starnes, Robert W. *Flag discovered inside U.S. embassy, Tripoli.* ©2004.

163   *Flag inside U.S. ambassador's office Tripoli.* 2004.

164   Starnes, Robert W. *Flags displayed inside ambassador's office in Tripoli.* ©2004.

165   Starnes, Robert W. *Picture of President Nixon inside embassy, Tripoli.* ©2004.

166   Starnes, Robert W. *Caskets inside embassy, Tripoli.* ©2004.

167   Starnes, Robert W. *Gaddafi's bungalow, Tripoli.* ©2004.

168   Starnes, Robert W. *Surface to air missiles, Tripoli.* ©2004.

169   Starnes, Robert W. *Picture of President Carter inside embassy, Tripoli.* ©2004.

170   *Al-Saadi Gaddafi,* "N.d." Shutter Stock. Used witih permission.

171   Starnes, Robert W. *Camel lot, Tripoli.* ©2004.

172   Starnes, Robert W. *Libyan toothpaste, Tripoli.* ©2004.

173   Starnes, Robert W. *Tripoli street market, Tripoli.* ©2004.

174   Starnes, Robert W. *Boat builder, Tripoli.* ©2004.

175   Starnes, Robert W. *Museum, Tripoli.* ©2004.

176   Starnes, Robert W. *Museum ship mast exhibit, Tripoli.* ©2004.

177   Starnes, Robert W. *Libyan food game, Tripoli.* ©2004.

178   Meehan, Dan. *Tunisian Barber, Tripoli.* U.S. Department of State. 2004.

179   U.S. Department of State, *Moussa Koussa* (cropped). 2010. Flickr. *http://www. flickr.com/photos/statephotos/5013202545/* Web. 01-Nov-2017.

180   U.S. Department of State, *Secretary Clinton and Moussa Koussa* (cropped). 2010. Flickr. *http://www.flickr.com/photos/statephotos/5013202545/* Web. 01-Nov-2017.

181   Egghead06, *Former Libyan embassy in London.* 2012. Wiki Media. *https:// commons.wikimedia.org/wiki/File:Former_Libyan_Embassy,_St_James%27s_Sq,_ London.JPG* Web. 01-Nov-2017.

182   *Officer Yvonne Fletcher.* "N.d." Courtesy of the Mayor's Office of Policing and Crime, London City Hall. Used with permission.

183   U.S. Department of Energy. *Libyan uranium centrifuges.* 2007. Wiki Media *https://commons.wikimedia.org/wiki/File:Libya_centrifuges_2003_(at_Y12).jpg* Web 01-Nov-2017.

184   *Libyan female soldiers.* "N.d." Shutter Stock. Used with permission.

185   *Col. Gaddafi and female soldier.* 1999. Rueters. Used with permission.

186   Starnes, Robert W. *Benghazi street vendor.* ©2004.

187   Starnes, Robert W. *Benghazi golf course.* ©2004.

188   Starnes, Robert W. *Benghazi golfer.* ©2004.

189   Starnes, Robert W. *WWII headstone in Benghazi.* ©2004.

190   Starnes, Robert W. *Omar Mukhtar memorial, Libya.* ©2004.

191   Etching by Joseph F Sabin from a drawing by Hoff. USS *Philadelphia frigate grounded by Tripoli pirates.* Circa 1803. Courtesy U.S. National Archives and Records Administration. *https://www.archives.gov/research/military/navy-ships/sailing-ships.html* Web. 01-Nov-2017.

192   Copy of etching by Chappel, Alonzo. *Decatur's Conflict with the Algerine at Tripoli.* Circa 1858. Wiki Media. *https://commons.wikimedia.org/wiki/File: Decatur_algerine.jpg* Web. 01-Nov-2017.

193   Waterhouse, Charles. Painting depicting Battle of Derna, Libay. "N.d." Wiki Media. *https://commons.wikimedia.org/wiki/File:Attack_on_Derna_by_Charles_Waterhouse_01.jpg* Web. 01-Nov-2017.

194   Peale, Rembrandt. Painting of Consul General William Eaton. circa 1813. Wiki Media. *https://commons.wikimedia.org/wiki/File:WilliamEaton.jpg* Web. 01-Nov-2017.

195   Unknown. *USMC First Lieutenant Presley O'Bannon.* "N.d." Wiki Media. *https://commons.wikimedia.org/wiki/File:PresleyOBannon.jpg* Web. 01-Nov-2017.

196   Starnes, Robert W. *Zeus Temple in Libya.* ©2004.

197   Starnes, Robert W. *American flag flown in Derna, Libya.* ©2004.

198   Starnes, Robert W. *RCC headquarters building in Benghazi.* ©2004.

199   Starnes, Robert W. *American cemetery in Tripoli.* © 2004.

200   Peterson, Jacob. *Painting of the frigate USS Constitution.* circa 1845. Wiki Media *https://commons.wikimedia.org/wiki/File:Jacob_Petersen_-_USS_Constitution_-_1845.jpg* Web. 01-Nov-2017.

201   Unknown, *Portrait of Francis Scott Key.* "N.d." U.S. Library of Congress. *ttp://www.loc.gov/pictures/item/2004672074/* Web. 01-Nov-2017.

202   Coyle, Wilbur F. *National Star Spangled Banner Centennial, Baltimore, Maryland.* 1914. Wiki Media. *https://commons.wikimedia.org/wiki/File:Fort_McHenry_flag.jpg* Web. 01-Nov-2017.

203   Starnes, Robert W. *Libya postal stamp depicting USS Philadelphia.* ©2004.

204   Starnes, Robert W. *American flag presented to Texas Governor Perry by Robert W. Starnes.* ©2004.

205   Starnes, Robert W. *Texas Governor Perry, David Armistead, and Robert W. Starnes.* ©2004.

INDEX

211 Crew, 189

Abu Ghraib prison, 303
Acheson, Dean, 257
Agência Brasileira de Inteligência
 (ABIN), 47
Aggie Grey Hotel, 176, 179
Aggie-Longhorn football game, 11
Agnew, Spiro, 287
Akatarawa Forest, 165
Akbar, Hasan K., 39
Akihito (Crown Prince), 243
Alfieri, Lincoln, 108–9
Alpirez, Julio Roberto, 127
al-Qadi, Marwan 'Adnan, 50
al-Qaeda, 47
al-Safadi, Marwan, 50, 51, 56–60, 95
Amazonian Guards, 312–14
American hostages
in Tehran, Iran, 2
American-Libyan relations, 265, 286,
 307, 316
Andean adventures, 155–60
Anthony, Dr. Kenny, 197
Apollonia, 325
Arajs Kommando, 93
Argaña, Luis María, 101, 103
Arizona, 187
Armistead, David, 249–57, 258–60, 332
and President George W. Bush, 255
Armistead, George, 332
Army's Criminal Investigative Command
 (CID), 38
Auschwitz concentration camp, 45
Austin, 3, 4, 11, 12, 24, 28, 30, 61, 62, 73,
 76, 196, 204, 207, 208, 212, 213, 217,
 218, 219, 244, 249, 251, 256, 257, 258,
 333, 343

auto-theft cartels, 149–53
Awethe, Ibrahim Malmood, 49–52

Bainbridge, William, 322
Baker, James, 127
Barbados, 191
Barbary Coast countries
 U.S. agreement and, 321
Barbary Wars, 315, 325, 329
Barbie, Klaus, 66
Barbie, Nikolaus "Klaus", 156
Barrios, Carlos Ortiz, 74
 of Baltimore, 332
Battle of Derna, 321
Bay, Michael, 167
Baylor University, 10
Belize and Guatemalua relations, 126
Benedek, Emily, 210
Benghazi, 315–19, 327
Benghazi Revolutionary Command
 Council (RCC), 328
Benghazi War Cemetery, 318
Bibb, Joe, 48
Bible, Dana X., 12
Bigbie, William, 192
bin Laden, Osama, 47
Bird, John (Byrd), 331
Bond, John, 31
Borisch, Tom, 203, 210, 211
Bower, Walter, 75
Boyd, James, 173
Brannen, Chris, 252, 254
Brigham Young University, 187
British Garrison, 192
broomstick
speeding, 5–7
Browne, Lewis
 Stranger Than Fiction, 287

Bryant, Bear, 10
bucket list locations, 325
Bush, George, 266
Bush, George H. W., 125, 306
Bush, George W., 196, 197, 255
Butcher of Lyon, 66

Capone, Al, 230
Capone-ized, 234
Capon-ized, 234
Carlson, Cody, 8
Carnes, Burt, 212, 213
Carr, Geneva, 188
Carter, Jimmy, 292
Cartisano, 188
Cartisano, Stephen, 187
Cartisano, Stephen, 184–85, 184
Cassidy, Butch, 156
ceasefire
    between Palestine Liberation
    Organization and Israel, 26
Central Intelligence Agency
    and Guatemalan politics, 131
Challenger Foundation, 184
Challenger Foundation Program, 187
Charles (prince), 27, 244, 249
Chase, Kristen, 187
Chase, Kristin, 184
Chicago Cold Storage Building Fire, 209
Chichicastenango, Guatemala, 158
Chilo
    encounter with a spider monkey,
    135–37
Chulabhorn Walailak (princess), 243
Cindy, 315
Ciudad del Este, 46, 51, 54, 55
Clancy, Tom
    Patriot Games, 33
claps man, 13
Clarkson, Jeremy, 160
Clements, Tom, 173, 175
Clinton, Bill, 51, 56, 125
CNPZ, 155
College of William and Mary, 244
Cooper, Gary, 176
Costa Rica, 187
counterintelligence
    and the DSS, 309
    coup d'état
    in Paraguay, 49, 33–34
Crider, Joseph Peter, 2–3
Crime Stoppers, 208

Crockett, Davy, 28
Cukurs, Herberts, 93

Dallas Cowboys Cheerleader, 12
Debayle Anastasio "Tachito" Somoza, 101
Decatu, Stephen, 322
Defense Criminal Investigative Service
    (DCIS), 235
Delancy, Bob, 178–80, 189
Derna adventure, 325–27
Derrick, Jim, 177, 179–80, 182–84, 186,
    283, 295
DeVine, Michael, 125, 126
Diplomacy for the '70s, 287
Diplomatic Security Service (DSS), 27–29
Diplomatic Security Training, 31
Dirty Martin's Place, 251
Dole, Bob, 56
domestic mission
    and the DSS, 30
Dorsett, Tony, 10
Drew, Charles William, 237
drunken sailors, 193–95
DSS Mobile Security Division, 52
DSS Office of Threat Analysis, 310
DSS Protective Intelligence
    Investigations (PII), 57
Ducote, Marion Joseph, 213–15, 215
Ducote, Marion Josephn. *See also* Love
    Bandit
Dudov, George, 217–21

Eagleburger, Lawrence S., 244
Eaton, William, 322–23, 330
Ebel, Evan Spencer, 173–75, 181, 189
El Al Israel Airlines office, 79
Elías, Jorge Antonio Serrano, 131
Elliott, Pamela, 187
Ellis, T.S. III, 239, 241
extradition
    of al-Safadi, 58
    of Fourie, 70
Ezekor, Peter, 225–29

Fadlallah, Sayyid Muhammad Hussayn, 47
FBI, 29, 59, 81, 82, 84, 85, 86, 93, 128, 131,
    132, 159, 203, 204, 210, 219, 220, 221,
    225, 226, 227, 228
First Barbary War, 297, 331
First Eagle Oil Production Corporation, 217
Fletcher, Yvonne Joyce, 306

FOPE, 52, 57, 82
  lockdown of, 110
FOPE's assistance and U.S. Embassy, 112
Foster, Jodie, 267
Fourie, William
  sentencing of, 76
Fox, Randy, 207
Fredericksburg, 3, 218
Friedman, Paul L., 98
Fuchs, Lois, 207
Fuchs, Lois Elaine, 204, 210, 211
  extradicion of, 212
Fuchs, Randy Lee, 204, 209
Fuller, Lonnie, 187

Gaddafi, Al-Saadi, 56–60
Gaddafi, Muammar, 2, 265, 269–73
Gaddafi, Munamar, 289, 312–14
Gannon, Matthew, 273
Gehrig, Lou, 9
Gentry, Dennis, 8
Gergen, David, 244
Germany, Düsseldorf, 219
Gilstrap, Howard Clifford "Bully", 11
Goff, Phil, 167
gold-leaf paintings, 14
Gorbachev, Mikhail, 243
Grassley, Chuck, 240–42
Grau, Raúl Cubas, 106
  resignation of, 115
Green Bay Packers, 7
Guevara, Che, 157
Gulf War, 128

haircut adventure, 300–303
Harty, Maura, 104, 112–16
Harvey, Paul, 194
Hawaii, 187
Hayes, Rutherford B., 39
Heartbeat (McGrath), 306
Heyn, Torres, 114, 116
Hezbollah, 25, 47, 50, 51
Hezbollah terrorist, 77
Hinckley, John Warnock Jr., 267
Hinds, Neil, 198
Hollingsworth, Larry Joe
  criminal activity of, 236–42
Hotel Corinthia Tripoli, 279–80, 293
Houston, 32, 37, 38, 70, 203, 209, 220,
  225, 226, 228, 229, 230, 231, 232, 233,
  234, 244, 249, 256, 257, 263, 273, 306
Houston, Sam, 257

Hudspeth, Michael, 57, 58–59
Hudspeth, Michael J., 95–98
human rights violations in Guatemala, 125
Hussein, Saddam, 128

Idris I (king), 270
immobilized Packer, 7
Inman, Bobby Ray, 27
Internal Revenue Service, 187, 215
Iran hostage crisis, 265
Iranian Shiite terrorist group, 51
Islamic Revolution, 292
Islamic terrorism, 26
Islamic terrorist operations in Paraguay, 37
Islamic terrorist support epicenters of, 47
Israel, 26
Israeli Embassy (Argentina)
  car bomb and, 48
Israeli Religious Community Building, 79

Jackson, Peter, 164
Jefferson, Thomas, 2, 322
Jewish-Argentine community center
  building car bomb and, 48
Joan Rivers Show, 210
Joint Terrorism Task Force (JTTF), 81

Kadi, Marwan Abid Adam, 50
Karamanli, Yusuf, 321
Keenan, John, 242
Kennedy, John F. statute of, 155
Kennedy, Lydia, 62
Key Bank, 188
Key, Francis Scott, 332
Khomeini, Ayatollah, 287
Kiser, Terry, 176
Koussa, Moussa, 305–7
Kramer, Mary, 196
Kyle Field, 11

La Belle discotheque bombing of, 272
Ladd, Austin, 3
Lagarto (Lizard), 91, 113, 116
Lake Titicaca, 158
Lanson, Mark, 204–6
Lariviere, Ronald, 273
law enforcement
  the unpleasant aspects, 13
Leavitt, Mike, 180
Lebanon, 25
Lee, Henry ("Lighthorse Harry"), 192
Lee, Robert E, 192

Leon, Nathan Collin, 173, 175
Lezcono, 105–6
Libya
    assignment in, 263–68
    reestablishment of dilomatic
      relations, 2
Libya adventure, 263–68
Libyan Football Federation, 293
lip vice, 7–8
living alarm system, 15
López, Francisco Solano, 103
Lord of the Flies, 182
Love Bandit, 204, 239
    male victim of, 208–9
Luckenbach, 218
Lunday, Paulina, 3

Macchi, Luis Ángel González, 108–9,
    113–15
MAGLOCLEN, 235
Makki, Bassam Gharib, 96–100
Makki, Mohamad, 85
Makki, Mohamad Gharib, 96
    posing as, 80–89
Mameluke sword, 323
Mancuso, Donald, 235–36, 240–42
Mandela, Nelson, 243
Marine Corps, 26
Marine Corps hymn, 323
Markle, Maryann, 204–6
Martinez, Estanislao Lesme, 68
Martinez, Pedro, 63, 101–3
Mastico, 322
McCaul, Michael, 333
McFarland, Stephen, 105
McGrath, Jim Heartbeat, 306
Mein, 125
Mein's, 128
Melnyk, Eugene, 194
Mengele, Josef, 45–46
Millar, Ray, 185, 186
Mohammed, Khalid Sheikh, 47
Montserrat, 195–96
Moseley-Braun, Carol, 176–77
Mukhtar, Omar, 318
Multi-Legal Assistance Treaty (MLAT), 214
multinational peacekeeping forces, 26

Nasrallah, Hassan, 81, 97
Nasser, Gamal Abdel, 270
national anthem, 332

National Automobile Theft Bureau
    (NATB), 150
National Science Foundation (NSF)
    Antarctica Program, 164
Nendell, Ed, 209–10
Néstor Paz Zamora Commission, 155
Nevis, 188
New Braunfels, 18, 218, 220, 221
New Mexico Bureau of Vital Statistics
    (BVS), 203
New York Yankees, 9
New Zealand, 125, 163, 164, 165, 166,
    167, 168, 169, 170, 171, 172, 175, 176,
    178, 180, 185, 186, 299
New Zealand Open (2001)
    security cost for, 172
Nixon, Richard, 289
No Double Standard policy, 171
Noor (queen), 243
North Africa inhabitants of, 277
North American Free Trade Agreement
    (NAFTA), 244
Nowlin, James R., 221
nuclear weapons program
    Libya, 312

O'Bannon, Presley, 322–23, 330
O'Connor, Daniel Emmett, 273
Ogden, Steve, 236
OJ, beware of, 14–16
Oklahoma, 188, 205, 206, 207
Olsen, Patrick, 9
Omnibus Diplomatic Security and
    Antiterrorism Act, 27
Operation Snowcap, 145–47
Ortiz, Dianna, 125
Ourisman, Mandy, 198
Ourisman, Mary, 197–99
overseas mission, and the DSS, 29
Oviedo, Lino, 49
Oviedo, Lino César, 103–15

Pacaya Volcano, 147–48
Pacific Coast Academy, 177–89, 186, 283
Pacific Coast Foundation, 188
Packer, immobilized, 7
Palestine Liberation Organization, 26
Pan Am Flight 103, 170, 265, 272
Paraguay, 33–34
    population of, 40
Paraguay Fuerza de Operaciones
    Especiales (FOPE), 44

Paraparaumu Beach Golf Club, 168
Parola, Wayne T., 85
passport fraud
    Larry Joe Hollingworh and, 239
Patriot Games (Clancy), 33
Peace Corps Volunteer (PCV)
    in Paraguay, 41
Pedernales River, 3
peeping Anne, 4
Pelé, 294
Perry, Rick, 256, 333
Peru, 220
Pflugerville, 218
Philadelphia Restaurant, 297–98
Pickersgill, Mary, 332
pink raccoon, 12–13
Pirates of the Barbary Coast, 2
Ponzi scheme, 217
Procter, Karen Sue, 207–8, 214
Puerto Rico, 187

raccoon
    pink, 12–13
Reagan, Ronald, 27, 265, 267, 272
Reagan, Ronald Wilson, 326
Record Breaker, 232
Red Castle Museum, 280
Redbook Magazine, 210
Revolutionary Command Council
    (RCC), 270
Revolutionary Nuns, 312–14
Rigby, 229–34
Rihanna, 193
Rio Group Conference, 107
Road Roaches, 3, 14
Rodriguez, Andrés, 103
Rodríguez, Andrés, 67
Rosebud News, The, 19
Rosenburg, Elizabeth, 206–7, 214
Ruggiero, Tony, 213
Ruth, Babe, 9

Sahara Desert, 276, 295
sailors, drunken, 193–95
Salt Lake Tribune, 186, 187
Samoa, 174, 175, 176, 177, 178, 179,
    181, 183, 184, 185, 186, 187, 188, 189,
    223, 283
Samoa, Apia, 185
Sartin, Darren, 73, 75
Sciocchetti, Tina, 98
Scotland Yard, 244

September 11 terrorist attacks, 165–67
Service, Robert, 51, 107
Shawn, 315
Sheikha Mozah (First Lady), 243
Sherrill, Jackie, 9–11
Shia Islamic terrorists, 50
Shiite terrorists, 25
Shultz, George, 27, 275
Shultz, George P., 156
Sievert, Ron, 213, 214
Slack, Craig, 73, 75
Smith, Anna Nicole, 197
Smith, Charlie, 70
Snake Farm Zoo, 18
snake-eaters, 53
Sorge, John G., 85
Southern Methodist University
    cheerleaders, 11
Spanish lessons, 14
Sparks, Sam, 76
speeding broomstick, 5–7
spider monkey encounter, 135–37
St. Lucia, 197
State Department
    U.S. Department of State, 127, 156,
    169, 170, 185, 188, 220, 228, 236, 292
Steinberg, Mark, 170
Stevenson, Robert Louis, 176
Stranger Than Fiction (Browne), 287
Stroessner, Alfredo, 46, 103
Stroock, Thomas, 124–25, 126–33, 152, 153
Sugerland Express, The, 6
suicide bomber, 26
Sundance Kid, the, 156
Swindells, Charles, 168

Tacumbú Prison, 69
Taylor, Phil, 139
Teaff, Grant, 8
Tehran, Iran, 2
Temple of Zeus, 325
terrorist attack
    on U.S. Marine Corps barracks, 25–26
terrorist attacks
    statistics about, 26
Texas A&M University, 9
Texas Governor's Protective Detail,
    249–60
Texas revolution, 27
Texas State Police Academy, 2, 3
Thatcher, Margaret, 244–46
Third Reich, 46

Thornburgh, Richard L. "Dick", 129, 131–33
Tiwanaku Aztec ruins, 158
Tonkin,, Tom, 126
Travis, Lilly, 62
tri-border area, 45, 50
Tripoli, 295
Truman, Harry, 131
Turkish bathhouse adventure, 299

U.S. Air Force, 187
U.S. Army's Airborne
    terrorist and, 38
U.S. Attorney, 62, 63, 88, 100, 128, 129, 133, 213, 219, 226, 237, 238, 242, 333
U.S. Department of Justice, 186, 188
U.S. Department of State, 32
U.S. Department of State Bureau of
    Diplomatic Security (DS), 27
U.S. Embassy
    in Tehran, Iran, 2
U.S. embassy (Paraguay)
    bomb threat and, 45–60
U.S. Embassy building (Libya)
    decommissioning of, 283–92
U.S. Embassy takeover, 267
U.S. Immigration and Naturalization
    Service (INS), 233
U.S. Marine Security Guard, 155
U.S. Marshals Service's Fugitive Task
    Force, 63
U.S. Postal Service, 187
U.S. Virgin Islands, 187
U.S. Visa Waiver Program, 218
Ugarte, Augusto José Ramón Pinochet, 67
United Fruit Company, 120, 133
United States-Libya relations
    reestablishment of, 305–14
University of Alabama, 10
University of Texas seal, 11
uranium, 311
USS Arizona Memorial, 167

USS Constitution Museum, 289, 331, 333
USS Intrepid, 322
USS Philadelphia, 298, 322, 333, 334
Utah, 187

Vance, Terry, 17, 18
Vienna Convention of Diplomatic
    Relations, 193
Vineyard Church members
    American missionaries and, 112
Violent Gangs Task Force, 225, 226
Voight, Jon, 186
Volcano Soufriere, 195
von Steuben, Friedrich Wilhelm, 332

War of 1812, 332
Warner, John, 244
Washington, D.C., 183
Washington, George, 191, 192, 331
Wasmosy, Juan Carlos, 103, 107, 113
Water, The, 3
Wells, H. G., 189
Weston, David, 187
White, Mark, 28
Who's Who in the Arab World 1971–1972, 287
Wilhelm, William E., 116
Williams, Steve, 168
Willy Wonka & the Chocolate Factory, 31
witch encounter
    in Bolivia, 157
    in Guatemala, 157–58
Witches' Market, 157
Wolf/Wolfman, 185
Woods, Tiger, 164
    threats against, 168–72
World Trade Center attack, 51
Wurstfest, 218, 220, 221

yellowcake, 311

ENDNOTES

[1] Carl W. Buehner, Second Assistant in the Young Men's Mutual Improvement Association.

[2] Les Stroud, Survivorman, Season 3, Episode 6, Paupa, New Guinea, aired December 19, 2008 on OLN.

[3] Roberts, Austin Ladd. "Every Song a Story Every Story a Conversation." Spoken Word. *http://www.laddroberts.com/spoken-word (accessed March 1, 2017).*

[4] Britannica.com/event/1983-beirut-barracks-bombings. *http://www.britannica.com/event/1983-Beirut-Barracks-bombings.*

[5] Colonel Charles Dallachie (Ret.). "Commentary: Remember the Sacrifices of Beirut." Marine Corps Times, October 22, 2015. *https://www.marinecorpstimes.com/opinion/2015/10/23/commentary-remember-the-sacrifices-of-beirut/*

[6] Contributor unknown. "Descendants of Capt. John Bond." *http://home.earthlink.net/~fbond/bond01/d1.htm*

[7] United States v. Murad. 1992, case no. 4:92-cr-00086, U.S. District Court, Southern District of Texas.

[8] Brett Barrouquere. "Appeal for soldier convicted in '03 grenade attack." Associated Press, August 27, 2014. *http://theleafchronicle.com/story/news/local/fort-camp-bell/2014/08/27/military-court-appeal-akbar-fragging-deaths-fort-campbell-ku-wait/14675557/*

[9] Paraguay-Latin America: The Case of Dr. Mengele (u). Declassified and released by the Central Intelligence Agency, sources, methods exemption 3B2B, Nazi War Crimes Disclosure Act date 2000, 2008.

[10] "A Global Overview of Narcotics-funded Terrorist and Other Extremist Groups." Federal Research Division, Library of Congress, May 2002, 6.

[11] Library of Congress. "Terrorist and organized crime groups in the tri-border area (TBA) of South America." A Report Prepared by the Federal Research Division, Library of Congress un-der an Interagency Agreement with the Crime and Narcotics Center Director of Central Intelligence July 2003 (Revised December 2010).

Additional Footnotes: Bin Laden Reportedly Spent Time in Brazil in '95," *Washington Post,* March 18, 2003, A24; "Bin Laden esteve em Foz do Iguaçu e até deu palestra em mesquita [Bin Laden Was in Foz do Iguaçu and Even Gave A Lecture in A Mosque], O Estado de São Paulo, March 16, 2003. [Estadao.com: *http://www.estado.estadao.com.br/editorias/ 2003/03/16/int026.html]*; and Policarpo Junior, "Ele esteve no Brasil" [He Was in Brazil], Veja on-line, no. 1,794 (March 19, 2003), *http://veja.abril.com.br/190303/p_058.html.*

[a] Additional footnotes: Reuters, "Bin Laden Reportedly Spent Time in Brazil in '95," Washington Post, March 18, 2003, A24; and O Estado de São Paulo [Internet version-www], March 9, 2003, as translated for FBIS, "Brazil: Terrorist Khalid Sheikh Mohamed's Passage Through Brazil Reported," March 9, 2003 (FBIS Document ID: LAP20030308000052); and A Gazeta do Iguaçu, March 10, 2003, 2, as translated for FBIS, "Brazilian Police: Khalid Shaykh Visit to Triborder in 1995 Unconfirmed," March 10, 2003 (FBIS Document ID: LAP20030311000123). [b] Kevin G. Hall, "Accused al-Qaida Ter-rorist Spent time in Brazil, Police Say," Knight Ridder Tribune News Service, March 13, 2003, 1. *https://www.loc.gov/rr/frd/pdf-files/TerrOrgCrime_TBA.pdf*

[12] Author unknown. "Terrorism: Bombings in Argentina." Jewish Virtual Library, May 2016. *http://www.jewishvirtuallibrary.org/jsource/Terrorism/argentina.html.*

[13] Argentine Secretariat of Intelligence submitted a 500-page report to the then President, Eduardo Duhalde, on the AMIA bomb-ing, asserting that the Hezbollah operatives used C4 plastic explosives that came from Ciudad del Este in the [AMIA] attack. A. F. Trevisi, Research Assistant. Assessing the Terrorist Threat in the Tri-Border Area of Brazil, Paraguay and Argentina. International Institute for Counter-terrorism. October 2013.

Additional Footnote: Raul Kollmann, "Responsibility for Argentine-Jewish Center Bombing Attributed to Iran," FBIS Document ID: LAP20030119000009, Página/12 (January 19, 2003). *https://www.ict.org.il/UserFiles/Trevisi%202013.pdf*

[14] Matt Levitt. "Hizbullah narco-terrorism - a growing cross border threat." HIS Defense, Risk and Security Consulting, Sept. 2012, page 38.

[15] Benedetta Berti. "Reassessing the Transnational Terrorism-Criminal Link in South America's Tri-Border Area." Terrorism Moni-tor, September 22, 2008, volume 6, issue 18. *https://jamestown.org/program/reassessing-the-transnational-terror-ism-criminal-link-in-south-americas-tri-border-area/*

[16] Andres Oppenheimer, "U.S. Fears Islamic Terrorist Influ-ence in South America - Training and Equipment Offered to Three Countries." Knight Ridder Newspapers, 01-Jan-1998. *http://community.seattletimes.nwsource.com/archive/?date= 19980101&slug=2726361*

[17] Renee Novakoff, Senior Analyst, US Southern Command. Islamic Terrorist Activities in Latin America: Why the Region and the US Should be Concerned. Air and Space Power Journal. July 2008. *http://www.au.af.mil/au/afri/aspj/apjinternational/apj-s/2008/2tri08/novakoffeng.htm*

[18] Staff Writer. "Paraguay Extradites Terror Suspect to U.S." Washington CNN, World News Story Page, 14-Nov-1996, viewed 25-Oct-2016. *http://www.cnn.com/WORLD/9611/13/briefs.pm/terrorist.html?_s=PM:WORLD*

[19] Library of Congress. Terrorist and organized crime groups in the Tri-border area (TBA) of South America. A Report Prepared by the Federal Research Division, Library of Congress under an Interagency Agreement with the Crime and Narcotics Center Director of Central Intelligence July 2003 (Revised December 2010) *https://www.loc.gov/rr/frd/pdf-files/TerrOrgCrime_TBA.pdf*

[20] US v. Marwan Kadi, case no. 96-CR-683-1. May 30, 1997; U.S. District Court, Northern District of Illinois.

[21] Chris Webb & Carmelo Lisciotto. "Klause Barbie: The Butcher of Lyon." Holocaust Education & Archive Research Team (H.E.A.R.T.) 2009. *http://www.holocaustresearch project.org/nazioccupation/barbie.html*

[22] US v. William Fourie, November 10, 1999, case no. A-97-CR-160(1)SS; U.S. District Court, Western District of Texas.

[23] U.S. Federal Prisoner file no. 79555-080.

[24] Stadelheimer Prison Memo, November 21, 1989, file no. IId-321/89.

[25] First Criminal Chamber of the Munich Landgericht vs. Bas-sam Gharib Makki, Bavarian Ministry of Justice, Judgment, December 4, 1998, case number Gz-9352-be-u-2580/98.

[26] Germany v. Bassam Gharib Makki, case no. Gz.1 KLs 112 Js 3948/89, pages 1–24. First Criminal Chamber of Munich Landger-icht, Judge Kliener, German court order dated December 22, 1989.

[27] *The Matrix*, directed by Wachowski, Lana, and Wachowski, Lilly. Cast: Keanu Reeves, Carrie-Anne Moss. Warner Bros. March 31, 1999.

[28] US vs Bassam Gharib Makki, case no. 98-334 (PLF), March 1, 1999, U.S. District Court, District of Columbia.

[29] Ibid (Hudspeth affidavit, exhibit 13, dated February 26, 1999).

[30] Ibid (Tripp affidavit, exhibit 24, dated March 1, 1999).

[31] Ibid.

[32] 47 F.Supp. 2d 25, *;1999 U.S. Dist. LEXIS 6982,**

[33] Ibid (Hector Rodriguez affidavit, exhibit 23, dated March 1, 1999).

[34] Association for Diplomatic Studies and Training, Oral His-tory Project, Charles Stuart Kennedy interview of Ambassador Robert E. Service, February 24, 1998. *http://adst.org/wp-content/uploads/2013/12/Service-Robert-E.pdf*

[35] U.S. Department of State; Country Report on Human Rights and Practices; February 23, 2000.

[36] U.S. Department of State, Country Report on Human Rights and Practices, February 23, 2001, updated September 10, 2016. *https://www.state.gov/j/drl/rls/hrrpt/2000/wha/823.htm*

[37] Ibid (Kennedy interview of Ambassador Robert Service) February 1998.

[38] U.S. government, CIA memorandum no. 0617/68, 29-Aug-1968, declassified Sept. 2001.

[39] Association for Diplomatic Studies and Training, Oral His-tory Project, Andrew Low Kennedy interview of Ambassador Thomas F. Stroock, November 27, 1993. *http://www.adst.org/OH%20TOCs/Stroock,%20Thomas%20F.toc.pdf*

[40] UPI, Jorge Banales, "Lawmakers Demand US-Guatemalan Papers." May 2, 1996. *http://www.upi.com/Archives/1996/05/02/Lawmakers-demand-US-Guatemalan-papers/6114831009600/*

[41] Casper Tribute, Made in Wyoming, "Truth, Justice and the Tom Stroock Way," by Dana Bieber, *http://www.madeinwyoming.net/profiles/stroock.php*

[42] Ibid.

[43] U.S. Department of State, Bureau of Diplomatic Security, publication no. 9869 "Significant Incidents of Political Violence Against Americans." 1990 edition, released July 1991.

[44] U.S. Department of State, Foreign Affairs Manual, Section 7, Chapter 050.

[45] John Strege. "New Details Emerge from Cyanide Threat at New Zealand Open in Which Tiger Woods Played in '02." Golf Di-gest, March 11, 2015. *http://www. golfdigest.com/story/new-details-emerge-from-cyanide.*

[46] Sports Illustrated, Vault, "This Week," by Sal Johnson, January 21, 2002. *http://www. si.com/vault/2002/01/21/8107749/the-week*

[47] James Derrick's personal diary, 2001. Courtesy of the Der-rick family.

[48] Christopher Smith. Justice Department Is Investigating Carti-sano for Teen Treatment Camp. The Salt Lake Tribune. 2002.

[49] Angela K. Brown. "Bomb-Making Materials Found in Evan Ebel's Car." Associated Press. *http://denver.cbslocal.com/2013/03/26/bomb-making-materials-found-in-evan-ebels-car. Last updated March 26, 2013.*

[50] George Washington's Mount Vernon. *http://www.mountvernon.org/george-washington/washingtons-youth/journey-to-barbados*

[51] cott Woodson Bigbie, The Descendants of George Bigbie of Virginia. (Lulu, 1994-2010), 28-29.

[52] Emily Benedek. "Love Bandit." Redbook Magazine, Au-gust 1992, pp. 98-101 and 118-120.

[53] Name and occupation changed by request.

[54] Ibid., 100.

[55] Ibid., 100.

[56] Melissa Moore. "Texas Love Bandit recognized as suspect-ed Louisiana swindler." Baton Rouge Advocate, page 1B, February 6, 1994.

[57] US v. John Doe; aka Randy Fuchs, case no. A-93-CR-11(2)JRN; September 16, 1993; U.S. District Court, Western District of Texas.

[58] Ibid.

[59] Rickie Windle. "Dudov guilty of federal money laundering charges." Austin American Statesman, 1994: A1.

[60] Ibid., A16.

[61] Ibid., A16.

[62] US v. Georg Peter Dudov; aka George Peter DudovA-94-CR-14JRN; March 2, 1995; U.S. District Court, Western District of Texas.

[63] "Nations Hospitable to Organized Crime and Terrorism," Federal Research Division, Library of Congress under an Interagency Agreement with the United States Government, October 2003.

[64] USA v. Ezekor, case no. 4:94CR00065-00; dated 21-June-1994; U.S. District Court, Southern District of Texas

[65] Unknown, "Nigerian gets jail in insurance scam." Houston Chronicle newspaper, 18-Dec-2007. *http://www.chron.com/news/houston-texas/article/Nigerian-gets-jail-in-insurance-scam-1992778.php.*

[66] Robert W. Starnes. "How Passport and Visa Fraud Relate to Identity Fraud." Diplomatic Security Service, remarks to the Texas State Senate, Infrastructure Development and Security Subcommit-tee, Austin, Texas, March 31, 2003.

[67] Senator Charles Grassley. Congressional Record. Vol 146.46. pages S2617-S2636. Statements on Introduced Bills and Joint Resolutions. 12-April-2000.

[68] US v. Larry J. Hollingsworth, case no. 1:96CR00014-001; 10-Jun-1996; U.S. District Court, Eastern District of Virginia.

[69] Congressional Record Report (S-13641, 11/02/1999). http://www.gpo.gov/fdsys/pkg/CREC-1999-11-02/pdf/CREC-1999-11-02-pt1-PgS13641.pdf, accessed March 3, 2016.

[70] Congressional Record Report, 106th Congress, 2nd Session, Issue: vol. 146, No. 5, daily edition, January 31, 2000, "The Penta-gon's Acting Inspector General," pages S130–S132.

[71] Corportationwiki, accessed 19-Oct-2017. *https://www.corporationwiki.com/Florida/Fleming-Island/larmar-enterprises-inc/25772467.aspx.*

[72] Margaret, The Lady Thatcher, Future Challenges in a Changing World. Speech during William & Mary College confer-ence, Quest for Western Security Amid Global Uncertainty. 11-April-1996.

[73] Texas DPS interoffice memorandum, Sgt. Escalante to Texas Public Safety Com-mission Chairman Allan Polunsky, dated July 28, 2008, *http://media.graytvinc.com/documents/DPS+Mansion+Fire+Report.pdf.*, accessed 2-Aug-2016.

[74] Author unknown. "Texas Safety Head Retires after Gover-nor's Mansion Fire." USA Today, July 11, 2008. *http://usatoday30.usatoday.com/news/nation/2008-07-11-texas-_N.htm*, accessed 2-Aug-2016.

[75] Sean Rayment. "Libyan cadet to train with William at Sandhurst." The Telegraph, 26-Aug-2005. *http://www.telegraph.co.uk/news/uknews/1497112/Libyan-cadet-to-train-with-William-at-Sandhurst.html*

[76] Bernard Gwertzman. "US Reports Shooting Down 2 Libya Jets that Attacked 2 F-14s Over Mediterranean." New York Times, August 20, 1981. *http://www.nytimes.com/1981/08/20/world/us-reports-shooting-down-2-libya-jets-that-attacked-f-14-s-over-mediterrane.html?pagewanted-all*, accessed 2-Aug-2016.

[77] Author unknown. "Text of the State Department report in Libya under Qaddafi." NY Times, 9-Jan-1986. *http://www.nytimes.com/1986/01/09/world/text-of-the-state-department-report-in-libya-under-qaddafi.html?pagewanted-all, ac-cessed 2-Aug-2016.*

[78] Arms Control Association, updated by Alexandra Schmitt and Yuta Kawashima, "Chronology of Libya's Disarmament and Relations with the United States," February 2014. *http://www.armscontrol.org/factsheets/libyachronology*, accessed 2-Aug-2016.

[79] Andy Carvin, "Hotel Sidi Driss," Wiki Commons, Nov. 2005, *https://commons.wikimedia.org/wiki/File:Hotel-sididriss.jpg*

[80] Robert Mendick, "Libyan dissident who photographed the death of Yvonne Fletcher speaks out against the Gaddafi regime," Telegraph New, April 17, 2011.

[81] Author unknown. "Weapons of Mass Destruction, Libyan Nuclear Weapons." GlobalSecurity.org, publish date unknown. *http://www.globalsecurity.org/wmd/world/libya/nuclear.htm*, accessed 2-Aug-2016.

[82] Martin Bright. "MI6 Halted Bid to Arrest Bin Laden." The Guardian, November 9, 2002. *http://www.theguardian.com/politics/2002/nov/10/uk.davidshayler*, accessed 2-Aug-2016.

[83] Mark Micallef. "Gaddafi 'raped' his female bodyguards." Times of Malta.com *http://www.timesofmalta.com/articles/view/20110828/local/Gaddafi-raped-his-female-bodyguards.382085 August 21, 2011.*

[84] Arwa Damon. "Libyan teen says Gaddafi's troops forced her to execute rebels." CNN, August 31, 2011. *http://www.cnn.com/2011/WORLD/africa/08/30/libya.female.fighter/index.html, accessed 2-Aug-2016.*

[85] The Friends of Valley Forge Park, The Valley Forge Mus-ter Roll Project. "Rolls of Regiment Commence," ID no. VA10067, 15-Mar-1778, *Valleyforgemusterroll.org*, accessed 2-Aug-2016.

[86] Iteration of a quote by Sir Isaac Newton. "N.d."

Robert W. Starnes is a retired U.S. Department of State, Diplomatic Security Service (DSS) supervisory special agent with expertise in international counter-terrorism, counterintelligence, investigations, and protective security.

Robert spearheaded the protective intelligence investigation in New Zealand after the U.S. Embassy received a death threat letter containing laboratory grade potassium cyanide targeting visiting U.S. golfer Tiger Woods.

He was a member of the first U.S. diplomatic envoy to return to Libya after a 24-year absence during the reign of dictator Col. Muammar Gaddafi.

Robert was stranded in Brazil with a high-ranking Hezbollah terrorist, he lead the efforts to disrupt and capture a Lebanese terrorist planning to attack the U.S. Embassy in Paraguay, and arrested a Pakistani military jet fighter pilot defector in Texas desiring to kill Americans when he was merely two weeks from joining the U.S. Army Airborne.

Robert rescued dozens of American juveniles from an abusive behavior modification camp in the island jungles of Western Samoa. He provided protective security expertise to revamp the Texas State

Police Governor's protective detail soon after the 2008 arson attack against the Governor's Mansion in Austin, Texas.

A serial adventurer, Robert W. Starnes shares life-threatening events during Guatemala's civil war, and managing civilian and military security assets during Paraguay's violent coup d'état. He has protected notable dignitaries such as; Nelson Mandela; Mikhail Gorbachev; Prince Charles; and Margaret Thatcher.

For excitement, Robert hunts Western Diamondback rattle-snakes, climbed an active volcano in Guatemala, visited the off limits volcanic ravaged Caribbean island nation capital city of Plymouth, Montserrat, traveled to the Israeli West Bank during Hezbollah rocket attacks, and has driven on the world's most dangerous road in Bolivia. Both native Texans, Robert and his equally adventurous wife Pam currently resides in San Marcos, Texas.

Visit his popular webpage at **www.nobilitypress.com**.

www.ingramcontent.com/pod-product-compliance
Lightning Source LLC
Chambersburg PA
CBHW050231270326
41914CB00033BA/1866/J